To:..

....

....

....

....

....

....

Signed..

About the author:

John Douglas was born in Birmingham in the '30's. He joined H.M.S. Ganges the day after his sixteenth birthday, and spent his time there training as a Boy Signalman. He served ten years in the Royal Navy, visiting twenty-two countries including several in the East Indies, Mediterranean and one or two within the Arctic Circle. His final posting was for two-and-a-half years in the Main Signal Office, Lascaris, Malta. ·

John has been writing for over twenty years; this is his fifth published book, as well as several items for radio and tv. He has also written, and had published, several poems and songs, including "Saturday night in the Bull-ring," a song depicting the days and nights in that old market-place in Birmingham.

A fluent speaker, conversationalist and story-teller, he has guested over 400 radio programmes, mainly **Radio WM** and commercial radio, **BRMB**, both in Birmingham, and several tv spots when presenting and promoting his books.

Married, seven children, all grown and flown, he now lives in Cornwall with his wife, Joan.

i

About H.M.S. Ganges:

H.M.S. *Ganges* - the naval establishment for training boy entrants into the R.N. - was situated on the tip of the Shotley peninsular, ten miles seaward to the east from Ipswich in Suffolk, and across the harbour from Harwich and Felixtowe.

Ganges was famous, or infamous, it was an excellent training establishment - which many claim, turning boys into men and producing the finest seamen in the world. Or perhaps it was the notorious harsh and strict place in which young sailor-boys were bullied, harassed, cruelly punished & brain-washed into obeying any orders immediately on command - or be subjected to barbaric punishments! Perhaps it really *was* the place where `shipmates` became `whip-mates,` as someone once suggested.

To it's debatable credit, H.M.S. `Ganges` produced leaders by way of Petty Officers and Chief Petty Officers; some eventually made it to the Wardroom.

To it's equally debatable adverse, there were young boys who committed suicide, or did themselves deliberate physical harm, hoping for medical discharge, rather than continue with the rigours of the training of that place. One, at least, died whilst undergoing punishment; another drowning whilst learning to swim; yet another jumping from the mast, the only way out; or failing to return from leave, having despatched themselves into the grave by hanging rather than return to *Ganges*.

However: Agree or disagree, you will read the following pages and, whichever conclusion you may reach, it will be absolutely right for some, wrong for others, and vice-versa for both!

You can only draw your own conclusion!

H.M.S. GANGES
Tales of the J.R.O.G.'s.
by

John Douglas

ISBN 0-906816-05-X

Published by Second City Publishers, Douglas Hse. Penmarth. Cornwall TR16 6NX

Set in **Times New Roman**, *printed by Troutbeck Press & Bookbinders Ltd. Antron Hill, Mabe, Penryn. Cornwall.*

Main illustrations by... John Wheatley

(34 Trinity Vicarage road, Hinckley, Leicestershire.Tel: 01455 616206.)

Ganges Association

The Ganges Association was born as a result of it`s first re-union of old Boys brought together by the author, John Douglas in May, 1981. Anyone interested in joining the Association and/or contacting old Ganges shipmates, can apply for a membership application form:

Douglas House. Penmarth. Redruth. Cornwall. TR16 6NX
A stamped, self-addressed envelope should be enclosed..

A short extract about **Ganges`** *mast is taken from* **"Way Aloft!"** *by John Webb. Copies available from that author: 71 Kingsland, Shotley. Ipswich. Suffolk. IP9 `ND.*

Contents

Page iv....The Legend of H.M.S. Ganges.

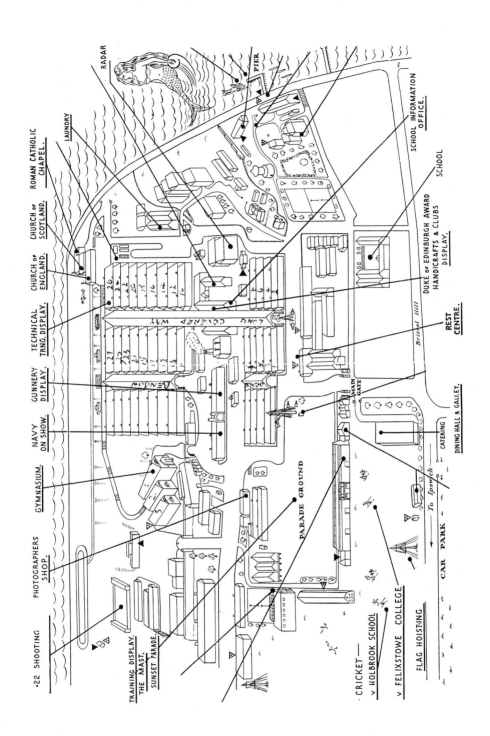

·22 SHOOTING   PHOTOGRAPHERS SHOP.   GYMNASIUM.   NAVY ON SHOW.   GUNNERY DISPLAY.   TECHNICAL TRNG. DISPLAY.   CHURCH OF ENGLAND.   CHURCH OF SCOTLAND.   ROMAN CATHOLIC CHAPEL.   LAUNDRY   RADAR

PIER

SCHOOL INFORMATION OFFICE.

SCHOOL

DUKE OF EDINBURGH AWARD HANDICRAFTS & CLUBS DISPLAY.

REST CENTRE.

DINING HALL & GALLEY.

CATERING

MAIN GATE

Bristol Hill

To Ipswich

CAR PARK

PARADE GROUND

TRAINING DISPLAY. THE MAST. SUNSET PARADE.

CRICKET —

v HOLBROOK SCHOOL

v FELIXSTOWE COLLEGE

FLAG HOISTING

LONG COVERED WAY

CANTEEN

26 24 22 20 18 16 14 12 10
27 23 21 19 17
9 7 5 3

V

The Legend of H.M.S. Ganges

There's a village they call Shotley to the east of Ipswich town,
The port of Felixstowe across the way.
There's a stone-built frigate, *'Ganges'*, near the Orwell flowing down,
And skirted by the shores of Harwich Bay.
Well, we joined as Nozzers new, the 'sailor-boys' in blue:
And punched our oppo's teeth out in the gym.
We marched and doubled - fast! Then we climbed that ***bloody*** mast;
The Foreign Legion ***never*** was as grim!

Ten Divisions - Admiral's all - parade-ground, Nelson Hall,
And Nozzer's Lane tucked out of sight away.
There was Collingwood & Blake, there was Benbow, Hawk & Drake;
And Grenville - down the long, Long Covered Way.
The 'dabtoes' learned to sail a boat, correct a starboard list,
And take evasive action from the bombs,
They could 'bend' & 'splice' & 'hitch,' they could knot a 'monkey's-fist,'
There was semaphore and flashing for the 'Comms.'

Down Laundry Hill on jankers, tin-hat shades the sweating frown,
And bayonet bangin' 'ard against the thigh.
Rifles chafed our collar-bones, the hot sun scorching down,
From inverted bowl of blue, the summer sky.
"Do just as you are told, lad, make do with what you got;
Obey the orders, Boy! No 'if's' or 'buts!'"
The discipline was 'hot,' and some went *'on the trot,'*
But they dragged 'em back and lashed 'em with twelve 'cuts.'

We had **Faith** and we had **Hope**, we had **Charity** as well;
But these were not just *virtues* - as you know!
We stumbled and we fell, - on those concrete steps to Hell,
Our souls were signed to *Ganges* - *be it so.*
What faith? What hope? What charity? Was there really *no* comparity?
As we staggered up those steps with muscle-pain?
We-e-ll, we knew we'd had enough - but assumed that we were tough -
So they made us double up and down again!

GANGES motto states at length, that *'Wisdom, it is strength!'*
*Is there **one** of you who wouldn't go agen*?
Tho' you flogged us an' you flayed us, by the livin' God what made us;
You took us on as boys - **and made us men!**

Copyright: <u>John Douglas.</u>

From the book:

'HMS GANGES' (Roll on my dozen!) (1978.)
By <u>John Douglas. First published by Roundwood Press.</u>

Chapter one
H.M.S. GANGES.

Where it was, what it was, and what they say about it...

'It was the first, the last and the *only* concentration camp in Britain.'
'Discipline was on a par with that of Cap'n Bligh of the `Bounty.`'
'Ganges was a holiday camp..'
`They say Ganges turned out the best seamen in the world - that was just a `con` to get young boys to join..`
'Discipline was brutal in the extreme..'
'It was the blue-print for the German P.O.W. camps...
'I hated it!'
'I loved it!'
A short history..
H.M.S. Ganges, the ship, which had sailed around the coast from the harbour of Falmouth where it had been for many years, was anchored in Harwich Harbour from 1895 to 1905. In that latter year the boys came ashore to establish H.M.S. Ganges the 'concrete frigate,` and the teak-built training-ship, the last wooden-hulled vessel to carry an Admiral to act as Flagship, was taken to Chatham, renamed and used as a tender to R.N. Barracks. She was later towed to Plymouth for breaking up.

Ganges, or what remains of it, is now a Police Training College; it may be gone from sight but not from the memory of hundreds of thousands of boys and men who spent several months training as Boys, or Instructors or as members of the staff. The memories it provoked, etched indelibly, marked for all time in thousands of minds, are often good, but most times bad. There are stories of compassion and kindness. Not all Instructors were bullying sado-masochists, and the latter trait was definitely *not* a qualification to become an Instructor, but it *was* brought out in some when they realised the magnitude of the mostly unquestionable and, in some cases, limitless power they held over two thousand boys. Some stories conflict with others, proving that some opinions can be guided, and affected by what happens to us or what we see happening to others.

It was planned to write a book of entertaining laughter-provoking anecdotes: '*The humorous tales of H.M.S. GANGES.*' But this one contains only a small fraction of the humour which had been anticipated. It was, initially, envisaged as a documentary of nostalgic humour of the days of a well-spent or miss-spent youth, depending how the reader observes it. The unfortunate result is that it includes sado-masochism, bullying, humiliation, with an occasional injection of spite, self-importance by persons with inferiority complex problems; humour, though little of it; pathos and sympathy, spiced with rare humanitarian actions of kindness by a few who cared about others. What a pity. It was meant to be about humour.

Worse than that; some stories contradict others. As the wise and ancient poet, `Jadie` said:

'It does not follow that whatever happened to us, must have happened to everyone; and if it did not happen to us, it does not also follow that it never happened to others.'

The extracts at the beginning of this chapter - disproportionately in favour of the good rather than the bad - are taken from letters about H.M.S. Ganges. It`s reputation varies greatly, depending upon who is relating the story, how they were treated by their Instructors and their contemporaries, their mess-mates, the boys themselves, who, in some cases were equally guilty of 'man`s inhumanity to man.' Some letters praised all the Instructors and say nothing but good about them, though it is not totally inconceivable to understand that the writers could not have first-hand knowledge of *all* the Instructors who passed through Ganges. It will be seen that so many ex-Boys, when relating their stories, continually use the word, `sadistic.` Some other phrases are also used several times and it is difficult to alter the wording and retain the original meaning. The comments on good or bad Instructors are mostly generalised in both cases, based mainly upon personal experience and seldom that of others; which seems to be *the* method of assessing situations as is usual and common to human nature. At the lower end, some tales are horrifying, bordering on the likeness to prisoner-of-war camp atrocities, though not to the extremes of Belsen or even the infamy of the `Bridge on the River Kwai` story.

One boy, now a retired police sergeant, thought Ganges was paradise. "It was," he said, "Absolute heaven to lie asleep, knowing I did not have to listen to the clumsy footsteps of a drunken father clumping up the stairs to drag me from my bed to thrash me for no reason." For no valid reason except to satisfy a lust for power over others weaker than himself, a situation which some

2

Instructors - and Boys who had been promoted over their mess-mates - illustrated by their own bullying actions. There are stalwarts who defend the reputation of Ganges defiantly and gallantly. There can be no doubt that certain aspects of the Ganges regime gave rise to atrocities, unfair and unjust treatment, barbaric punishments, bullying sadism and masochism - according to the letters which follow, including several from ex-Boys who returned later as Instructors, and one at least who returned again as an officer. Although a few liked or loved Ganges, others hated and feared it so much they tried to bring about their discharge by deliberately wounding themselves to a point where they could be discharged because of ill-health, or some deformity brought about by their own desperate actions. Most Boys took Ganges as a sufferance to be endured and got rid of, to make way for the obvious good things to come. The reputation of Ganges as a paradise, holiday-camp, hell-hole or simply a training establishment for Boy Seamen, was therefore relative to personal opinion.

At the height of the Ganges' training schedule, there was accommo-dation for two thousand boys and several hundred staff. Place those two thousand boys in the same situation, in the same place at the same time, ask them to relate their experiences - and the result is two thousand differing versions, each one in total belief that his version is the true one, and the versions of others, if they differ greatly, are accused of being suspect for varying reasons. There is also a strong-minded, one-track, self-opinionated section who were treated well by the Instructors and Instructor-Boys, later known as Junior Instructors, and refuse to believe that anyone could have been treated less than fairly and justly. A similarly biased view is held by those who's Instructors and Instructor-Boys were 'little Hitlers,' - and that was being lenient with their opinions - who cannot believe that anyone could have been treated, in the very least, any way but harshly, unfairly and unkindly. In the stories which follow the reader should ignore claims that Ganges was all bad or all good. It should be understood that not all humans are average, nice people. There are those who have been bullied at school and could not retaliate because of their lack of courage and/or stature to fight back. They get their revenge later, in adulthood, by treating those beneath them in like manner. There are those who's ego is so large that they have to impose their thoughts and beliefs upon others; conversely, there are those who have massive inferiority complexes and have to put down others to make themselves look big, clever, smart and all-powerful.

Several stories herein are related by ex-Instructors. They convey a feeling of responsibility and anxiousness to see the job through, and to do that job most efficiently with great consideration to their Boys. One chapter, in particular, is devoted to ex-Petty Officer Frank Henry Austin and his story: **My finest hour...**

Ex-Instructors, who made the similar collective comment: 'I was a Boy at Ganges and later returned as an Instructor and got my own back,' when asked to elucidate upon that statement, remained jointly silenced. Only one, a Junior Instructor, elucidated upon it.

We are all the centre of our own world, and, as such, most people are convinced that their own personal views are right, and the opposing views of others are completely wrong; the intelligent person will look at the situation from both sides and concede that some could be right and some could be wrong. Neither side are completely right or wrong. To compile an unbiased opinion of Ganges, apart from my own observations and comments on some stories, I tried again to get other points of view - from the Instructor's side, or from those who had stories to relate about kind, caring human Instructors. I wrote to the *Ganges Gazette*, the quarterly magazine of the *Ganges Association,* asking for stories about the kindness of Instructors, and contacted ex-comedian Charlie Chester, who has a two-hour spot on Sunday evenings on Radio Two, inviting ex-Ganges Boys to write letters of contradiction to the general 'sado-masochistic Instructor' theme.The meagre response of just one letter from each source was disappointing, especially as one admonished me for saying Ganges wasn't as bad as I said - then explained how bad it *really* was!

As the author of this book and to be fair and impartial, in defence of most of the Instructors, P.T.I.'s and officers, I have to say this: In the seventeen months I spent at Ganges, I never experienced any atrocity, unfair dealing, cruelty, sadistic bullying by any Instructor Boy, Leading Boy, Petty Officers or Chief Petty Officers, Wardroom Officers or P.T.I.'s, with whom I had personal contact. Therefore, I could not say that atrocities and mis-use of power by Instructors, did, or did not take place. Tales of atrocities did filter through at the time, most were not rumours, but provable facts: a comparable instance is the boy who, with his fellow janker-pals, died by being forced to double up and down Laundry Hill. Unknown to himself, or anyone else, his physical condition concealed a serious ailment or deformity which had not been discovered by previous physical examinations. After several dozen up-and-downers on the notorious and dreaded Laundry Hill - the tortuous hilly-route of many painful memories of jankers and Shotley Routines - he began to approach the point of near-collapse. Faint and weak by this time, he told the Instructor-in-charge that he felt ill; the Instructor ignored his plea and ordered him to keep doubling. Shortly after, the boy dropped to the ground unconscious. The Instructor, according to reports, kicked him and ordered him to get back onto his feet. The boy was unconscious. The Instructor continued to poke him with the toe of his boot; then, realising that the boy was not shamming, he ordered two other boys to escort the boy to the sick bay. The boy died later. The Instructor had a nervous break-down. That was true; but it was more likely that his break-down was caused by the incessant barrage of vociferous boys who threw away all caution to deride that Instructor from the safety of distance as they hurled vocal insults and accusations at him wherever he walked in the Ganges enclosure. Within three days of the luckless boy dying, the Instructor was removed from Ganges to elsewhere.

The foregoing tragedy was brought about by the seeming uncaring attitude of an Instructor who had one purpose in mind: 'These boys are under punishment, it is my duty to punish them, and punish them I will.' The boy claimed, and stated, that he was unwell. He was not believed. It was very obvious that the Instructor thought the boy was pretending to be ill to get out of the punishment.

You will read many complaints about the P.T.I.'s, physical training instructors, but the P.T.I. of my division, Grenville, was no less than thoroughly likeable, understanding and friendly. It is a suspicion I have held for several years that some aspects of Ganges which caused pain or fear would eventually give rise to a total hatred of Ganges itself. Those same aspects could, conversely, cause some ex-Boys to actually herald the praises of Ganges. The aspects which come to mind, three of them, are climbing the mast, swimming and gymnastics. If there is a fourth it would be taking part in the many types of sports which Ganges had to offer..

From my own point of view I loved climbing the mast, I excelled at swimming, I was good at gymnastics - near the top of the class but not outstanding, apart from boxing, and rope-climbing, and I was good at running. Some of these sports contain a high element of fear, particularly in the case of swimming and climbing the mast if the complainant has a fear of heights and/or water. Other sports, gymnastics, football, cricket, rugby, etc., contain pain-inducing activities which are ignored by the lovers of those sports as 'par for the course.' But if a boy is not the sporty sort, and is forced to learn to swim, climb the mast, take compulsory lessons in gymnastics and sports, then he might blame his hatred for those things entirely upon Ganges - and therefore he would hate Ganges.

Unbiased view

Some of the stories provoke disgust, and the only intervention by the author is to make an appropriate comment, assuming the stories are true. My personal view of Ganges, is, therefore, unbiased. Any comments made before, during, or after a story, is made only upon the contents of that story. I have no personal gripe against Ganges - I made at least two life-long friends whilst there - but if I was urged to make some complaint, then it would be this: I was once hit over the head with a rolled-up map by an Instructor, but this was part of jocularly-friendly banter which was taking place between us both in the class-room. It didn't hurt - although it came as a mild and unexpected shock - and when the Instructor left, half-way through the course to be demobbed, I was as sorry to see him go as the rest of the class - except perhaps the WRN he was having an affair with. Our main concern was because we were anxious that the Instructor taking his place would turn out to be as good - or not as bad, depending - as the one who was leaving.

Chastising tender young bottoms..

There was one Instructor, a Lt. 'Schoolie,' who took a gang of us lads for a week-end camping at Pin Mill, two miles along the river; a welcome week-end away from the pomp, bullshine and discipline. It was rumoured that the 'Schoolie' liked the look and feel of the tender bottoms of young boys. From a true incident which follows, he also liked to chastise those tender bums with semaphore-flag-sticks on the slightest excuse and personal whim. Two others and myself were observed by an uncaring cottage-dweller scrumping mouldy wind-falls from her overgrown orchard which was ankle-deep in rotten apples. She voiced her complaint to the 'Schoolie' who's soft, brown eyes sparkled with expectation at the thought of being able to scourge the bums of the scrumping young scamps. By surreptitious questioning of a few 'stool-pigeons' who toadied to him by 'grassing us up,' we were soon unearthed as the culprits and sentenced without trial to three whacks of a pair of semaphore-flags across the buttocks.

The other two took their punishment meekly, 'tho timidly and fearfully, without protest or questioning of his right to do so.

Then it was my turn - but I was determined not to be beaten by a perverted 'poof' of a cow-eyed 'Schoolie.'

I said: 'No, sir, you're not allowed to hit us. Besides, we only picked up what was nearly rotten apples.'

He didn't know what to do or say. Here was a cheeky young, fresh-faced Nozzer, actually defying the high-blown, unquestionable authority, which he thought, up to that point, was infallible.

"I said: bend over!" he demanded sternly; "And touch your toes."

I shook my head: "No." I had reached the point of no return and was determined to see it through. I warmed to my new-found bravado, realising by the look on his face that he was near defeat, not quite knowing how to handle this young, persistent upstart. "You're not allowed to punish us without a fair trial." I realised then that it sounded a bit melodramatic, and wondered in the following split-second what would happen - obviously, being an officer he could not back down in the face of insubordination.

I held his gaze, thinking perhaps I had better bend over and take my punishment before this simple charade of bravado might end in Commander's report and six whacking cuts delivered by 'Creeping Jesus,' the beefy R.P.O. But I obstinately refused to bend over so that my tender young bottom could be chastised by *anyone* just to satisfy his homosexual tendencies.

'Alright,' he said. 'Report to the quarterdeck when we return to Ganges and I'll charge you with direct disobedience of orders and insubordination, including dumb insolence. Take that defiant look off your face, Douglas, and go and collect some firewood for the fire." His 'face' had been saved but his threats never came to fruition. I reported to the quarterdeck, waited, but he didn't appear. Even to this day I still marvel at my courage as one of the absolute lowest of naval ratings, opposing such great majesty as a Royal Navy Lieutenant. I felt as if I could have said, 'Balls!' to the skipper and got away with it.

Back in the mess, as the tale was told, my esteem rose to the highest levels of admiration. At a height of five feet two inches I was the tallest in the Division for several weeks and someone to be wary of. Who would dare to antagonise he who defied authority?

There are stories which follow that prove several boys, who were given the same ultimatum, `my punishment or Commander's report?` would have been punished more leniently, or not at all, if they had opted for Commander's report. It makes one wonder just how many boys would have escaped illegal and harsh punishment if they had stood their ground, or reported those unofficial and oftimes barbaric unjust treatments. There are several stories on that theme.

My own Instructors were never guilty of the statement, 'Commander's report or my punishment?' None of my Instructors ordered us out of bed at 0100 or 0200 to satisfy a drunken urge to show us they were closely blood-related to Hitler or any member of the S.S., determined to prove their superiority. But according to letters received, there were those who did. It makes sad reading.

Unlike the stories of long, sweaty hours on punishment routine, we were not made to double up the three flights of concrete steps jokingly called `Faith, Hope and Charity` in an attempt to teach us how to read morse-code at a speedier rate, or more efficiently. We *did* perform a few strenuous sinew-stretching muscle-cramping up-and-downers on that tortuous stretch of concrete steps, not because we were slow in learning, but because of some minor breach of rules, regulations or discipline, and which we probably deserved. There were some Instructors, according to the stories, who suffered the affliction of conspicuously apparent brain-thickness, believing with old-fashioned Victorian reasoning, that physically and painfully punishing slow-learning, back-ward boys, would actually cause them to learn more quickly!

Isn't punishing a person for being unable to learn quick enough the wrong way to teach? Punishment for being lackadaisical, sloppy, or lazy, or being *deliberately* slack in learning, is a totally different matter. Brutality and humiliation does not earn respect, it breeds fear, and only fear. Fear causes a person to react quickly because of nervousness; it leads to inaccuracy, causes mistakes and sometimes total inertia. The old saying: `more haste, less speed,` is as true to this day as when it first stated. Kind treatment can lead to respect, and respect will lead to the person respected being obeyed by their subordinates - *that* is discipline. Fear sometimes has the same result but not the same respect for the mentor, and mistakes are often caused by the nervous hurriedness which fear brings.

None of my Instructors tried to teach by terror. We were never made to put bed-chocks down our pyjama-legs, button an oilskin on

8

back-to-front and run around the parade-ground until we dropped. But because those things never happened to me, I cannot honestly swear that they did not happen to others. In fact, so many say that it did, they must be believed. There are several extracts from the letters sent in by ex-Instructors who were ex-Boys. They also tell of, and thereby confirming, the unnecessary brutalities and bullying by *their* Instructors when *they*, the story-tellers were boys.

One ex Boy is **Ronald S.C. Robinson**, a one-time member of Drake Division, 1936, retired now as a Lieutenant Commander. Despite his rise through Petty Officer, Chief and finally to the wardroom, he has always been stoically cynical. His following statement, as an ex-officer, ex-Ganges Boy, simplifies what H.M.S. Ganges, when all it`s aspects are whittled down to basics, really meant to those who considered it`s purpose and meaning in greater depth than most:-

"What I recall most vividly," reports Ronald, "Was the irrelevance, not only of Ganges, but the Royal Navy in general. I can remember becoming, even at that early age, an expert on practices that would never be of the slightest use to me at sea. It did irreparable harm to me in that it bred a cynicism that even now is not fully eradicated. This was the product of the realisation that, there was I, in a navy that had no concept of its relevance or function, had no intention of finding out, and, confronted with it`s sobering reality, *would probably have tried to polish it.* It also created in me a lot of good, a resolve to counter both bullying and gross inefficiency at any level to which I might be advanced.

We became highly proficient at diverting attention from our inability to do something - by doing something else, and doing it well. In taking part in that diversionary, protective hypocrisy, we were merely copying what the whole of the service was up to.

Some of the stultifying orthodoxy is still doctrinal: From time to time, I wonder if, perhaps, there might be a Rosetta Stone somewhere that I`ve not been able to decipher. As an example: the significance of proficiency at `*Horse Hockey*` in determining fitness to command still eludes me."

Chapter 2.
We joined the navy.....

Peter Dolphin was conned into joining:
"I joined the navy at the age of 15 on August 24th, 1964. My mum
and dad drove me to the recruiting office. Crying wasn't really on, as
I was to become a man very soon, so I was glad that my mum stayed
in the car. Outside the recruiting office my Dad said: 'As far as I'm
concerned, this is as far as I'm going. If you want to change your
mind, this is the time to do it. There'll be no disgrace, no regrets,
nothing.'
'No, thanks,' I said. 'I'm going to join the navy.'
The next few hours are hazy. I must have travelled in some sort of
shock. I was still numb as we were herded into canvas-topped lorries
outside Ipswich station and driven off to Shotley. I thought, *'where
the hell are we all going?'What the hell have I done?'*
So here I am, in this big hall in Ganges, a canvas sail draped across
the room, and a voice the other side called my name. I went to the
other side of the sail and sat in front of an officer who kept saying:
'Do you agree with this - do you agree with that...' and so on. I said
'yes' to everything. Then he shoved a bit of paper towards me, and
asked: 'Will you sign on for 12 years?'
I said: 'No way, mate. I'll sign for three years and see how it goes
from there.'
He said: 'I see. Why don't you go outside and consider it?'
Well, I sat outside on the steps, chewed some gum, had a smoke, and
thought - *twelve years!   Shit! I could die in the navy and no-one
would know where I was!*
A shadow fell across my face; I looked up and saw this tall, thick-set
smart-looking chap with black gaiters, shiny boots and a big smile.
He said cheerfully: 'Hello, son!'
He seemed quite a nice sort of chap, smiling and genial. Older than
me. Father-like.
I said 'hello' back, and he said: 'What seems to be the problem?'
'That chap in there wants me to sign for twelve years but I don't want
to do that - I don't mind three, then I'll have another think about it.'
'I see,' he said. Then proceeded to tell me what a wonderful life it
was in the navy. Good pay. Good mates. Foreign travel and so on. He
made it sound so good, and I felt a lot better about it, especially as
everyone seemed so friendly and helpful. What could I lose? I'd
already made one good friend. I stood up, dogged my cigarette,

thanked him very much, walked off and signed away 12 of the most important years of my life. I went outside again and my new mate came over to greet me, the cheery smile still upon his face.

'Well, son,' he said. 'Did you sign?' Still chewing the gum, I said: 'Yes I did matey, thanks a lot for helping me out.'

Talk about Jekyll and Hyde! His nice attitude changed suddenly. He screamed: **'Well spit that f.....g shit out of your f.....mouth! You're in the f.....g navy now!'** *The 24th of August, 1964, is a day I shall always remember!''*

'You're in the navy now!!'

JW 1955

Report: A truly magnificent specimen of a 'spindly-legged, typically narrow-minded, ugly-faced, self-opinionated bastard of a <u>very</u> 'petty' Officer.'

The minimum age for joining the navy as a boy entrant was fifteen years and three months. The required minimum height was five feet two inches, and the stature of the recruit should at least be normal. Not too fat, nor too thin; eyes and ears, as well as teeth, were also inspected, and those of sub-normal featuristics were rejected, but the strictest of rules were sometimes relaxed, and a few who were sub-standard of stature, height, weight and intelligence, were allowed in - if they looked serious enough to join. Sometimes the rules were very strict, depending on the idiosyncrasies of the recruiting staff at the recruiting station. One boy was refused admittance until he had his uneven teeth straightened, another, in the 1940's, had a full set of teeth but one of them was bad. He went away, paid seven shillings and sixpence - a lot of money fifty years ago - went back to the recruiting office and was accepted; but any owner of a pair of flat feet was refused entry into the Royal Navy; and spectacles, if worn, was a guarantee of immediate return to the rigours of civvy-street and most certainly not allowed into the elite communication branch; good eyesight being an obvious `must` if they were to be called to the bridge to read a flashing light, semaphore or a flag signal from several thousands of yards away.

There are many who would agree that the 'unlucky' ones who were refused entry into Ganges were really the lucky ones - taking into consideration the rigours of that place which the reader will learn of later in this book. Some branches accepted short-sighted sailors, Sick Berth Attendants, Stores staff, Writers, but not seamen or communicators. An intelligence test had to be taken to join the Navy but a few, a very surprising few, of lesser-intelligence, did sneak through.

In my first class, 243, of 33 Mess, Benbow Division, we had an `Ambling Alp` type - although he did try very hard to give a reasonable impersonation of his close relatives, Homo Sapiens. We called him, 'Blossom.' It was at the time when a film called, 'The Hasty Heart,' starring Richard Todd as a soldier-about-to-die, had a grudge against mankind and was generally nasty to everyone who tried to express sympathy. One of the unforgettable characters was a tall, slow-moving and slow-of-wit person, resembling the `Ambling Alp` in his movements, tho` not his stature, who attempted to show a kindness to Richard Todd, but was brusquely rejected. The rejected one knew only one word of English: 'Blo-summ!' He spoke that one word very slowly, breaking the syllables with a jerky hesitation: **'Blo-summ!'** Someone once asked our `Blossom,` cruelly, but in jest: "Blossom, are you a member of Homo Sapiens?"

His reply was: 'Naah. Not meee! I only loikes wimmin!'

We marvelled, not at his answer, but at the fact that he had been able to distinguish the difference between 'Homo Sapiens' and 'Homo-sexual.'

At an unbelievable boyish age of fifteen and a half year's old, he was six months younger than myself, but against my five feet one and seven-eights, and bordering on the challenge for the seven-stone-weakling title, he was almost six feet tall and weighed about twelve stone, slightly sub-normal in appearance - and supposedly in intelligence. From behind, when he had stripped for the shower, he resembled a soaking wet gorilla. His head was massive, and a seven-and-a-quarter-size hat, the largest available, was very much too small. It was unfortunate that his over-size head did not hold an over-large brain; it was more to the adverse and his many fiery-red pimples contrasted with, rather than complemented the blackheads, both contained in the setting of his puffy, pasty-white face; his massive arms and shoulders almost split the seams of his number three suit. He had a mystifying type of arm which had been broken during childhood and badly re-set, giving it a crooked, hind-leg-of-a-dog appearance. Passing over all the foregoing, he was harmless and affably genial with a pleasant character which gained him lots of friends and earned him no enemies. Everyone liked him. He was the `farmer's-boy` type, likeable and good-natured; at meal-times he had the endearing and comical habit of making the same humorous observations upon any meal laid before him, and would make the following comment in a booming, stentorial voice which seemed to emanate from the depths of his great hairy belly:

"Moy fav`rit meal!"** - a long, hesitant pause as he slowly sucked a stupendous amount of air into his massive lungs, staring at his plate: **"Is braaahn sauce - sloshed abaaht on mooshee peeeees!`

No one laughed in derision;no one jeered, most smiled in sympathetic understanding. But, proverbially speaking: *He stood out like the proverbial tanner on the proverbial sweep's arse.* He did not conspire to the normal type of boy which the navy needed, to mould to their own specifications, and, to get rid of him, the navy had to find a feasible excuse to dismiss this genial misfit, who had, somehow, in his innocence, deceived the intelligence-test which is needed to pass for the superior intelligence of the Communications Branch. Could he have been a genius disguised as a country bumpkin? It is possible, but because of his badly re-set arm he was unable to send semaphore messages properly, his arm actions being obviously mistaken for something other than what they were supposed to be. The correct solution was to transfer him on the same level to the telegraphist branch, or, failing that, down to the seaman branch. But one evening he was asked to pack his kit- bag, told to ask no questions, and, next morning, he was awakened quietly by a Patrolman, warned that he should make no noise, not even a reference to `braaaahn sauce on moooshy peeees!,` and he and the Patrolman pussy-footed down the length of the polished deck, as quietly as anyone could `pussy-foot` with clumping great hob-nailed boots worn by both parties, and he had gone. No-one knew what happened to him. He was never heard of again and it was amazing to think that he had to pass one intelligence test to get in, and another to enter the Communications branch, and yet was discharged after only a few weeks as unsuitable - if that was the case.

Difficult To Join.

It was difficult to join, but more difficult to get out if you didn`t like it. Three months after the initial medical exam, any volunteer would be invited to attend the Recruiting Office where he was escorted with others to a train station and taken to Ipswich or Harwich for final embarkation to the Ganges Annexe where he spent the next six weeks being kitted-out, innoculated, vaccinated and indoctrinated into the Ganges regime. He would spend weeks sewing his name with red chain-stitch in several dozen pieces of his kit, learning to march, trying his best to knock his oppo`s teeth out in the gymnasium, climbing the mast, and most-times being shouted at, sworn at, threatened, berated, cajoled and, according to some of the stories, beaten into submission and finally humiliated.

The Boy Seaman, for that is what he now is, has to clean the communal bedroom, the mess-deck, wash his own clothes and learn how to look after himself in every way - and accustom himself to a new language: the ceiling becomes the `deck-head;` the floor the `deck;` the walls the `bulkhead` and the toilet the `heads.` He will not wash his clothes from the moment of ingestion into the Annexe but he will `dhobey` them.

Most boys, after surmounting several awkward moments, adapted fairly easily to the completely different way of life, some could not tolerate it at all, some rebelled and some ran away. Depending on who they were, how tough or how weak they were, they have varying stories to tell.

One boy would run away two or three times, take six, nine or twelve cuts for doing so with no ill-feelings and claim that `Ganges was not too bad,` or even admit that he deserved the punishment.

One boy, after relating tales of horror and torment; hours of Shotley Routine, dancing bare-footed on bed-springs, holding his hat-box or suit-case out in front of him and receiving vicious swipes of a cane, or, in one case, a spanner, would say that Ganges wasn`t **too** bad. Another, in the later years before the closing of Ganges, complained of being deprived of watching the World Cup final between England and Germany because he had not yet gained the honours and passes needed to obtain the privilege of watching tv. Times was `ard indeed! The opinion of Ganges is sometimes strongly related to what was liked or disliked. Stories in this book represent the various quirks of sadistic and masochistic tendencies of Instructors *and* boys.

On both sides there are those who liked to dish it out, and those who loved receiving it. Not that *all* Instructors were bullies or that *all* boys liked to be humiliated. But Ganges was not a prime or typical example of a perfect world.

The tales before they became T.R.O.G.`s

It is appropriate that we start on the joining stories with an anecdote which began before actually joining - the medical room of the recruiting station. We`ve all been through a similar experience.

Ray Dunwell: "I was wandering around the city with my mate, Dave, when we came across the Naval Recruiting Office. It had a display in the window, depicting what a wonderful life for a boy it could be in the R.N. We went in, had a chat with some very nice men and we decided to join and went through the usual preliminaries of filling in a form. Later they sent for us to attend a medical. There must have been about twenty boys, all shapes and sizes in attendance, we were ordered to strip off all our clothing except our trousers. Then it started: hair, eyes, ears, teeth, a tap here a tap there, breathe in, breathe out, after each examination a brief comment to the matronly old dear who was seated behind the desk making notes. When we had gone through this ritual the next order from the Doc: 'Line up facing the desk and drop your trousers' We hesitated, not wanting to embarrass the old dear behind the desk. He repeated his order in a much louder voice: **'Drop your trousers!'**

Slowly, down came the trousers, all eyes on matron. She raised her head from the desk, pen poised, and looked, not in our eyes, but a bit lower. Her eyes travelled slowly along the line, pausing every now and again to have a longer look at those who were better and larger equipped than the others. Then the Doc came along the line. Even he is having a look. At the same time, placing his fingers underneath the testicles, asking the boy to cough. *'What can he possibly find out from that?'* we ask ourselves. The final order; 'Bend over and touch your toes.'

Round the back he goes and has a good look. 'Right,' he says, 'That`s all, get dressed, go home, you will be informed.'

The Doc and the matron gather up the papers and leave the room leaving us in a state of bewilderment. My mate, Dave ended up at that other place, H.M.S. Bruce."

Most can equate with Ray`s tale. The same experience happened to me, with the exception that when we stripped off we had to do split jumps, legs apart, arms out sideways, feet together, arms slapping thighs, then again for about twenty times, our private parts bouncing and flopping about, the more well-endowed flopping much more on a pro-rata basis. The female audience at that time consisted of several delicious young typists watching with broad smiles and wondrous eyes from an office-window across the street, James Watt street. Most of them probably gained more knowledge on the varying sizes and odd-shapes of the male organ then, than at any other time during their lives.

The stories move on, most of them mentioning just briefly the trauma of having their crowning glory shorn to the bone and several other items including the issuing of kit and the sewing-in of names upon it. For some, it could be most traumatic, the mere joining of Ganges was a culture-shock. Mummy wasn't there to do the dhobeying, and Father was not available to supplement the meagre pay of a Boy 2nd Class.

John Sallis, who joined the Andrew at the recruiting office in James Watt street, Birmingham on June 7, 1949, gives a typical true-to-life view of how most of the new-entries, the Nozzers, attempted to gain the title of Trained Ratings Of Ganges - of which TROG`s is a mnemonic - and saw their first view of the Annexe.

"When we arrived at the entrance to the Annexe, a large Petty Officer asked everyone on the bus: 'If any of you has any doubts about joining the navy, and wants to change his mind, now is the time to say, because once we are through the gates it will be too late.'

None of us seemed to have any doubts. If we had had the same option three weeks later I think most of us would have left there and then."

In the Recruiting Office in Birmingham, back in September, 1947, I and others received the same ultimatum. I remember thinking at the time: *"You are going to remember this moment for many years to come."* And I was right, but at the time I was young, adventurous, and the momentum of the start of the excitement and prospect of actually going to sea - *which I had been looking forward to for several years,* was under way. If I had been told truthfully what to expect, and between twelve and eighteen months to experience it, I think I would have opted out and hired a rowing boat on Handsworth park pool and be immediately promoted to Vice-Admiral.

"We were allocated our various messes," continues John Sallis, "And I was in Beatty I. In charge of which was what I thought was a monster of a Chief Petty Officer, C.P.O. FINCH. I remember thinking, *'I`m no longer a person, I`m just a number.'* The first night I lay on a very hard bed in a mess with all these other boys from all different back-grounds and different parts of the country. The first night was not easy and doubts began to creep into my mind. *Had I done the right thing?* I had never been away from home before.

Lights out at 2100. An Instructor Boy paced up and down telling us what we were in for, Instructor-Boy Braybrook. He really put the fear of God into me, and most of the others, with all these tales of the terrible things that were about to befall us. On reflection, neither C.P.O.Finch, nor Instructor-Boy Braybrook were the monsters that they first appeared to be. I got to like both of them. The harsh reality of life for a boy seaman was clearly meant for us. We had to learn to wash our own clothes, something which I was not prepared for. We went to the laundry for the first time. In charge was a retired Marine Corporal, a real bully of a man. His job was to instruct us how to wash our clothes and he would then inspect the finished article. I've rarely seen such terror in boy's faces than that of a boy who failed to meet the standards of this brute of an Instructor. For reasons I never quite understood, we had to strip naked to do our washing. The ex-Marine would deal out punishments with his cane or stick, which he called his 'Percy,' to anyone who crossed his path. He would delight in humiliating any boy in front of everyone. He would say: 'If I find any Admiral Brown on your under-pants, you will get a thrashing.' And, sad to say, many boys did. This sort of thing, in the first few days of joining the navy, made boys think they would do better by leaving, however, there was no way out. I understand that this Marine Laundry Instructor and his stick, 'Percy,' were later dismissed for brutality."

If I may stop the story here and make a comment: I left Ganges in February, 1949, and I recall an ex-Marine in charge of the Annexe Laundry when I joined in September, 1947. I assume it was the same person. If it was, then my view and opinion of him is very different. He was slightly taller than my five feet two inches, but obviously not a tall man himself. He was rather rotund and spoke with a country-fied accent, all `ohh-arrrs` and `oi be's` and so on. My own confrontation with him went like this: It was Jellicoe One's first dhobey-day; another new experience to be looked forward to. The navy had only three sizes of kit-issue, small, medium and large, men's sizes. There was no lee-way for the shorter boys, so my `small` kit was a little too large. This resulted in my pyjamas, and not the only item of kit, to be too long in the arms and legs. The arms I could cope with. I folded the cuffs back, but the legs, even though turned up, would eventually, with the help of gravity and the strenuous rigours of a young man's energy in dodging about the mess before 'lights-out,' would unfold to the point where the backs of them would be trodden under-heel. The result was that the bottoms of the pyjama-legs would become much more dirty than the rest of the outfit. No amount of scrubbing could remove the grime. The ex-Marine Laundry-man noticed this, and proceeded with a lecture.

"Now, then," he said, in his Norfolk or Ipswich country-fied accent, whichever it was, "Oi can tell by the looks o' these 'ere leg-boddoms

BOYS IN THE LAUNDRY R.N.T.E. SHOTLEY

that you're a young lad what loikes a skoi-laaark!"
"Not really," I said, "How can you tell?" Wondering how he had arrived at that conclusion by inspecting my pyjama-bottoms. His accent was funny and I couldn`t help smiling. He peered at me and saw a cheeky, fresh-complexioned, baby-faced, blue-eyed blond young boy who looked about twelve.
"We-e-e-ll!" he said, vehemently and passionately, "Oi can tell, because boys what`s got dirty 'jarma boddoms, goes round skoila-a-a-a-rkin' a-a-a-rter loights-out when they should be in bed. Roight?" And he **was** right.
I remembered that I had been doing a bit of running around, but it was *before* 'loights-out,' not after. I already knew by this time that there was no point in arguing with the naval or civilian-staff. One just could not win, except by devious means of which I became efficiently self-taught later. I nodded, smiled sheepishly, letting him think he was right, and beamed a smile up into his face.
"Goo on," he said, nodding his round, red face, his fat jowls wobbling like a bulldog`s chops in a force ten gale. "Goo an' do 'em agen. An' do 'em proper this time or you`ll be `ere all bloomin' day!"
There was only five minutes to go before dinner-time so it was impossible for him to keep me there all day because (a) he had to break for dinner, and (b) another class would be in after dinner, and (c) we had an appointment with the Sick Bay for jabs. He was bluffing, so I called his bluff, pretended to scrub my 'jarma-boddoms' and followed the others out when the period ended. I have always considered him as a figure of fun, rather than a sadistic ogre, and I cannot recall him hitting anyone - if we are talking about the same person. But everyone`s opinion is not the same, it depends how one faces it or interprets it.
Garry Owen, 1933-34, has a much milder view of his Laundry supervisor: *"The civilian, a very fat man, was an ex P.T.I. His call was, 'Any more for the hydro!?' The hydro was a very large machine which spun the water out of the clothes prior to putting them into either the pull-out drying cabinets or the convector-type heater."*
John Sallis continues: "I was sorry to leave the Annexe, our Instructor, C.P.O. Finch, was no monster, in fact quite a fatherly figure and a gentleman. Not so for certain other Instructors!
P.T.I.`s were expert bullies...
One day we had to double over to the main camp to the Gym. The P.T.I. kept us doubling round this Gym. I had never seen the inside of a Gym before. We ran around for what seemed hours until eventually one or two of the weaker boys showed signs of distress. It was one of the worst cases I remember of bullying. P.T.I.`s were

very good at this sort of thing. I used to think these men were specially chosen to break any spirit a boy might have. By this time I was planning the best way of getting out of the navy as quickly as I could. Many boys were of the same mind, including, I later found out in conversation, Instructor-Boy Braybrook. The thought of being in until I was 30 years of age terrified me. The routine was quite hectic by most standards. We used to feel so tired at the end of the day that early to bed was about the only thing we were good for. The harsh discipline of Ganges life came very hard to me. I remember when we were waiting for meals we would fall in outside the mess while the cooks of the mess would go to the Galley to collect the food. Many is the time I've spent doubling round the parade-ground because the P.O. caught someone talking in the ranks. When we were allowed back into the mess for our meal it was often cold and very little time to eat it.

Instructor Lt. was a bully...

One of our Instructor Lieutenants was a real bully in the class-room. As A.C. Boys, we were expected to be well-versed in everything academic, however, this was not the case as far as I was concerned. Instructor Lt. P...'s favourite pastime was to stand a boy out in front of the class, chalk out whatever theory we were being taught on the blackboard and bang the boy's forehead against the blackboard so the imprint of the chalk was on the boy's forehead.

'Now boy!' he used to say, 'You won't forget it!'

At the school I attended we had never done electrics, magnetism or mechanics, so I had a lot of catching-up to do. This Instructor Lt. P... put the fear of God into many a boy. I have to say this however, he used to give us sailing lessons, whalers mostly, and he almost became human. He once produced a packet of wine gums and handed them around, much to the surprise of everyone. My Divisional Officer in Drake was Lt. Cdr. Johnstone. NICE CHAP. Our Chief was a fellow name of Green, again, a nice fellow. In my early days at Ganges I think a lot of the bullying came from amongst the boys themselves. Boys who had reached the end of the initial training would pick on newcomers and make their lives a misery.

Shotley Joe, the barber, was one of the best remembered characters of my year. Years later when I returned with my wife to Shotley we were having a drink in the bar of the Bristol Arms and I got talking to someone, it was Shotley Joe. He told me about the demise of the Marine Corporal Laundry Instructor. We had quite an interesting chat.

The best seamen in the world...(1)

It has always been said that Ganges produced some of the best seamen in the world. I'm sure that's right, however, in my case I shall have to say in fairness, it failed. Some of my class went on to H.M.S. Hawke for Officer training, but I very soon realised that I was not suitable officer material, either from back-ground or academic point of view. Anyway, daddy never read The Times!"

John Sallis mentions buying himself out, which he did later. Before John's time, and during mine, it was impossible to do that. At least, we were not told that we could if we wanted to, it was kept secret. One would think that if it was known that it would be possible to purchase one's release from the navy, that life could be made easier by the comforting thought that at any time the contract of 12 years could be terminated at fairly short notice. After the initial training in the Annexe, a boy could decide if he wanted to make the navy his career, or give his notice to leave. It could be construed that if that was the case, most boys would have opted out and exchanged their naval kit for a 'civvy suit. A few years ago there was a short series on television called, I believe, 'Nozzer!' It was about the training of boys in the R.N. Each episode was, very obviously, played soft and safe by the Instructors, but, as obvious as their acting was, their true real bullying natures came through at the end, when one boy decided to opt out. The Instructors issued degrading and humiliating remarks to the effect that his, the boy's, opting-out was for the best because he was not man enough to continue in what was a man's navy, wimps not included or welcome. Later in this book, one ex-Boy admits that almost half of his class had bought themselves out by the end of the course.

"A WRN grasped my testicles.."

Back to Birmingham Recruiting office with ex-Boy **Nick Nicholls,** 1957, now an Aussie. Nick tried to join Birmingham Police force as a recruit but was a quarter of an inch under the required height of five feet eight. Despite many attempts to gain some height, which included getting his brother, David, to hang from his feet whilst he was suspended from the Anderson air-raid shelter at the bottom of his garden it didn't work, not surprisingly, so Nick joined the navy:

"The R.N. recruiting office was in James Watt street, Birmingham, and part of the criteria for entering consisted of an intelligence test and an alleged medical examinanition. Part of the physical test consisted of sit-ups, touching one's toes, etc. At this point, as we were naked, a sick-berth attendant would peer up our back passages with the aid of a torch. I never discovered what he was looking for. We also had to do chin-ups on a bar, whereupon, a large WREN would grasp our testicles. I don't recall the reason for that, but her cold hands still linger in my memory.." There's also lots of other things which linger in Nick`s memory; they are told elsewhere in this book.

"The best seamen in the world! (2)"

Andrew Motte- Harrison, now of Waira Rapa, N.Z., relates a clear example of kitting-out, the story is submitted by Mrs. Marguerite Strathow, probably from the writings of Andrew:

"On the counter, striding up and down it, waving a yard-stick, was the awe-inspiring figure of the Stores Chief Petty Officer. Absolute silence reigned. Fifty new-entrants, `nozzers,` stared as the Chief and the 'Jack Dusties,' the Stores Assistants, waited expectantly. We were the third 'issue' of the morning, and there was an awesome sense of occasion matched only by the over-powering smell of moth-balls.

'Right!' roared the Chief, making us all jump. 'I am the Chief Petty Officer, Stores. I WILL issue your kit. YOU WILL keep SILENT! The only voice I want to hear is MINE! GOTIT?!'

Nobody said whether they had or hadn't 'gotit', and, after a dramatic pause: 'Right then! We will start at the top. `Ats!..'

And, so saying, he tapped the first boy, me, non too gently on top of the head with his yard-stick, and pronounced: 'Six and seven eighths,' and, as the other boys came after me, 'Six and five eighths, seven,! Six and three-quarters,' in a continuous bellow. Behind him a muted, and seemingly well-rehearsed, flurry of activity sprang to life as the 'Dusties' tried to get the right size hat atop the right-sized recipient. In all, some seventy items of kit were issued to each of us in this manner. The Chief would not tolerate any interruption to his flow of eye-measurements from hat to boots, especially by such heresy as the suggestion of a wrong size.

It was at this point that I learned that Naval Stores Clothing had just two sizes, too big and too small. My boots, I discovered later, were date-stamped 1918. To his credit, our mess-Chief, over the ensuing week, managed to get any grossly ill-fitting items changed, by threat or coercion, we never knew, but I shall never forget my first traumatic meeting with a big, loud-mouthed Chief Stores 'tiffy."

It could have been worse, like a 'butch' CPO WRN Stores 'tiffy, as **Pete Spamer** found out.

"That day was full of shock and trauma," he says. "I shall never forget it; I was a fifteen-and-a-half-year-old innocent schoolboy looking forward to joining Ganges. The great day arrived at last! It had been like waiting for Christmas when I was a child, but at last the time had come. I had a new set of clothes, a jacket, grey flannels, shirt, tie and shoes. I felt so very proud and smart. I set off, feeling keen, excited and thrilled and only a little apprehensive.

*Er. please miss,
none of it fits..*

Shotley mag.

It all suddenly and very dramatically changed on arrival at New Entry. We met our Instructor who turned out to be a very hard and sadistic man. CPO Hancock. He had grey hair and a mean face. I had seen him countless times before in movies, wearing a black uniform, an iron cross and a death's head skull insignia.

We were ushered into a classroom and signed a form, committing us to twelve years service. As I signed the form I felt, for some uncanny reason, like a nobleman in medieval times, signing my own death warrant. My first-day nightmare then began. The second person I met was a *CPO Wren with a moustache, built like a rugby prop-forward with arms and legs to match. We had to stand on a long bench and this 'female' began to throw us an enormous amount of kit which we had to stuff it into a large, stiff canvas thing we later found out was a kit-bag.* All the time CPO Hancock screamed at us to get a move on.

Then we went to the mess. It was spotless: A thought crossed my mind: *I wonder who cleans this place up?* Well! Guess who?

From there we were rushed off to the barber with CPO Hancock still screaming, where I experienced the fastest and shortest hair-cut in my life. At the speed in which those electric clippers sped over my scalp I am sure I could smell hair burning! From there to a queue for vaccinations; the sounds of the cries of pain, the smell of methylated spirits. I got three injections in my left arm and four in my right. God alone knew what terrible diseases were lurking around Shotley? With my arms about as much use as two lumps of lead, I was ushered into the dentist and had three teeth removed and four fillings. I was totally lost, miserable and felt like a production-line chicken. It put me off dentists for the rest of my life.

We had been given half-an-hour to pack away our new kit and then report to the dining-hall for dinner, but I forgot to ask where the dining-hall was, and the person I asked, a Scotsman, seemed to speak a foreign language, and he thought the same about me, but we wandered around together. I had lost a lot of things, including my teeth and my dignity, but I still had my sense of smell. Following our noses where the smell of food came from, we eventually found the dining-room where I sort of sucked at my meal, thanks to the demon dentist. I didn't really taste it, which may have been a blessing as it looked and smelled like school dinners. Then back to the mess where I suffered the final indignation of having to parcel up my new clothes which my Mum and Dad had saved up for. The next time I had a chance to try them on they didn't fit, I had out-grown them.

Finally to bed, feeling lost, home-sick, sore, tired, still hungry and thinking to myself, *'What have I done, surely things can't be as bad tomorrow?'* I was wrong! CPO Hancock was still screaming!!"

The next letter mentions the same CPO Hancock of the Annexe. The writer is **G.D. Searle,** and he is annoyed at the contents of my letter, which asked for humorous stories about Ganges. He obviously did not comprehend and understand the letter properly. He writes:

"I was a TROG (Trained Rating Of Ganges) and I was a bit annoyed at the reference to a concentration camp and 'internees.' To me it gave unknowing people the impression of being a form of a Borstal, and that all who went there were sent by the courts."

I wouldn't say that, G.D., it's really a matter of opinion and, as I will be accused of that many times throughout this book, the phrase: *'Ganges was the first, the last and the only concentration camp in England,'* was not, *repeat,* not mine, I merely referred to it. The phrase recurs voluntary by many other writers of letters in the book, and other, more vehement phrases are used in place of it. In any case, the remainder of **G.D. Searle's** letter, as follows, relates very much more of what happened in Ganges and *could* relate to concentration camps much better than most letters received about the Ganges regime, and, as for Borstal, the Borstal authorities who inspected Ganges when it was up for sale in the late 70's with a view to using it for that purpose, said it didn't match up to their high standards of accommodation!

G.D. continues: "Writing this I am thinking of all the high-lights and low points of my time at Ganges. *'The Pink Cafe'* at Harwich where a lot of us went at week-ends. I remember CPO Hancock of the Annexe who used to wake us at 0600 by throwing metal spit-kids and the dust-bin into the middle of the mess. There was one trainee who tried to work his ticket by hanging himself with a lanyard in a grounds-man's hut, but the structure of the hut was so rotten that the whole thing collapsed and nearly killed him!'

It is difficult to believe that the latter tale is by the same person who wrote to the 'Bush Telegraph' in his local Evening Telegraph saying that Ganges was definitely **NOT** as he himself admits that it is! And if those in charge of the Borstal dormitories were to use those spiteful and bullying methods of waking the in-mates, there would be protests in Parliament.

It is said that we tend to forget the bad times and remember only the good. As an instance, the summer days of our childhood school-day holidays were always bright and sunny. It never rained, and we remember them with wistful nostalgia, wishing for those good old days to return once more, if only to re-live the experiences of our youthful innocence. In some cases this is true for most of us, but where H.M.S. Ganges is concerned, the rule seems to be: The bad times were so bad that the good times have difficulty getting a mention, or remembered at all. Although H.M.S. Ganges is strenuously defended by those who love discipline, pomp and the bullshine, the smart and efficient guard-parades, the feeling of being able to overcome the atrocities, the harshness of the sometimes unfair discipline, the bullying Instructors, Instructor-Boys, and of the boys themselves who bullied their contempories in an attempt to be top-dog, the conspicuous fact which remains is that Ganges, whether or not it was intended, bred bullies - and bullying - they were condoned by the few who had sadistic and masochistic tendencies, making out that their policy of strict regime and harsh punishments were right, and those who oppose it are lesser persons. Most agree that Ganges deserved the title of 'concentration camp,' if only for it's infamy in the treatment of it's 'inmates.'

Bill Chapman, joined 15th January, 1946, writes: "It was interesting that Ganges has been called a concentration camp, my feelings exactly. It is said that, looking back, you will always remember the good times in life and forget most of the not-so-good. My memories of Ganges are quite the opposite. I remember the bad times very well and remember the good only vaguely. Two exceptions to this; I still have fond memories of the lads I served with, one in particular, Harry Edmunds. We met the day we joined and kept in touch over the years. The second is, I think, we were the first post-war Horn Pipe display team, performing at Christchurch Park, Ipswich, and, the crowning glory, Wembley Stadium.

My memory of the first day was that after all the joining routine, we had our first meal. I felt like Oliver Twist except that I didn`t ask for more, in fact, I didn`t eat any of the slop that was dished up. The second day, after 'stand-easy' in the canteen, the Instructor-Boys were shouting their heads off, telling everyone to get out. There was a rush for the narrow door as two hundred boys tried to get through at the same time, except me and my mate, Harry. The badge-boy shouted: 'If you don`t move faster you'll get my foot up your arses!'

I stopped, turned around, and told him what I would do to him if he did. He reported me and this led to an 'off caps' session before the Divisional Commander who said: 'This not a very good start to your naval career.' So I was punished.

The P.O. in charge of our mess was a Canadian. His punishment for me was two bed-chocks down the leg of the bell-bottoms and a full kit-bag of our brand-new kit on one shoulder, doubling up and down behind the galley."

Jack-booted Instructors.

"I still remember the experience today, travelling down to London with my empty suit-case, bound for Shotley. First time I had been away from home in my life; how nice everybody seemed to be in those first few hours," says ex **J.R.O. Proctor, 1963.** "We were bunked down in the Annexe with boys from all walks of life, everybody watching everyone else to see who were the strong and who the not-so-strong. Little did we know that even the strong would become meek at the hands of those jack-booted, white-gaitered Gestapo Instructors. Uniform was issued, all civilian trappings sent home, now we knew the reason for the empty suit-case which we had been told to bring along. Only the boys from Ireland were spared this indignity. They retained their 'civvies' to travel back home on leave to a country which, at the time, was hostile to England. Then the final ceremony where you signed your life away to something that could have been on a par with Hitler's youth, followed quickly by a standard hair-cut of very short back-and-sides which was repeated at regular intervals. I don't believe my hair ever recovered from this mauling. Days spent embroidering names onto uniforms, every last man thrown into the boxing ring, whether you could box or not. They wouldn't dare put an ABA champ with a no-hope wimp from Surrey would they? Yes, they would, and did. Today this would probably be looked upon as some sort of sexual hang-up. Group photographs at every opportunity, and you *had* to have a copy because money was stopped direct from our pay, and anyway, the camp photographer was in with all those Gestapo men. The ultimate make or break, climb that damn mast, go over the top and stand by. Anybody who chickened out was punished. Skinny-dipping in the swimming-pool, but not by choice. Everybody in the raw, off the top board, whether you could swim or not. Don't worry, that nice P.T.I. will pull you out with his pole, but not before he had bashed you around the head with it. Six weeks later, a triumphant march over to the Main Establishment. Things could only get better. 50 pence per week pocket money to buy everything you needed down to toothpaste, this was really the Big Time! Accommodation which was pre-war, living in the drying-room to keep warm in winter, polishing those wooden floors that shone like glass. We spent hours on the parade-ground doing drill or doubling round it late at night with your bedding on your head because some prat spoke after lights-out. Or doubling up and down the Long Covered Way for some obscure misdemeanor which someone else had committed. We also had to endure the 'cuts' of the cane for those more serious offences. What would be said today about such acts of barbarism?

Boys went to Ganges as toughs, scruffs, rough-nuts, or wimps. 99% of those who finished the course came out as proud young men, ready to charter their course in the world as independant individuals. Sure, there were bad times, but the 'ups' out-weighed the 'downs,' and the wimps had become strong and the rough-nuts stronger but tamed, and it was a strength that was used to good effect, not for bashing old ladies over the head for a few pounds. We stood on that parade-ground on passing-out day, not as individuals, hell-bent on destroying everything, like today, but as a team, having endured the rigours of being trained to take our place in society. What a pity society today would not tolerate such an establishment, and yet it tolerates such mis-guided and mis-directed hard-ship, violence or what-ever.

I would do it all again tomorrow."

Record jankers.

G.H. Padley has a nice sense of humour. His story is one of injustice, humour and joining. It would fit all three, but because it is about the first day in the navy, it belongs here:

"I joined the Ganges in July, 1926. I shall never forget the first day. 0645 on the parade-ground for half-an-hour`s run round. The second time round I dropped out and slipped into the toilet. I had no sooner got my trousers down when - BANG! - a slap round the ear. I was taken on the quarter-deck to the Officer of the Watch. That nearly frightened me to death. I received seven days jankers for being absent from post of duty. Dinner-time I had to go to the galley for the dinners. The Petty Officer who was supposed to let us into the galley arrived late, so when he did arrive everyone booed him, but only in fun. Some fun! We all got seven days jankers for 'unbecoming conduct!'

The sweet that day was an apple. Someone threw an apple core across the mess, just as P.O. Williams walked in. The whole mess got another seven days jankers.

I thought, *'Well, that was that. I can`t get into any more trouble now, I`ve had the lot!'* But during the first part of jankers, running round the parade-ground, with me, muggins, in front, someone, who I thought was our Instructor, yelled: 'Come back you stupid bastards!' I, being green, thought he meant, 'Turn around!' So I did an about-turn, and bumped into the bloke behind me. Needless to say, I got another seven days jankers. The first twelve hours in the navy, I got a total of 28 days jankers, just for being green!"

Someone else who was green in more senses than one, is **Jimmy Green:** Ron (Jimmy) Green, September, 1946, says he was luckier than most because he had been able to look after himself at home and had worked away for a short while. Other boys, he goes on, had a mother or family to look after them and found Ganges a very hard and traumatic experience. Despite that, the Annexe still gave him a few surprises which he didn't expect.

"We arrived in the late evening and were taken to the dining hall where we greeted with a meal of dried-up chips, fish, and peas like ball-bearings. This was served on steel plates which smelled of kippers and washing-up water. These steel plates had the remarkable quality of storing odours deep into the metal and, combined with the steel mugs, made for an interesting gastronomic experience.

After the meal we were herded to a building and allocated a bed, told how to undress, clean teeth - even urinate - and warnings of 'no noise, no talking, and definitely no leaving the building.' To the average fifteen or sixteen year-old-boy, came the sudden realisation of a great mistake: *Devil's Island, Alcatraz, Dartmoor...Oh, mother, what have I done?* The next day we met our Petty Officer. He came in at six o'clock and it was like a cyclone had struck. About three weeks later, at about nine o'clock in the evening, we were made to wash, put on our pyjamas and sit to attention on the end of our beds. One of our Instructors was holding court and we all listened intently, not daring to do otherwise, and the Instructor told a some-what feeble joke. There was a polite titter all round, but I, having a strange sense of humour, and finding it quite funny, laughed uproariously.

Oh, you stupid boy. What have you done? I thought.

The Instructor ordered me to stand in front of him.

'So,' he said. 'You thought that was funny did you?'

Fool that I was, I said: 'Yes, sir,' and smiled.

The Instructor grimaced, and went several shades redder in the face.

'Bend down, boy,' he suggested, fairly quietly, I thought.

I bent over and he kicked me up the backside with his booted foot.

Bloody hell! That bloody-well hurt!

After three or four kicks he said: 'Did that hurt?'

Like an idiot I said: 'Just a bit.'

'Well see if this hurts a bit more then,' he said and started kicking me again. I counted fourteen times in all, and though I was very close to

28

tears, I did not want the rest of the boys to see me cry. I think he realised I had had enough, and probably his bloody leg ached anyway, so I was allowed to return to my bed. I thought twice about laughing about anything that anyone said after that. This was just one incident that occurred whilst I was at H.M.S. Ganges, but maybe it made us more able to accept the discipline that was demanded of young, or indeed, all boy seaman at that time. It certainly made one appreciate the easy-going life of a civilian..."

"I have no individual stories that I can recall after this lapse in time," writes Ex P.O. Electrician, previously P.O. T.I. **N.O. Baker** of 1937. "What does still stand out is our first introduction to the rigours of the Shotley concentration camp during our first week's stay in their first-class accommodation. We were lodged in the Annexe before transferring to the 3-star section of the covered way.

Someone inadvertently spoke after 'lights out.' This was not to the liking of our duty P.O.'s, their names: P.O. Foulger & C.P.O. Battler, so we were requested to adjourn to the parade-ground with our new stiff oilskins put on back-to-front, new kit-bags on our backs, fully loaded, and made to double around the parade-ground until such times as three or four of our happy band collapsed from exhaustion. To appreciate this, one must realise that none of us were more than sixteen years of age and the first time away from home. Pay-day meant we were richer by two shillings and sixpence; that afternoon was one of glutting. A bottle of pop and a couple of 'charlies,' one penny each. In Yarmouth, my home town, they were called 'Nelsons' and made of stale cakes in a sort of bread-pudding mix. I still like them to this day. Another recall; early morning trips over the mast; in the Laundry, on hands and knees with a bar of pusser's-hard, washing your blanket; polishing the long mess-deck floors. Great days!"

Were they *really* `great days?` Do you **really** mean that?

Michael Pratt, the next story-teller, thought so, but he by-passed Ganges, thanks to the foresight of his caring parents who had probably heard of it's reputation.

The one who didn`t join.

Michael Pratt was 15, going on 16, in 1934 - going on 1935, and he lived at Diss: "I was mad about the Royal Navy," Michael says, "and I used to cycle from Diss to Shotley on Sundays, a round-trip of about 70 miles, just to see the boys in their uniforms, and wishing I was in there with them. It was not to be, my parents were adamant that I should not join the R.N., at least, not as a boy. But I did join at 18 at Chatham as a 'sprog' Stoker, and left 27 years later as Chief Mechanician. The happiest days of my life. I still go down to Shotley, by car now, and have a meal at the 'Bristol,' visit the Marina, and have a look at the photo's of Ganges in the bar entrance."

Time does indeed dim the memory - it not only dims the memory but stretches the imagination - or distances from one place to another. For one ex-boy, **Syd Baker,** 1949, time increased the length of the Gunnery School in distance from the main establishment. In my time I recall it could have been not much more than about 600 to 800 yards. Syd claims it was two miles. But then, he had reason to believe so. According to Syd: "The Gunnery School, which was roughly two miles from the main camp, was a favourite of the Instructors. While they walked there, the class was made to double, then, when far enough ahead, the Instructor would order them to 'About turn!' So, in fact, the class ran more than ten miles before starting a rigorous Gunnery Class."

Chapter three

ᎧᎻᎬ ᏜᎯᏚᎧ!

It is surprising how memories of the past which leave indelible impressions upon our minds, and sometimes, with devilish deviation, displaces their position to elsewhere, enlarges it`s height, or sometimes diminishes it. One ex-boy writes claiming: *"The mast was in the corner of the parade ground."* Oh! Was it? No, it wasn't. *"In the centre of the parade-ground was the mast,"* corrects **George Skidmore**.

It was, and still is, and always will be - as a protected monument - situated at the extreme edge of the parade-ground perimeter at the quarter-deck end. This estimated position takes into account the space needed to accommodate the safety-net and provide an equal net area on all four sides. It is, therefore, located several feet *inwards* for that purpose.

The height of the mast varies, depending which version one reads about it. The booklet, "`Way Aloft!" a history of the Ganges mast by John Webb, states: `The overall height is 143ft." That figure comprises of: *"Lower mast, 75ft, Topmast 47ft.6ins., Topgallant mast 45ft. Lower Yard 68ft., Topsail yard 56ft. 5ins., Topgallant Yard 42ft., Gaff 49ft."* Then some interesting information that: *"The mast is set in concrete some 18 feet deep. A further sixty tons of cement anchors the shrouds and stays, in the form of clumps and pickets. There is approximately one mile of rigging, ranging in size from four-inch steel wire ropes down to half-inch wire ropes used for stays, lifts and braces."* That is as near to the exact truth as possible, but observed at different angles and personal points of view, the dimensions change:

"I believe it was 175 feet high and a real old-fashioned 18th century Main Mast with rope rigging," continues George Skidmore, continuing his description of the mast with a commendable, dramatic account of the traumas which confronted young, innocent and very frightened boys, some who were terrified beyond the point of vertigo. "Part of our training was when the Instructor ordered us to line-up against the rigging; six boys across, facing the rigging. The command, 'Go!' was given, and we had to clamber up the rigging and race upwards to the Devil`s elbow. Then, as we negotiated the elbow, pulling ourselves up by our arms, our feet and legs would leave the rigging, leaving us dangling about sixty feet from the deck, and we then had to haul

ourselves up by our arms again to the next part of the rigging. Further upwards, the rigging got quite narrow as it reached the half-moon platform, so that fewer boys could proceed, then the top, where just one boy at a time could squeeze over for the downward journey, harrowing, scaring, frightening, it was a nightmare for heights, but grit your teeth, think of England and when you touched the ground how relieved you were. This was done every day for weeks on end until you completed the climb in under 3 minutes. The record was 1 minute 14 seconds. What seemed impossible at the start, was gradually conquered. As regard to safety, there was none. Remember, we were young boys, soon, I may add, to become men."

There *was* a safety-net, raised about eight feet from the ground, and it saved many lives. One boy fell from the yard-arm, landed on the safety-net and bounced up and away to land again and fall through the roof of the parcel-office on the corner of the Short Covered Way. And, according to the book, "Way Aloft!" it was not unknown for boyes to dare each other to leap from the lower yardarm to land on the safety-net. Some boys loved the mast, some hated it, most conquered it. Only a few refused to climb it and most of those were discharged to civvy street.

Unfair criticisms of Ganges

Bitter criticisms about the rigours and unfairness of the Ganges regime can, in some places, be reduced to trivial complaints of being deprived of certain diverse privileges such as being unable to watch television on certain memorable sporting occasions, or having to attend classes for the terrors of being `*taught to swim.*` The latter complainants were non-swimmers. The worst and most real terror was a fear of heights, particularly when the vertigous victim was forced to climb the mast. Comfort could be sought in the swimming-pool by a non-swimmer, knowing there were several P.T.I.`s present, But when you are aloft you are the only one you can rely on.

Mast-class took place at various intervals for every mess at certain times. Not many looked forward to it, but some of the boys always did. No-one is brave who perform feats of which they are not nervous about. The brave are those who are terribly frightened and force themselveto do what they are afraid to do.

In the lifetime of Ganges the mast was three different things to various people: those who liked to climb it; those who appreciated and loved it`s artistic lines, but suffered from vertigo and dared not to master it`s terrifying height and climb to the button. The third are those who could climb it but did not appreciate it`s beauty and soporific influence. All parties loved it, it gave them the joy of pleasure, and another, different pleasure, that of fear and the conquering of that fear, and those who loved it because the mast was Ganges. Those two latter ones were, and are, inseparable even to this day. The mast is now a protected monument and the Ganges Association of Old Boys contribute to it's upkeep. It seems that it will always stand as a nostalgic reminder of the old days. And so it should be.

Euphoria!

K.F.D. Bushnell, of North Humberside, who exclaimed: - 'I loved it!' - not only loved it but he was so enamoured that it imposed upon him a state of euphoria, oblivious and deaf to the outside world, including unheard tannoyed instructions during inclement weather, rain, hail, snow, mist, fog, to "Clear the mast!"

"One of my greatest pleasures whilst at Ganges was climbing the mast," says K.F.D., "And, in particular, sitting on the button, admiring the wonderful all-round view. So there I was, above the cloud of mist, totally in a world of my own enjoying the solitude and tranquillity, unaware that I was being surrounded below by an incoming sea-mist. Unknown to me, due to the weather conditions, the mast had been cleared by a Leading Patrolman from the Main Gate. Thirty minutes later I descended, feeling light-headed and happy with myself having enjoyed yet another visit in the sky. I can only describe the moment my feet touched the ground as one of the memorable and momentous times of my life at Ganges.

On descending the mast, looking up through the safety netting, my thoughts were, 'Another safe landing.' But then I was confronted by a somewhat irate Leading Regulator who had spotted me descending. Standing there, literally shaking in my gym shoes, the dialogue, minus foul language, went like this:

'Where the hell have you been!!?'

'Up the mast, sir.' *I thought it was obvious; where else could I have been?*

'I know you've been up the mast. I cleared the mast thirty minutes ago. Where the hell were you?' Another silly question. *There was only one place I could possibly have been.*

'On the button, sir.'

By this time, steam was venting from beneath his hat.

'Another so-and-so wise-cracking answer like that and you will feel the so-and-so end of my so-and-so boot!'

After a lengthy ticking off on so-and-so safety, so-and-so mast-

climbing and so-and-so weather conditions, he sent me on my so-and-so way with a flow of so-and-so's ringing in my ears. Walking back down the Long Covered Way, I can remember quite clearly talking to myself, thinking, *how else could I have answered him when it was very obvious, and he knew very well where I had been? Up the so-and-so mast all the so-and-so time!*
I must have had a smile on my face for a week. More to the point, I bet the Leading Patrolman must have had a good laugh back in the mess."
Another ex-Boy who loved it is **Robert W. Hind** of the mid-sixties. He also experienced the euphoria of the solitude of the mast, but enhanced that euphoria by lounging around on the main yard-arm reading the Sunday newspapers. "I used to climb the mast on a Sunday morning and climb through the rigging to nestle myself on the main yard-arm under the fighting-top to lean on the massive chain, and there I would read the Sunday paper in peace. I remember one morning an officer, looking up, and calling to me:
'What are you doing boy?'
I replied: 'Reading the paper, sir!'
With a look of complete bemusement he said: 'Very well. Carry on.'
I remember a stoker named Morgan, who came from Bristol. One Thursday he climbed the mast, stood on the button, and saluted the four points of the compass, north, south, east and west. I loved the mast!''

'I **hated** it!'

Charlie Kent, one of the brave `cowards` who has other stories elsewhere, tells of his fear of the mast and how he overcame it.
"On arrival at Ganges, it was early morning of November 12th, that Bill Webster, my mate, on being informed that the biscuits and cocoa was our breakfast, we decided to go home. On walking towards the Main Gate, what do I see but this awesome-looking thing, the mast, my first thought was to get going fast away from it, for I know if I stayed I would be expected to climb it at least once. This was not for me, heights and I don`t get on. We were stopped from leaving and the next day we were expected to climb it. I said to my mate: 'I shall never climb that.' I knew in my heart that I was going to flinch out of it, and this is what happened: there I stood, ashamed, feeling so cowardly, in front of all. The Instructor shouted: 'Alright, Kent! Away aloft!'
'No, sir,' I pleaded. 'Please don`t order me away aloft,' and I stoutly refused the order, ready to accept whatever punishment may come

my way. None came, but the stigma of being a failure was awful. One or two of the lads felt for me, especially my pal, Bill. And what a pal. He suggested that he and I should have a go at it each day. This we did and with the feeling of terror inside of me, I made it, then twice more, but each time it drained me. How the young chap, the button boy, could climb to the button, stand upon it and send semaphore to the RAF at Felixtowe across the harbour, I will never know. But a proud moment came for me when my two P.O. Instructors complimented me for doing it and overcoming my fear of the height, but I have never got over height, even today. I still live in fear of it.

Years later, I returned after many years to Ipswich with my wife, and it was whilst my wife and I were travelling back to London, we decided to go round to Shotley. As we approached the Ganges we could see the Mast. She then said: 'There's your friend.' I nearly said a very rude word about it, but the words never came. On entering the Ganges, my wife and I just stood there, gazing up. And then she turned to me and said, 'You climbed that?' knowing my fear of height. She squeezed my hand, and I felt so proud, tears arrived, the thought came over to me: 'I nearly beat you, you so-and-so, if I had only made it to the button, what a feeling that would have been.'

Brains spilled out

Tug Wilson joined in October, 1939. "The only thing that sticks in my memory after all these years, while climbing the mast, a boy above me fell onto the safety-net. I looked down and thought his brains had spilled out but it turned out he had only been sick."

"I joined Ganges in November, 1945," says **A.L. Walton.** "I was in Hawke Division over-looking the parade-ground, Nelson Hall and the mast. I had a good view of those on number 11a doing jankers and was unlucky enough to join them on a few occasions with the infamous Petty Officer Delarue, who made them frog-hop with a .303 rifle held above their heads until they keeled over.

'Cruel and barbaric.'

In our mess were identical twins called Tompson. They came to Ganges from Hospital Training Ships as did quite a few. One of them would go up the rigging of the mast, about twenty feet, and go no further without the other one, who wouldn't get on the rigging at all. You don't leave Ganges 'til you have been over the mast, so there was a problem which was solved by one of the twins going over twice, impersonating the other. Ganges was hard, it was cruel and barbaric, but I'm still proud to be an ex-Shotley boy."

Cameron, V.C.

Tony Worthington, March, 1949: "I remember my first Divisional Officer, after three weeks basic training, was Lt. Cdr. Cameron, VC. He won his Victoria Cross taking part in the midget submarine attack on the Tirpitz in a Norwegian Fjord. If one was sent before him for some minor misdemeanour, the trick was to get him on the subject of submarines. He either forgot what you had been sent for or he let you off lightly. I have a vivid memory of climbing the mast on cold and frosty mornings. The Instructors made a race of it, and if we did not go over within a set time, we were made to climb it again. I remember a young Welsh boy named Dewe Williams who climbed half-way up and froze with fright. He could neither go up nor down. I and another boy were instructed to go up and bring him down. It was quite frightening as the poor lad was hanging on for dear life. To make matters worse, other boys were still engaged in racing over the mast, resulting in a violent shaking of the rat-lin's. It took us quite some time to get him down."

Piddled on from a great height..

J. Whittle, 1939: "Times were really hard. It didn't matter whether you were good or bad, the whole mess suffered if someone put a foot wrong. We were called at five in the morning and marched to the mast. The dress was shorts, shirt, no underwear. Then it was, 'Off shoes and socks!' And then a check for anyone wearing under-wear. The snow was six inches deep. The next order: 'First six up the mast and over the trucks, not under the truck.' I'll always remember this as when I approached the truck, a little ginger-headed boy called Proctor above me, was shaking with fear, and, as he went out and over the Devil's elbow he piddled all over my head. Down we all came and fell in; next order: 'Pick up your shoes and socks and double across the parade ground to the swimming bath, strip off and jump in the deep end, out the other and into the cold showers' Then back back to the mess for one dog biscuit and a cup of cocoa."

The 'ginger-headed boy' obviously had a lot of guts - good job he didn't let those go as well!

Return trip

"I remember one occasion when C.P.O. Cubitt caught a group of us pillow-fighting in our mess after 'lights out,'" writes **John Graham,** June, 1951. "As punishment," he continues, "The entire mess complement was fallen-in outside in our pyjamas and oilskins, marched from the bottom of the Long Covered Way to the parade-ground and ordered to climb the famous 148ft high mast in the dark and the middle of winter. After completing the climb, which left us blue with cold, the Chief asked us if we still felt boisterous, and, unfortunately, someone sniggered. You can guess the rest. We were sent back up the mast and eventually back to our mess. How no-one suffered from exposure that night is one of life's mysteries."

"Burst into tears..."

"My name is **Joe Ray** and I joined as an ex-internee in 1958, Drake, 39 mess. When we came over to the 'Main' after six weeks in the Annexe, every boy had to go over the mast. When it was our mess to go we all lined-up in rows at the bottom of the rigging. I was in the second row of four, terrified out of my wits, thinking, *'There is no way I am going up there.'* To this day I have never been so frightened. Anyway, I kept dodging back and back until I was in the last row of four. As we got up to the rungs, I burst into tears. A certain Petty Officer Ling, bellowed in my ear: **'What's a matter with you, lad?!'**

I stood there, tears streaming down my face. I said:

'I am frightened I will fall off, sir.'

His reply was: 'There is no chance of that, lad. None whatsoever!'

Me, thinking he knew something I didn't, I said: 'What makes you so sure, sir?' I blubbered, sensing a ray of hope. 'BECAUSE YOU WILL BE HOLDING ON TOO BLOODY TIGHT TO LET GO! NOW GET UP THERE!'

I did finally go over the mast, and I will never, ever forget that experience. I don't know if you will find it as funny as I do."

No, not funny, Joe. Courageous. But, not trying to detract from that courage, were you more frightened of the P.O. than the mast?

There was always one kindly person to encourage the timid by frightening the life out of them. **Stanley Hunt:** "It was war-time and I was on a Naval Division Class in 1943. We all had to climb the infamous mast. We had to go round the shoulders and not through the 'funk-holes' of the platforms. I was scared but there was no way I could get out of it. I voiced my feelings to a Chief P.O. who looked like the Ancient Mariner who was standing nearby. He looked old enough to be a refugee from Trafalgar, he was watching from the foot of the mast. He said, gruffly: 'Don't worry, lad. If you fall off there's a safety-net. Trouble is, if you hit that from the top, you pop out underneath as chips....' I was even more scared, but I climbed it."

Heavenly choirs from above

Jolly Jack always triumphs with his exuberance, boyancy of spirit and cheerful, positive thinking. A war-time Hostilities Only rating,

Sandy Powell, (*mind my bike!*) 1940, sets the scene as precisely as only a matelot returning from shore-leave, with a skinful of booze beneath his belt, could do so:

"H.M.S. Ganges, 1940. Parade ground. Returning from a run-ashore in Ipswich and crossing the parade-ground in the dark, I could hear singing from above. I didn't quite catch the words, but it certainly wasn't hymns, more like the singing of a sods-opera and other obscenities in the Fleet Canteen. Was I going barmy, or what? The war-time beer was not all that strong, surely?

There was a sudden, far-off sound, gradually increasing to a tumultous crescendo, and I realised, out of the darkness, there were several Crushers charging across the quarterdeck towards the mast. I knew then that the Heavenly chorus from above was coming from several drunken matelots perched in various positions in various places upon the mast. The Crushers stood at the bottom, shouting and bawling for the matelots to come down, which they eventually did. They were all ticked off by the Officer of the Watch and let off. It was war-time and sometimes discipline could be relaxed.

Owing to continuing air-raids we spent nearly every night in the shelters. Bunting Tossers and Sparkers were falling asleep during the afternoon, so the Instructors and us were all shunted to Higham Court, under canvas outside Gloucester. We complained about no toilet paper in the Heads and next day two Spitfires flew over and dropped toilet rolls all over the site! Also at Higham Court there was a big, craggy Lieutenant Commander named Sylvest. He was six foot five inches tall. I thought at the time he was the one in the song, 'My brother, Sylvest, who has a row of 40 medals on his chest!'" **Gordon (Sandy) Powell, H.O. 1940.**

The final story also takes place during the war. **Joe Carroll,** ex-Stoker 1st class, was not a Ganges Boy, but his story illustrates the dedication and concern for their Boys by some Instructors:

"At the end of the war I was serving as a one-badge Stoker on BYMMS 2252. We were tied up third in a 'trot' at Parkestone Quay, Harwich, doing an engine-oil change. The easiest way to get the oil aboard was to throw the 30-gallon drum in the river, tow it round the stern of the ship, remove the guards rails and lift the drum inboard on the derrick. This we did, but on swinging the derrick inboard, the clamp on the wet drum slipped off. The drum came down like a bomb. I jumped back out of the way, but fell over the bollard behind me. The rim of the drum hit my outstretched leg, almost severing it. Feeling numb and shocked, and standing where the paravanes were, minus guard-rails, I just toppled overboard into the river. On surfacing between the ships I managed to hang onto a slack stern line which was trailing the water. Help arrived and I was dragged out with a broken tibia and fibia. I was shipped across the river to Ganges, there to be plastered and put to bed. Now, at this time, the navy had just started taking in boy sailors again. After a couple of days in bed, a Petty Officer was brought into the next bed to me with lacerations all over his body. It turned out he had been training the boy sailors to climb the mast. One of them got to the top, lost his nerve and daren't come down again. The P.O. went up, and, cradling the lad inside his body, he said: 'Come on, we'll go down together.'

They got half-way down over the Devil's elbow and, with their backs to the ground, the lad lost his nerve again, let his legs slip from the rigging, and knocking the P.O. completely off the mast. Hence the lacerations. He bounced off and hit all the rigging coming down, struck the safety net and rebounded out onto the concrete below.

The irony of it was, the lad managed to climb down on his own. That P.O. must have been hardy: in a couple of days he was out and about drilling the lads again.''

There was at least one deliberate suicide; a Boy leapt from the yard-arm onto the parade-ground. The following illustration, taken from a Shotley magazine, is not , and is not intended to be, related to that latter incident.

I'LL HAVE HIS SUPPER !

Chapter four
"Britain's Naval Penitentiary..."
"As men we were treated like boys..."

Ex. Tel. **F. Weddell,** Feb 41. "I was a member of that establishment, Ganges, so aptly described as *Britain's Naval Penitentiary.* I had volunteered in 1940 for the Royal Navy as a telegraphist. In February of 1941 I entered the Annexe at Shotley. A brief stay, and a rig-out, and, with great anticipation, along with other excited recruits, we entered the Main Establishment, H.M.S GANGES two weeks later. I felt now I was in the *real* Navy! It was an unexplainable sense of excitement.

Two colleagues, whom I had be-friended, and myself set out to explore this fascinating place with the huge mast and the many buildings from where all types of sailors and Petty Officers seemed to be coming and going. We left our mess, 25 mess, Grenville, near the bottom of the Long Covered Way, and went for a walk.

Our first shock was when, coming out of the Covered Way and admiring the ensign flying from a gaff, and calmly walking towards the parade-ground, a loud voice bellowed: 'YOU RATINGS! - COME HERE!' Being eighteen years old I was petrified when returning and confronted with a stern-faced Petty Officer.

'Who the hell do you think you *are*? <u>Walking</u> across the quarter-deck?' This to three rookies who naturally just thought it to be a wee short-cut through an ordinary roadway. We learned later that there was nothing 'ordinary' about anything at Ganges. I spoke out with one of those 'lost in the throat' voices:

'I'm sorry, sir, but we have just come from the Annexe and were unaware this was the quarter-deck. I'm really sorry, sir.'

'Don't call me 'SIR!' he shouted, without relaxing the intensity of his voice. 'Only *officers* need to be called *SIR!*' he thundered: 'The flag in this establishment always flies on the quarter-deck. When you arrive at the quarter-deck you stop, salute smartly, and double across. Now then! The three of you, about turn, and smartly *double* across. *Double!'*

Being our first day it was a criterion of what to expect - discipline to the extreme. Though this was war-time, the recruits were given the same treatment which younger Boys got before us. 5.30 a.m. Backward swimmers to the baths. Cold shower and P.T.I.'s with belts to whack our buttocks if we did not cold-shower first. I'm certain we had the cream of sadistic P.T.I.'s over-lording us.

And so life went on. Christmas leave with T.A.B. in one arm, vaccination in the other, going back to the backward-swimmers class, cold water, wet duck-suits, pale blue lighting in the pool, making it look like a big ice-berg, which it was. Two minutes to get dry and dressed, fall in outside and God help the last boy out.

Boat pulling on the river, wind, snow, hail - made no difference, bumped into a moored submarine one day. Thought, *'This is it. The Tower at least, pictures of jankers, running around the parade ground with a rifle for ever.'* But the sub turned out to be a wooden decoy.

I don't remember making any friends at Ganges, it was just survival! No, that's the wrong word, *'endurance of the regime,'* knowing that it had to end sometime, and eventually a ship where life would be better. It turned out that the regime continued at sea with a horror of an Instructor. Men's work for Boys' pay. We left Ganges early 1940 and went to H.M.S. Impregnable, Plymouth. Two rows of bell-tents, overlooking the school; watched bombs falling on Devonport; barrage-balloons being shot down, all very exciting to us. Planes flew low, machine-gunning between our two rows of tents. So we moved again. One week's leave, then reported to Liverpool for passage to Isle of Man to Cunninghams Holiday Camp in Douglas. Eventually went to sea on H.M.S. Hermoine."

Never stopped crying for a week...

R.F. Beales, May/June 1947: "I remember every morning in the Annexe we were awakened with: 'Wakey! Wakey! Hands off cocks, put on socks!' Then up and over the 180ft mast. A rude awakening for most of us. One big lad, I recall, never stopped crying for a week and was sent home."

G. Blackburn tried to join, November 1939, with about 20 other boys. "We arrived at Harwich in the late evening, and boarded a small ferry for the trip to Shotley. Then the order came: 'Everybody off!' So back we clambered onto the jetty. The Petty Officer in charge of our party threatened us with a fate worse than death if we wandered off. 'I'm going to find out what's happening,' he said, and came back later to our party saying: 'This boat is needed for rescue work. A destroyer has struck a mine just outside the Harbour.'

I think it was the `Gypsy,` so he took us along the front where we could see a lot of activity going on a short way off-shore. Searchlights, shouting, boats bobbing about. To most of us it didn't mean much, just a bit of excitement. We were taken to a Y.M.C.A.

Hostel and given a meal, then we bedded-down upon mattresses on the floor. Breakfast next morning onboard our boat, over to Shotley, and so started our training.

Two weeks in the Annexe, nightly air-raid practices and down the shelters, pyjamas, oilskins, football boots for grip, and a foot of water in every shelter.''

G. Blackburn's ship was later torpedoed, but he survived to tell the above tale.

Jack Thwaite: "What a change there was when we returned to Ganges after Easter Leave, 1940. 'Hostility Only' ratings were joining; buses renovated into ambulances lay alongside the drill shed to be used to ferry to the mortuary bodies of the crew of *H.M.S. Gypsy* and passengers from the Dutch Merchantman *Isaac Swears* which had been sunk by magnetic mines when entering Harwich. I will never forget the sight of the pathetic bundles of men, women and children laid out in rows by the Methodist chapel when my mate and I, against orders, sneaked down to satisfy our curiosity. A month or so later Holland fell to the invading armies and it was decided to remove all the boys from Shotley. It must have been decided at very short notice; our class was marching down to the signal school when we were suddenly ordered to return to our Mess. We changed into working rig and were doubled down to the jetty and spent the rest of the day, and well into the night, loading kit-bags and hammocks into lighters, taking them across the river and loading them into railway waggons for onward transporting to an ex-Holiday Camp on the Isle of Man."

Sandy Burgess of Falmouth recalls the 'Gypsy' hitting the mine. He joined in May, 1939. "The first thing to catch my attention was a bunch of 'old hands' who had been in the navy at least four weeks, jeering and shouting: 'NOZZER!' at us. I remember being given a kipper to eat along with a mug of cold tea, followed by a lecture by a Petty Officer, then off to bed. *I admit I cried that night.*

Next morning I came face-to-face with the stark reality that I was in for twelve years after the age of 18, and resigned myself to whatever was in store. Boys who joined up at this age, 15, before the war, could be put in one of four categories. Some came direct from boys' training establishments, i.e. Barnardo's, Arethusa, etc., others from very poor families, some, who had fallen foul of the law, and were encouraged to join the services - or else, and those who just joined for adventure and to see the world. But we were all the same from day one and treated as such. The months that followed was high-pressure intensive training with a little time for recreation, but hardly any time to think or get homesick - things were even stepped up after the war was declared on 3rd September.

I clearly remember Shotley Routine, and took part in it on several occasions - this was a special routine devised by some sadist in which an entire class of 60 would be punished if one of that class committed an offence, this in itself was a killer and was designed with one aim - to make or break.

In the early days of the war, when my class was approaching the end of training, we were called out in the middle of the night. A Dutch ship, called `Simon Bolivar,` which was carrying a large number of passengers, had struck one of the new magnetic mines and sunk off Harwich. We manned the cutters and were towed out to sea by a pinnace to spend the rest of the night recovering bodies from the sea - mostly women and children - we were growing up quickly! Shortly after this incident, *H.M.S. Gypsy,* a destroyer, hit a similar mine when entering harbour. She broke in two and one half finished ashore at the Harwich side and the other half was beached on the Felixtowe side near the Sunderland flying-boat hangars."

Sandy survived the war and was finally promoted to Chief. Unlike most others who went to Ganges, and decided they had suffered or not suffered, but still held some, if not a lot of affection for the old place, Sandy did not seem to have any affection at all for Ganges. Unfortunately Sandy died in April, 1994 before this book, and his story, was published. His wife, Pam, still lives in Falmouth.

A.W. Buxton, 1939, presents a couple of horror stories but says: "If I had my time over again, I'd still go back. I was in 44 Mess, Collingwood and life was hard, but after a couple of months I did not mind it too much. I did not like early morning bath, getting up at five o'clock and going down to the bath-house for a luke-warm or cold shower. The duty P.O. sitting at the desk with his book of names, then standing in front of him with arms out-stretched. If he did not feel too sharp he would cut you across the arse with his lanyard with the words: 'Go back and give yourself another scrub!'

We were always hungry but looked forward to pay-day for our shilling pay. With that we used to buy a couple of 'Charlies' three-ha'pence a go. Smoking was absolutely forbidden.There was a Royal Marine who used to prowl around during the afternoon and dog-watches, trying to catch boys smoking. The first offence was six cuts dished out down at the guard house on Saturday morning. The Crushers were experts at laying them on about an inch apart; the marks used to stand out like red fingers on a boy's bum. One of the boys in the Mess had to be circumcised. When he came back from the Sick Bay, we all had a look at the result. It looked as though he had been to the butchers, but everybody agreed he had gained an inch!"

Knowing Jack-me-Hearty and his usual pre-occupation with his private parts, it is surprising the whole mess did not immediately volunteer for the same operation!

'Cried all night..'

John Beeley relates: "I joined Ganges on 13th February, 1934 - the date is etched on my brain - wearing my best blue pin-striped suit, what a mistake! I was disgorged onto Shotley pier from the steam pinnace which had brought us over from Harwich, where the half-dozen of us were fallen in by a very self-important Instructor Boy, and doubled all the way up to the Nozzer`s mess. There, we were met by an old P.O. Instructor who marched us to the clothing store and issued with the essentials of loan clothing. Our 'civvies' were bundled up, labelled, and put into a steam chest where they were cooked overnight. My suit, when I got it back some three months later when going on leave, was ruined; so shrunk and creased that it would only have fitted a pygmy. By the time we got back to the mess it was dark. We were among the last arrivals, most had been there a few days, and the sight of those chaps in their ill-fitting clothes and shaven-heads was pretty shattering. There was one chap who cried all night, and all the next forenoon. He was sent home the next day. Another wouldn't, or couldn't climb the futtock-rigging on the large mast in the main establishment, and despite much goading from the Training Officer and the Commander, who were both up there with him, threatening everlasting jankers, cuts, and anything else they could think of, he just would not budge. He was sent home the next day.

We eventually went over to the Main Establishment where I was put into a Communications class as a telegraphist. For rifle drill we had a seaman Chief Gunnery Instructor who didn`t like Communications classes, and always greeted us, 'Ah! We`ve got the intelligence department today, have we?' Some seamen always resented the fact that to be a communicator you had to have a higher-than-average I.Q. We didn`t like him much either! However, I do not recall that his grudge went further than the above remark. He treated us fairly.

Smoking was forbidden, as was the possession of cigarettes or matches. But there were some boys who went to extreme risks to sastisfy their addiction; how they came by their meagre supply of smoking material I shall never know. Lack of a match was no handicap because there were fuse-boxes in the mess, and withdrawing one of the fuses slightly would cause it to arc, thereby giving a spark to light the cigarettes from. Three or four 'draggers' would share a cigarette, or part of one, with a look-out posted to warn of the approach of authority. Penalties, if caught, were severe: 14 days jankers, or, if you were a persistent offender, you got six cuts admistered by a Crusher in the Guardhouse. Although sometimes fierce, our Instructors did have their human side, and I remember a couple of occasions when out sailing, the Yeoman pulled a box of 'Players' out of his pocket and gave us a cigarette each when the coast was clear. Great care had to be taken not to drop ash or cigarette-ends in the boat in case it was noticed by alien Crushers or Marine Corporals. I left Ganges on 3rd March, 1935 and left the navy in 1948 as a Petty Officer Telegraphist. In civvy street I became a Works Manager and later served part-time in the RNZS as an MFV skipper and then a small minesweeper. I never re-visited Ganges, not that I hated it, but there has never been an opportune moment, and, having spent ten years working out of the Port of Liverpool I consider that all the seamanship I learned at Ganges was not wasted after all."

The 'Tiddley-suit' tailor...

"I can't remember the name of our Instructor Boy," remarks **Dick McBurney,** July, 1948, "But he did a roaring trade in selling us a variety of naval badges to which of course we were not entitled. More about those later.

My memories of the Annexe are dominated by Welsh rare-bit, which was our first meal, and the boxing bouts in the Main Gym, where I was pitted against Boy Prince. He was a hefty street-wise dark-skinned lad from Glasgow. The whole intake was relieved that they hadn't drawn Prince as their opponent, and the bout caused a lot of interest. I had never fought or hit anyone before, and all I can remember about the fight was that it was stopped once to see if I wished to go on. I must have said, 'yes.' Afterwards, I   got commended for trying, if nothing else.

No complaints

Our P.T.I. was Marine Sgt. Nelson and our 'Schoolies' were Lt.'s Holt and Shackleton. None of our classes had any complaints about treatment from any of the staff.

We soon discovered that the issued uniform was not the best of fits, nor did it, in our opinion, look the most tiddley. So we did our best to make it look tiddley for leave, called 'Tids for leave!'

The hats were normally oval-shaped, and real sailors wore round-shaped hats. The O.K. thing to do was to soak an oval hat then loop a lanyard round it, pull it tight, tie it and hang it in the drying-room to dry. The result was a mis-shapen, warped and mangled-looking hat which we thought real sailors wore..

The next thing we attacked were the bell-bottoms. Real sailors had 21/22 inch bell-bottoms which could be made to swing from side to side if one walked with the appropriate seaman's roll. Our issued bells were only 19 inches wide, if that, like drain-pipes. The solution was to soak the bells in water and, using one's own small brown attache' case, and another borrowed from an oppo, push one up each trouser-leg and force in some wooden bed-chocks, one on each side of the cases, then hang them up to dry out. The result was: trousers which went more-or-less straight down to about the ankles, and then flared out in the most extraordinary square-shape. If the word, 'cool' had been in use then, we would have used it!

The white front with which we were issued was not, of course, white, it was a sort of porridge-colour and very hairy with a thin, oblong-shaped black strip around the neck, along the top. Our mates in the *real* navy wore snowy-white fronts with a light-blue edge.

There were two solutions to remedy this deficiency; one was to scrub the existing front with tooth-paste in an attempt to bleach the thing, but this tended to result in a striped, or sort of rag-rolled look. The other was to make a dickie-front from a handkerchief with a strip of blue-jean sewn along the top. This contraption was tucked in under the jumper and tied around the chest to keep it in place.

Our issued lanyards were thick, rather like thin rope, so

TID'S FOR LEAVE!

Collars bleached - 2d. Bells widened - 6d.
Assorted Destroyer's cap tallies - 2/6.

these were washed and hung up to dry with the heaviest item we could find tied to the end. The result - a very long and very thin lanyard, more like a piece of parcel string.

The black silk scarf, or simply 'silk,' as it was called, when folded the proper way, was about an inch and a half wide and about four folds thick. We adjusted this so that it was much narrower and cut it in half so that it was only two folds thick.

The black tapes which held the silk in place had two ends cut in fish-tails and were supposed to be the length of the width of the palm of your hand. We made these longer - much longer. We hid most of these adjustments in our cases, and the big transition from 'Pusser' to 'Tiddley' came about in the train home. Cap tallies were taken out and put on our hats. Instead of '*H.M.S. GANGES*' we would have tallies like: '*HM DESTROYER*' or the names of such ships as we could get hold of, all purchased at great prices from the old hands in Ganges.

I should just mention one refinement which some of us added to enhance the rig. Along the inside-edge of the top of the white-front we carefully sewed a length of small sisal rope which we had teased out, so that when the front was worn, the hairy fibres of the rope all protruded above the tops of the white-fronts, giving the impression of a hairy and manly chest. So there we were, before arriving in the big Smoke, a dozen or more fifteen-year-olds, with incredibly hairy-chests, strange, mis-shapen bell-bottoms, three good-conduct badges sewn, with any luck, on the correct arm, indicating twelve years' good-conduct, but, probably to the discerning observer or astute mathematician, that we could have only been three years old when joining the navy!

I also remember one of the Instructors, who was going on leave with us to Belfast, saying to me: 'You, lad! Carry this case, look after it, and give it back to me when we get to Belfast.'

I discovered, on arrival at Belfast, that I had left it on the ferry. The Instructor was mad, to say the least, but he did not want any tracing action taken. It turned out that it was full of contraband 'Tickler' tobacco."

"Reading your letter about Ganges brings back memories, not all printable,'' writes **Ken Pantling**, a retired schoolmaster. "As an Instructor Boy in 1946, it was part of my duty to escort the Nozzers from the Harwich boat to the New Entry Division. Many had fresh hair-cuts ready for joining the service, but unfortunately their ideas of

49

a hair-cut fell very short of the Navy's ideal, as they learned the very next morning. However, they soon bonded as a group and looked forward to joining the main 'Ganges' after basic training. I have never regretted Ganges, and look back with pride and fondness to the time spent there."

Perhaps he did, but **Charlie Kent's** first experience of Ghastly Ganges was not impressive, 'specially when his crowning glory was shaved and shorn.

`Petty Officer Boys Drunk with power`

Charlie Kent had the type of humour one needed to survive the disappointments, shocks and the rigorous routine of Ganges. He could laugh at his own downfall(s) at the hands of his Instructors. Charlie had a good head of hair, and, at 81 he claims that he still has. However, the first Ganges hair-cut left him devastated and deprived of his fine head of hair - it also broke his heart.   Here's Charlie:-

"When I joined I had such lovely hair, cut just right, made to look so nice, the cut was great, the hair made to look so good, aided by the help of Brylcreme, Vaseline, and, in the case of dire-need, lard, margarine or best-butter when times were hard. Anyhow, it came to pass that myself and the Petty Officer Boy had a few harsh words. Some Petty Officer Boys were ruthless, drunk with power, and treated us worse than the worst Instructors treated us. But this one, suddenly changing his tune, remarked how nice my hair looked! I was chuffed. I thought: 'Oh, I've won this argument.'

In his next breath he yelled: 'Get your @/+%@ hair cut!'

''What for?' I said, indignantly. 'It's alright.'

Again, he said: 'Get yer 'air cut! And when you get down to the barber's shop at 7.30 tomorrow morning, ask to see Mr. Sweeney Todd.'

So I enter the barber-shop next morning. I make my way to see Mr. Todd and I walk across the shop and see a man standing there.

'Good morning, sir,' I said. 'I have to report to a Mr. Sweeney Todd for a hair-cut.'

A man who had been standing by, and having the appearance of a Demon Barber, heard me and bellowed out: 'I'll give you Mr. Bloody Sweeney Bloody Todd! Sit down here, you miserable little so-and-so!'

'Well, sir, isn't your name Mr. Todd?'

Again, a louder roar: 'No, it f...... well ain't! I am not even a 'Mister!'

I am a Royal Marine. Now, you little bleedin' Nozzer 'orror, what style would you like?'

'Just ordinary, please, sir. I had a hair-cut last week just before I joined.'

'Well, sonny,' he said, 'Try this one!' **Whoosh! Whoosh! Whoosh! Whoosh!** Jesus! I'm naked!

It is now November the 18th, and Christmas leave is coming up. What will all the girls think when they see what the navy have done to my hair? I am now none too keen for leave, but I go, wearing my cap as much as possible. I am ashamed; my friend, Rodney, suggested that I put a bandage round my head and mark it with a spot of red paint or ink and pretend I'd been wounded. Yes, you guessed it, I did. What a response I got!

'He's only been in the Royal Navy a month and he's been wounded already!' I felt such a wally, because when I was on leave I ran into a three-badge Patrolman in the town.

'What's happened to you?' he asks.

I could have said I fell off the mast, but I hated that bloody thing too much even to mention it. If only I could have made it to the button, this would have been happy memories. I gave the only excuse I could think of: 'I fell off a horse, sir.'

He must have believed me because he went away.

Admirals fought over me, I was gorgeous!

On going back to Ganges, I ran into 'Sweeny Todd.' He gave me a nasty look, as much as if to say: '*you have a few more visits to me.*' I'm sure he was gloating, but then I found out he was never there on Thursdays, so I always requested to have my hair cut on Thursdays. The other barber who cut my hair came from my home town. We townies always respect our township. Also, he remembered me, that at the age of 14 years I fought and beat the Territorial Army boxing champion. I also think he must have had a word with Blue-beard, our Instructor, and he actually *did* have a blue beard, and he would always pass the time of day with me. But I would not chance my arm for another hair-cut by 'Sweeney,' and today, thank goodness, I have still got a good head of hair of my own. But a few teeth are missing.

But that hair-cut: I just thought it would never grow again. It was horrifying, for I was a handsome fellow. Oh, dear, what conceit! Here, in this place where I work, whenever I have shewn the fellows and girls photo's of me as a young man, they say: 'Were you really as handsome as that?' Of course I was, and I often remark, in a joking way: 'Bloody Admirals used to fight over me. I was gorgeous!'

It causes quite a laugh."

George Skidmore: aged 15 years and 8 months, December, 1935.
"It was a cold, wet evening. I got my first look at Shotley Barracks after landing from the tug, About twenty of us were marched into the bathroom and told to strip off and shower. Then, in a single file, we were ordered to raise our arms above our heads for inspection by our Petty Officer, a man, nick-named by us, as 'Killer Stevens.' He was about 38 years old with 1914-18 war ribbons. He was a right Gestapo-type, with a flashlight in one hand and a stonnicky - a length of rope, in the other.

'Back foreskins!' he roared. I blushed, but did as I was told, only to be belted around the buttocks with the stonnicky and ordered to go back and shower again. I was usually picked on because of my size: I was five feet ten inches and weighed 12 stone; quite a big lad for my age. In bed, later, after kitting-out and a cup of greasy cocoa and some dog biscuits, at 9 p.m., I tried to sleep. We had just two blankets and a hard mattress. It was rough and uncomfortable. I almost cried myself to sleep - and to think I had signed up for 12 years.

Brutal... discipline was on a par with Captain Bligh.

I had been in the Boy`s Brigade and learned how to march, but a boy named Bell from Cork, in Ireland, just couldn't tell his left leg from his right. Poor old Tinker Bell. He was hit, insulted, even had his left arm strapped to his left leg to try and make him march properly but somehow, when the P.O. Instructor said: 'Quick march!' the left foot goes forward and the left arm goes with it. He looked like a waddling duck. All the shouting and hitting, and I mean hitting, made no difference. The P.O.'s felt no pain when belting any boy with a stick, or their hands. It was really brutal at times, we lads were tough, discipline was rigorous but we were considered as the lowest of the low. Discipline was on a par with Captain Bligh!

Morning came, the dormitory doors would open and a P.O. with an overcoat and leather sea-boots, armed with a broom-handle, would put the lights on and shout: 'Out you bastards! Get out, and fall in outside. **Now!!**'

It was a cold December morning and we had to connect up hoses in the covered way. With our trousers rolled above the knees, the cold water would freeze our toes and feet and each one of us had to wield a large, stiff broom. The order would be shouted:

'Form a single line and scrub the stone deck!'

If the P.O. was in a bad mood he would make us use the Holy Stones, large, white bricks of coral, well-worn, and we would be on our knees scrubbing and scrubbing, hoping and praying for the time to come when we could stop.

Smoking was forbidden, and if we were caught we were punished by seven days jankers which meant we had to fall in on the parade ground. Then, with a long pole about four feet long and two inches in diameter, held above our heads, we had to double until we dropped from exhaustion. This would take about an hour, the poles weighed about four pounds.

If we were caught swearing, the whole class would be mustered to witness us eating a bar of soap. After just one mouthful and a chew of it we would feel terrible and vomit. The P.O. would grin and say: 'If your body is dirty, you wash with soap, so if your mouth is dirty, it shall be cleaned.' *(Some of the Instructors had the foulest of mouths.)*

If anyone failed to wash properly he would be ordered to wear his oilskin coat back-to-front with a broom stick threaded through the arms, like a scare-crow, then the class-mates were ordered to scrub his face, legs, body with brooms, while another sprayed him with cold water from a hose-pipe. They were never dirty after that.

Kit-musters were once a week and if the kit of any boy didn't meet with approval, two lines of boys were formed. Each boy was ordered to take off his belt and the culprit had to run the gauntlet, his ankles were tied together, which meant he could only move slowly and kept falling over, thereby received more beatings from his mess-mates as he tried to get away from this punishment.''

Proud to be a Ganges Boy...

Roy O`Connell says: ''I have always been very proud to tell people that I was a Ganges boy. The whole system of training at that establishment was archaic and very tough. The place had an atmosphere unlike anywhere I had ever been, or have been to since. It reeked of history, pride and patriotism, and I would never have missed it for the world. I have been a Police Officer since 1978, and always wanted to visit Ganges again, and recently, whilst on a motor-cycle course, I was presented with the opportunity to do just that. From Ipswich I took the lead on my BMW K100 police-bike and led all the way to the main gate of Ganges - or the Shotley Gate Police Training Centre, as it now is.

I have rarely felt so emotional as I sat astride my motor-cycle on the Quarter-deck, looking up at the old mast-head. As my colleagues ate lunch, I went off on my own to tour what was left of the old Ship.

Benbow Lane, the Long Covered Way, Short Covered Way, Laundry Hill, the Drill Sheds, were all gone. Bulldozed. I couldn't believe the destruction. Virtually everything on the river side of the parade-ground, except for the water tower, had been demolished. I took photographs of what remained of the Long Covered Way, a single tree-stump marked what was left of my old mess, 21 mess. I have never felt so gutted in a long time. To have seen that once-proud establishment, which had turned out generation after generation of sailors, many of whom had served with distinction in war-time, including Boy John Travers Cornwell, VC, battle of Jutland fame, and the youngest sailor to win the Victoria Cross.''

(Boy Cornwell was not at Ganges, although most ex-Ganges Boys are of the opinion that he did because his portrait hung in Nelson Hall.)

''Ganges was reduced to rubble. A piece of our national heritage had been lost and cannot be replaced. I am proud to be associated with H.M.S. Ganges and I mourn it's loss. But I hadn't always regarded it with such affection, especially the day I joined, 2nd September, 1975. I had been accepted for the Royal Navy and I still remember how proud I felt on my journey from home to Ipswich station, to be carrying on a family tradition with the Navy. Most of my ancestors had been navy men, Merchant or Royal. My grandfather had sailed with the tea-clippers, including one spell on the Cutty Sark, and his brother was decorated during the first world war for taking command of the ship in action when all officers were either dead or seriously wounded. His actions led to the destruction of an enemy U-boat.''

An illusion is suddenly shattered

''So, it was with great excitement that I stepped onto the platform of Ipswich Railway Station to be greeted by a Leading Rate, Hooky, as he told us to call him, and then to be shepherded onto a waiting R.N. bus. On the journey from the station to Ganges, I suddenly realised, *'This is it!'* I was in the Navy! The Leading Rate, obviously a former pupil of *Heinrich Hermans School of Charm,* decided that he wanted to inspect the *'queer's overalls'* - as he termed it - of the entire complement of recruits on the bus. It was not performed without a considerable amount of hustle and bustle, and many Anglo-Saxon expletives, that we finally managed to produce an array of various styles of pyjamas, ranging from Conservative Cotton through Paisley Pattern to outlandish bri-Nylon. Some of us were singled out for derisory remarks about our choice of bed-wear, and culminated in one individual having his pyjamas thrown from the moving bus. I do not know what prompted such reasons for producing the garments in the first place, or for the strange actions of the Instructor-Boy.''

The reason is obvious, a cowardly, big-headed Instructor Boy with a massive inferior-complex and overlowing ego, was showing the New Entries just how mighty and important he was - determined that they shouldn't miss the chance of finding out just _how_ important. It was also the first indication of what was to follow later.

''We arrived, finally, at the Main Gate where we were de-bussed and lined-up, two ranks deep, outside of the initial intake blocks in Benbow Walk. A Fleet Chief Petty Officer appeared, and from the attitude of the other N.C.O.'s present, I decided that this large man was obviously second-in-charge to God.

I don't remember much of what the Fleet Chief had to say in his opening address, but I do remember that we were constantly called 'Nozzers,' a term I later discovered referred to new recruits. ''

(The word, 'Nozzer' derives from an Instructor from years back called Parker. All 'Parkers' were nick-named 'nosey.' It was Nosey Parker's job to train the new recruits when they were stationed in the main establishment before the Annexe was built. 'Nosey' was slurred and shortened to 'Nozzer,' becoming Nozzer Parker. Nozzer Parker's recruits - which was further shortened to 'Nozzer.' They did their training in a road which ran across the bottom of Benbow Lane and the Long Covered Way. It was known as `Nosey Parker's Lane` or Nozzie Parker's Lane,` or, shortened further, without the `Parker,` 'Nozzer's' Lane. Another version of `Nozzer` is, again, a corruption of the phrase: 'No, Sir!' Take your pick!))

Roy O'Connell again: ''Having received the wisdom of Solomon from the Fleet Chief as to how we would conduct ourselves, and a brief resume` of how our training would be carried out, we were divided into small groups according to which mess we were to occupy. I was allocated number one mess in Benbow Walk which was nearest to the parade-ground and the other amenities.

We were introduced to our respective C.P.O.'s who were in charge of our mess-deck. Ours was C.P.O. Critoph, with whom I was immediately impressed. He was Royal Navy down to his toe-nails. He was, as I remember, quite a large man in his forties, with a full set - beard, well-trimmed and, I think, sandy-haired. He was as smart as a carrot and his over-all appearance was quite fearsome. We learned very quickly however, that he was not at all fierce, but good-humoured and very patient. My God, he had to be! He, and a Leading

Hand, who's name I have now forgotten, had the unenviable task of turning a cartload of scruffy teenagers into a smart band of sailors who would be a credit to H.M. Royal Navy. As with any collection of people thrown together, there are the odd-balls and idiots, swots, blots, crabs, skates, schemers and the rest. I shall refrain from naming names from here on when a particular misdeed comes to mind, but I am sure that any of your readers will remember and identify them, or those known to them. We went through all the usual steps of joining, but one thing stands out in particular - the hair-cut! We all went into the barber's as individuals with individual hair-cuts, and came out looking like clones of each other! Peas out of the same pod! There is a saying: *'what is under your cap is yours, the rest belongs to the king or queen* - and off it comes!

That first day over, we turned in. We still regarded the whole thing with some hilarity. One boy, after 'lights-out,' started throwing Maltesers about; other boys threw them at others and so on. The noise built up to a crescendo of riotous hilarity.

Suddenly, the mess door burst open and in marched a C.P.O., unknown to us, who was bristling and steaming with rage. We were ordered from our beds, those too slow in complying were physically tipped out. We were made to put on boots and gas-masks and ordered to pick up our full kig-bags, formed into three ranks and doubled to the 'Hill,' Laundry Hill, and for the next hour or so were doubled up and down. This then, was summary justice as meted out by the Royal Navy. I forgot to mention that all this took place with us wearing pyjamas - except one Boy. His pleas that he didn't have any pyjama's - *they had been thrown out of the window of the bus* - was met with a sympathetic, 'Tough shit!' He had to perform in the nude.

Kit musters: The worst case I recall was when a muster of kit was called by some jumped-up, self-opinionated L.R.O. a Leading Junior, the day before the D.O.'s rounds and kit-muster. We wrongly assumed that the reason for this was to make sure all our kit was up to scratch. But the devilish L.R.O., or Hooky from Hell, entered our mess like a whirlwind and upset everyone's kit by pulling out the bed counterpane upon which the kit was laid, and shooting it all over the deck. That was an exception, mostly they were quite civilised affairs with only the occasional bulled boot being stamped upon and the odd white front rubbed over the deck, or the offending socks/underpants being consigned to the gash bin.

We later finished up in 21 mess, and we were quite accomplished at most things. But we had a handicap in the shape of an overweight youth who had not endeared himself to his fellow recruits for a number of reasons. One being his lack of ability to perform any physical activity or display any team spirit. With the day of the final assault course fast approaching, our slovenly friend still refused to do his bit. I am ashamed to admit it, but a conspiracy between myself and the other members of 21 mess was hatched, and, during a practice session on the assault course, our 'friend' mysteriously fell from the top of one of the wooden walls and broke his collar bone. This resulted in admission to the sick-bay for our 'oppo' and back-classing to the following intake. But it resulted in 21 mess winning the assault course finals.''

That was Roy O`Connell of 1975, who left the navy to become a Police Officer in 1978. Roy did not, after all, follow in the footsteps of his predecessors, his sea-going, sea-faring ancestors, but he set a family precedence by becoming, perhaps, the first of the O'Connells to join the Police force.

Here follows another Connell, without the `O` - and four-and-a-half decades before Roy: -

Ron Connell, April 8th, 1930, tells a similar joining-story, travelling a great distance to join his projected hopes of future exciting adventures, only to be disappointed with the final culmination of buoyant expectancies, which proved to be a personal disillusionment. It could be an exact copy of the experiences of many boys who joined Ganges, not knowing they would have to suffer or enjoy that establishment for many, many months before embarking upon a Jolly Jack-type career. Arriving at the disappointing and drab frugalities of the Annexe would burst the most colourful bubble of even the greatest of optimistic imaginations. However, Ron shows unusual leniency in accepting whatever Ganges had to offer with extreme optimism and forgiveness, even though his first impressions were discouraging.

''We had come a long way,'' explains Ron, ''and it was evening when we arrived at Harwich. We were met at the station by a Naval officer and some Petty Officers, and marched down to the pier where we boarded a pinnace to take us across the bay to Shotley. It was fairly late in the evening and one of the Petty Officers said: 'The war babies are coming!' We had all been born about the beginning of World War One.

Next morning, at 0500, we were marched down to the swimming

baths to pass the swimming test. It was fre-e-e-ezing. We had to strip and put on a duck suit each, which were hanging on the clothes-line outside. The duck-suits were frozen solid and, if we held them at the bottom end, they stood straight up!

Instructor threw his bayonet at us..

I could swim quite well and passed the test, so did some of the others, but some boys could not swim at all. They were instructed to jump in at the deep end and grab hold of a pole which was held out to them by the Physical Training Instructors. The Instructors would pull the pole away, but they would not let anyone drown, and they soon taught the boys to swim. Discipline was very strict which was very good for us because we all knew what we could and could not do. We had two Instructors, gunnery Petty Officers, one wasre-knowned throughout the establishment. He was very strict and he seemed to have eyes in the back of his head. He used to carry the thick end of a billiard cue around with him, and if any of the lads were doing anything wrong he would turn around and give them a whack with his club. He was known as the **Shotley Terror.** When he took us for rifle-drill on the parade-ground he would say: *'If you see me doing*

anything slovenly, YOU can do it slovenly, but while I do it smart, YOU will do it smart!' And sometimes, when he was feeling nastier than usual, he would throw his bayonet at someone. We had plenty of sport and once I won the half-mile running-race. I won a leather cigarette-case - *even `tho we weren`t allowed to smoke!!* If a boy was caught smoking he would receive six cuts for the first offence and if he was caught again he received twelve. The culprit had to put on a pair of duck trousers and lean over a box-horse and the Master-at-Arms used to lay it on with a cane. The victim would have stripes on their backside for weeks afterwards.

"Hooky` Walker."

Our Commander was Commander Walker, he had only one arm, he had lost the other in a raid on Zeebruge in World War One. He had a brass hook in place of his left hand, hence his nickname, 'Hooky Walker.' After him, anyone called `Walker` joining the navy was automatically nick-named `Hooky.`

One day a Marine Corporal saw me in the doorway of our mess and came and sniffed and smelled smoke on me. He said: `Have you been smoking?' I said: 'Yes, sir.'

He said: 'Right, stand by to doff your lid on the quarterdeck.'

I was put on Captain`s report and he said to the Corporal:

'Did you see this boy smoking?'

'No, sir, I did not.'

'How did you know he'd been smoking then?'

'I suspected it, sir, and asked him outright, and he admitted it, sir.'

The Captain said: 'I am pleased that you have spoken the truth, and, because of that, instead of six cuts, I am going to give you a `caution.''

When I went out of the Captain's room the Master-at-Arms and the Regulating P.O. were waiting to pounce on me. They had the shock of their lives when I told them that I had got a 'caution' Such a thing was unheard of for being caught smoking.

Instructors were not always ogres. A lad in our mess was very nervous and afraid to go up the mast. He eventually got over his nervousness through the kindness from our Instructor who rewarded him with sixpence for his bravery. My time at Ganges was from 9th April, 1929 to 3rd September, 1931. The discipline would have done some good to the youth of today.

Another memory I have is the toilets. They formed a line of about a dozen cubicles with a long trough running beneath the length of them with running water taking away the waste. Occasionally, when all the cubicles were full, except the end one where the water came in, someone would light a bundle of newspaper and send it floating down the trough, burning a few hairy bums and other `dangly` things in transit.''

Ex A.B. **Fred Webb**, *D.S.M.*, had a night to remember after turning in on the late evening of his first day:

"During the first week the duty P.O. would turn out the lights, prior to 'pipe down,' but one night, someone shouted out: 'Put those f.....g lights back on!'

The P.O. said: 'Who shouted?' No one answered, so we were told to fall in outside and everyone started to put on socks and trousers. The P.O. said: 'As you are!' None of us had pyjamas, pyjamas were for officers only, and we duly fell-in outside. He asked us again:

''Who shouted?' No one answered, so he marched us to the quarter-deck and reported us to the Duty Officer who gave us all Commander's report. This led later to Shotley Routine for the whole mess. In the meantime, the P.O. marched us back to the mess.

Next morning we were woken at 0500 hours and given one hour's extra drill. We made darn sure that the offender kept his trap shut in future! Standing around half-naked on the East coast in February is no joke. We were all the same colour, blue!

In the drill-shed, I believe it was known later as H.M.S. Nelson Block, *(Nelson Hall)*, there were three twelve-pounder guns and limbars. We were asked if any of us had been in the Home Guard, Sea Cadets, or other units. I had been in the Sea Cadets and put my hand up and was told to fall in by one of the guns, two others, who had previous experience, were also standing by the guns. We were in charge and had to take responsibility. Then the P.O. detailed 36 volunteers, split three ways, making 13 of us to each gun, then we were given instructions how to maintain it, handle and work it.

At eight o'clock, 2000 hours, we were told to fall in by the guns and

61

each unit was given six blank shells. The shell cartridges were loaded with cordite, no actual shell-heads, but they were still lethal at close range. That night we went on a Home Guard exercise. We had a hell of a job pulling and cursing the guns across a ploughed-field and lining them up. The enemy, the Home Guard, attacked and were getting close, so close in fact, that they were almost upon us before I yelled: **'Fire!'**

A bloody great flame, about six feet long, shot out of the muzzle and frightened the lot of us to death. It also scythed through the Home Guard's ranks, scattering them like chaff in a force ten gale. After firing all six of our shells each, eighteen shells in all, we hitched up the guns and trudged our way back to barracks. The next morning we had the biggest bollocking ever. The P.O. shouted: *'You are not supposed to wait until you see the whites of their eyes, you stupid bastards! You nearly blew their bleedin` `eads orf!`*

Dave Walker, May, 1965: "On joining we were given a haircut, medical and a dental inspection. I told the dentist: 'I don't need any treatment because I've just finished a course of treatment with the family dentist before joining.' I should have known better, the dentist stated that I needed five fillings. This was done without any pain-killing treatment. I never told the dentist his job again. I also recall that anyone who didn't keep his kit clean had the whole lot put into a dust-bin full of water and he had to wash the whole lot."

Bungy Williams, as he signs himself, gives his address as: **'H.M.S. Ganges, Concentration Camp, mess number 19, 1933/34.** ' Bungy says: "A very apt name and description. The first shock was the rude-awakening on the first morning in the early hours. Then to be given a mug of revolting cocoa with no sugar or milk, and a dog-biscuit. We little thought that in a few weeks we'd be trying to pinch the same dog-biscuits from the bakery. The second shock was to be marched to the swimming pool before it had time to warm up, we had to don an old duck-suit which had been drying outside, and tie it around our waist with a piece of wet rope. The first of many hair-cuts came before kitting-up. The Royal Marine barber would ask each boy: 'How would you like it cut, sir?' Then starting at the front with clippers, giving a convict's hair-cut down to the scalp. Ironically, the comb issued with the kit had teeth about an inch long. That, and the hair-brush, were *never* used during the whole training period.

Some ex-Borstal boys wished they were back in Borstal, as our P.O. Instructors were much more brutal than what they had been used to.

62

Our Gunnery Instructor caught a lad smoking; he made him eat the fag-end while dancing up and down, bare-foot, on his bed-springs, being encouraged by the frequent use of a steel rifle-cleaning rod slashed across his legs which he called 'Percy Vere' by the P.O. who owned it. The victim was then marched before the Officer of the Watch for Captain`s report and received six cuts of the cane.

The food was terrible and would probably cause a rioting in a modern prison. One revolting meal for dinner was called the 'Shotley Mystery,' even the cooks were not sure what they had put in it; minced-meat and any left-overs from previous meals, including sweet. All eaten off tin-places and bowls. You will see that Ganges imprinted itself in my mind for sixty years now.''

Don Winter: ''October, 1936, a momentous year for Great Britain, King George V died, and boy 2nd class, D. Winter joined the Royal Navy to be welcomed with less than open arms into H.M.S. *Ganges*. No sooner were we innocent beings through the gates than all hell seemed to break loose and the process of brain-washing began. Ganges has been compared to a concentration camp, and I'm sure it was the blue-print for Germany's notorious camps, but be that as it may, I survived a year's training there and was a *very, very* happy Boy 1st class when I finally left.

The first day of our induction was a shock; a visit to the barber who cut our crowning glory down to the scalp, next, to the doctor, who certified that our limbs were present and correct. We then showered, stone cold water, and issued with old uniforms, worn by our predecessors, and doubled away for our introduction to the navy's idea of food. A baked potato, a slab of meat, beetroot, a cob of hard bread and a one-inch square of marge. To ease down this sumptious riposte`, a half-pint of cocoa, less sugar or milk. We were then lectured by an Instructor who's attitude boded ill for our immediate future under him. After that homicidal lunatic had finished his sermon, we received a long, yellow, woollen shirt known as a night-shirt, and, at last, blessed oblivion in a cast-iron bed with a cast-iron mattress to match. But that did not matter. We were so knackered, we died before our heads hit the cast-iron pillow. We ended up as 36 class, Collingwood Division, old salts now, who were soon to descend to earth with a crash. Our Instructors made themselves known to us at this stage, Petty Officers Bond and Tusker, the first to teach us seamanship, the second gunnery and it`s attendant pleasures. Every class had two Instructors, and as far as I could see ours followed the same pattern, with the seaman Instructor nearly humane and the gunnery P.O. a pure hundred percent, dyed-in-the-wool sadistic swine who, in my case, was responsible for one of my claims to fame, a record second-to-none for jankers as he and I differed in our ideas of discipline. Needless to say his ideas had an unchangeable force of argument and I spent my days contemplating the error of my ways. For even the most trivial offence it was Divisional Officer's report, and that individual considered even a dirty look as a henious threat to the navy. It was Captain's report for his sentence, usually a period of 8a's as it was called. This consisted partly of galloping up and down Laundry Hill and the concrete steps. Faith, Hope and Charity for two hours every afternoon with a 4ft 6in pole above our heads. I saw many boys pass right out during this harrowing pastime and I'm sure it was one of the causes of numerous cases of nervous breakdowns among the boys. Every Wednesday we used to see an ambulance, called by us the 'happy waggon,' it's sole purpose was taking those sick boys to what we referred to as the 'funny farm.' They were probably the only happy boys at Ganges. My second claim to fame was the setting-up of a new record for ascending and descending the old man-of-war's mainmast on the parade. We climbed six at a time, thoughtfully assisted by the Instructor's rope's-end called a stonnicky, and timed by a Marine with a stopwatch. I believe a couple of fatalities occurred in my time, but I wasn't witness to them.

We looked forward to leave, and freedom, but the last two days were marred by the thought that we had to return to Ganges. And we *did* return, I never heard of anyone absconding in my time and can only put this down to fear of the consequencies as **no-one in his right mind could ever be fond of Ganges.**

There were certainly characters at Shotley, and of these, two survived through each generation and became a part of Shotley naval folklore, 'Creeping Jesus,' and the 'Shotley Shadow.' These two gentry had been a misery for generations of inmates, and in my time the first named was a Royal Marine who patrolled the Long Covered Way and seemed to materialise out of thin air whenever anyone was violating any of the naval commandments. The other unsavoury being, the 'Shotley Shadow,' was a repulsive gunner's mate who was a regular sadist who laid about him quite happily with his stonnicky for no reason, and you soon learned to vacate the area when he was around.

We used to like 'workship.' It meant two weeks from most of the discipline and routine. Blessed he was who copped for cleaning duties in the Wardroom or Chief's and P.O.'s messes with the opportunities for cigarette-end gathering out of the ash-trays. A good haul and you were the most popular boy in the class, but the penalty for getting caught was pretty hairy - flogging no less, but not the Nelsonian idea of flogging, ours was administered in the gym with the unfortunate offender strapped over a vaulting-box wearing only a pair of duck-trousers, the seat of which being dampened to make sure it was taut. The actual cuts were delivered by a Royal Marine Sergeant. I could reminisce about Ganges at greater length because it was a very traumatic experience, but before I finalise I would like to pose some questions and opinions: did the harsh regime produce the wonderful adult seamen it was credited with doing? *I don't believe it did;* my opinion is that *the products of Ganges were automatons conditioned into the navy's idea of performing, mainly by fear, and were no better or worse than other seaman trained in other, more humane, naval establishments, i.e. St. Vincent. Discipline by fear is always self-destructing.* There were two paintings in the drill shed at Ganges, one of Boy Seaman Jack Cornwell, V.C. the other of Rear Admiral Sir Thomas Lyne who was the only boy to ever reach flag rank. Were those portraits there to inspire us? If so they failed because we cruelly ridiculed the first as a 'nut' *who was serving no useful function by hanging about at an out-of-action gun, who's entire crew had been killed.* I'm afraid we probably, quite unjustly, saw it as a *blatant recruiting piece of propaganda* and as for our gallant Rear Admiral, we asked ourselves, '*If only one boy out of hundreds of thousands of past and present boys can achieve flag status, we were flogging the proverbial dead horse to even think of emulating him.*' We formed the opinion that he must have been the world's number one creeper who's granny scrubbed the Admiralty steps.." *By that last statement, if we read it correctly, Don Winter implies that the Admiral's rise through the ranks was brought about only by the simple fact that his grandmother cleaned the Admiralty steps, thereby gaining favour for her grandson to attain promotion!* He continues: "I believe that the phrase: '*H.M.S. Ganges produced the navy's finest seamen in the world,*' was a deliberate fiction, fostered by naval authority to excuse the harsh treatment which it dished out. I modestly claim to be a fair judge of seamen as I served 51 years at sea in practically every type of ship afloat..."

Chapter five.
P.T.I.'s and Swimming

Were P.T.I.'s human? Yes, apart from the few who disgraced that profession. I can think of nothing to condemn them for.

Some boys were good at physical sports, some were mediocre, ungainly, and a few overweight, flabbily-muscled malingerers were disgustingly useless. Perhaps it is those who complain the most; but we have to consider that their stories could be true, especially as the difference between a bullying P.O.G.I. and a bullying P.T.I. is negligible. If one is not good at physical sports, and is encouraged, perhaps a little forcibly, to perform as well as others, would it be right to think that the boy on the receiving end could misconstrue the `encouragement` as bullying? Each Division had it`s own Physical Training Instructor. Sometimes, when the resident Instructor was on leave, or indisposed because of sickness or other reasons, another P.T.I. would substitute. Backward swimmers were, perhaps, among those who considered their treatment as unfair. They were continually being encouraged - or harrassed - to learn to swim for their own safety, and, if one is afraid of water, the trauma of the experience of learning to swim is magnified many times from the normal, and genuine efforts to `encourage` are mistaken as `bullying torture.`

Tom McGregor says: "Were the P.T.I.`s really human when putting boys through a shake-up in the Gym?" Another: "I was a faithful boy at Ganges," says **A. Gray** of 1942. "I well remember my clash with one of the P.T.I.`s in the swimming pool. Before going to H.M.S. Ganges, I was told that if I liked swimming, to tell those in charge that I was unable to swim. By doing so I would be able to use the pool more often, the only trouble was you had to do all your strokes beside the pool for two days. After that they would tell you to get in the water. Most boys in the class dreaded the thought. All but me. I completely forgot why I was in this class, being a good swimmer. I dived in and finished in the middle of the pool. By that time the roof of the pool almost came down on me. The P.T.I. had seen what I had done and called me everything in good naval language for wasting his time. He said: 'You, boy! Go and put on a duck suit!'

Before I could do that, he grabbed one and dunked it into the water. Then he said: 'Now do the swimming test. Swim to the end of the pool and keep afloat at the end.'

This I did. I got the letters, P.P.T. put in my pay book. This meant I could go ashore to Harwich on night leave. My sister was in the

WRNS over there, so it was nice to see her. I remember her coming over to Ganges with another WRN to see me, her Ordinary Seaman brother. I heard the pipe:
'Ordinary Seaman Gray report to the Guard Room at the double!'
My mess-mates all ribbed me about it. They thought I was in the rattle and some of them followed. Imagine their faces when they saw me chatting to two beautiful Leading WRNS. We still take about it."
In the 60`s when television was introduced to the boys` recreation rooms, if anyone had not passed their swimming test they were not allowed to watch tv or attend the film shows. At one time, when Harwich leave was allowed, boys not in possession of evidence of having passed their swimming test, were banned from the ferry.
Able Seaman `Rocky` Rock, 1949, had a similar experience re the swimming pool: "The only humorous story I can recall about that place of horrors was during the first few days the Divisional P.T.I. asked the question: 'How many of you are backward swimmers?'
I thought that was a funny question to ask but I held my hand up with several others.
'O.K.,' he said. 'Muster at the swimming pool immediately after afternoon divisions.' Which we did. He took us into the pool, told us to strip and don a swimming slip, which we did. Then he said: 'O.K. All of you, in the pool and line up by the side facing me. Chop, chop! Move!' We all got into the pool; some jumped in, some lowered themselves over the side, and one or two climbed down the steps. We lined the side of the shallow end, facing him
'O.K.,' said the Instructor. 'Go to it. Let go the side and we`ll see what you can do. Now! Go!' As I had been the back-stroke champion of the senior school, I held on to the side and immediately thrust backwards and did a very beautiful, very swift, very professional two-length back-crawl with a somersault racing-turn at the end of the first length. This was, apparently, watched in awe and wonder by all present. When I climbed out the P.T.I., who turned out to be a smashing Instructor, said: 'What the bloody hell do you think you`re doing, lad?'
What did I think I was doing? Well I was doing the back-crawl, that`s what I was doing. But I was a bit wary of his attitude and didn`t think it appropriate to say that at the time. I stammered: 'Er, the back-stroke, sir. You said you wanted people who could do the back-stroke.'
'Laddie,' he said, rather kindly, but dangerously softly. 'I said I wanted `backward` simmers. NOT f......g back-stroke swimmers! Now f... off!'
Our P.T.I. was a great guy, every time we had gym lessons after that

he used to refer to me as `The only backward swimmer who could swim backwards.`"

Whatever is said, and how many times it is said, in detrimental terms about Instructors and P.T.I.`s, there are those who will not believe it. Before the end of this book the reader will come across Petty Officers, Chief Petty Officers and officers themselves relating stories of harsh treatment to the boys, and to themselves, by Instructors. One of them is **Lt. Commander Thomas Reed,** 96 years old at the time of writing, joined Ganges on his 15th birthday, 5th October, 1914. He was a schoolboy champion diver and an excellent swimmer. Of Ganges swimming pool he says: "In those days you had to be able to swim, and if you couldn`t, well it was unfortunate. Those that couldn`t had a bit of a tough time," he puts it mildly. "I was fortunate that I was able to swim. Those that could swim lined up, swam one length of the bath and got out and were passed. The other poor kids that couldn`t swim, they had to start to be taught how to swim. They had Petty Officers along the side of the bath and they had a contraption like a long pole with a rope at the end with a sort of harness, a canvas strap in a loop, which they looped around under your chest, and then walked along the bath and you had to try to swim in that way or manner. I remember the screams, some of these kids were dead-scared of the water, had never tried to swim before in their life. I remember some of the kids screaming for their mothers while they were trying to learn to swim. We had to go up on the middle board, and could either jump off or dive off. When it came to the diving the Chief in charge of us said, 'Well, come on! All you boys that can dive, line up.' We lined up on the diving board and those that could dive dived off, the rest jumped in the water and we swam to the side of the bath, and that was the finish of it.

Some of these other kids, who were just learning to swim, when they thought they were proficient and could swim the width of the baths, the Instructors got them to swim a length. Then they had to come and do this diving test.

I remember I was down in the swimming bath a couple of weeks afterwards and I saw some of these kids doing their diving test. At that time we had a Lieutenant Commander in charge of all the swimming and he was a vicious bloke; he was Hogg by name and hog by nature. He was a shocking bloke and I felt really sorry for the young kids that were there who couldn`t swim, they had a hell of a time. This Lt. Cdr. used to carry a big black malacca cane with a silver knob on it. When a kid would walk out to the end of the board and stand there shivering, old Hogg would walk along the board with his stick and just push the kid in the back and knock him off the board. I thought that was terrible and the kids there used to scream their bloody heads off."

So they learned to swim and to dive. It probably saved some lives in later years...

One so-called 'non-swimmer' pretended he wasn't good-enough to pass the swimming test so that he could take full advantage of the facilities of the swimming-pool. **Mel Howden,** 1950: "The pool was of Olympic standard with a ten-metre diving-board. It had many other attractions. It offered relief from that cruel east wind that dogged us all with it's bone-chilling ferocity, and the water was warm - almost embryonic. To take advantage of these comforts, I was determined to delay the passing of my swimming test for as long as possible. I think we 'backward swimmers' were called around 0500 hrs. It was certainly about the same time as boys under punishment were called - probably to instill a sense of guilt. We would race across the frozen parade-ground in sports gear, dance and hop around the duty P.T.I. as he opened up.

'C'mon, sir, we're freezing!'

'Just you bloody wait,' he would grumble.

The lights flickering on, some of them buzzing until they also warmed up. The water was smooth and glassy, not a ripple to spoil it's appearance.

In the changing rooms the bathing slips, striped jean cloth with two white tapes at one hip. Normally we had to put them on wet, yuk, from the previous user, so we would jump in the water first and then put them on - until someone leapt in the pool starkers only to find it full of WRNS. In our case we found them where they had dried overnight. After our attempt at learning to swim the duty P.T.I. would squeak: 'Clear the pool!' Giving one long blast on his whistle.

But I was hanging back for as long as possible to oggle the Wrens as they followed us in. As I climbed slowly and unwillingly up the chrome ladder, my gaze travelled upwards, and standing there was the Chief P.T.I. fully dressed.

'You want to pass your test do you, sunshine?' he murmured.

'What, me sir?'

'Yes, you sir!' he replied calmly

Now let me say that I was quite a brave lad, but I had only just learned to swim. The test was to jump off the high board, swim two lengths and float for three minutes at the deep-end whilst wearing a duck suit. That high board was over thirty feet up - or down, whichever way you looked at it, and the side of the pool was quite high enough for me.

'No, sir, not me, sir,' I pleaded. 'Up there and jump!' he shouted. 'Not on your life, sir. You'll have to drag me up there screaming.' Not thinking that he would; he was fully-clothed and might have got his clothes wet if he came into contact with me.

'That's alright, son,' he said. 'That's already been taken care of.'

'OH, NO, SIR. NO NO NO NO NO NO!' I screamed as I was hauled bodily up to the top board by willing hands.

We stood together on the edge of that board, looking down into the pool. Already the Wrens were moving away from the diving area to the sides, and everyone was looking up and grinning at my terror.

'Jump!' he said. 'No bloody way!' I screamed. I was beside myself with fright. So he wrapped his arms around me, lifted me up, walked to the end of the board and just stepped off, taking me with him. As we arched out and away, he gave me a shove and I catapulted from him, yelling my head off. It must have looked like something out of the cartoon, 'Tom & Jerry' as I tried to scramble back up through thin air. I hit the water with an almighty, 'splosh,' and when I had risen from the bottom of the deep-end and spluttered to the edge, he was waiting for me, still fully-clothed and dripping wet: he had an evil smile on his face and he was holding a white duck-suit.

'Put this on, boy, and take your test,' he grated.

I took the test and I passed, just. The alternative, as you will recall, was to wear a 'life preserver' at all times 'til you did pass. Six soddin' great lumps of cork sewn within a life-jacket.

Amazingly, I went on to the famous training-centre in Pitt street in Pompey and became a 'clubswinger' too. So if anyone is thinking of trying it on as a backward swimmer - just watch it!''

Frank Phelps, September 1935: "P.T. was very hard indeed, although having done it at grammar school under an ex army P.T.I., I had a good insight into some of it. A large locker at the far end of the Gym contained dozens of pairs of gym-shoes tied together with their laces, and, on entering the gym we were given three minutes to change into our gym kit and put on a pair of these shoes, then fall in on our marks. Anyone not on his mark in time had to bend forward and receive a heavy blow on the back of the neck with a gymshoe from the P.T. Instructor. If someone in the class did not behave, we were all punished with exercises that left us with no strength in our bodies.

No smoking was the rule and anyone caught breaking it received six cuts with a cane across the buttocks. If they were caught a second time it was twelve cuts. Not many wanted a second helping. Anyone caught spitting received two hours punishment on the parade-ground for a week. The P.T.I.'s also took us for swimming. We were marched to the swimming bath at six a.m. There were duck suits hanging on the line outside, drying, and also frozen stiff. None of them fitted, but this did not matter as we had to wear them to do the swimming test. The two P.T.I.'s in charge got us to undress and don these frozen duck suits. It took your breath away.

'All those who can swim,' the order was given. 'Jump in at the deep-end, swim three lengths of the pool, and then tread water for three minutes at the deep end. Go!'

We didn't like this very much; the water was cold, our limbs were frozen, it was like a death sentence - but we did it!

All the non-swimmers were laughing at us - but then they were also ordered to jump in at the deep-end. Some of them tried to run out of the baths, to no avail. They were made to jump in and were stopped from drowning by long poles held out for them to hang on to."

"I was a good swimmer," **Alan Ross** states. "It was an aspect of Ganges I enjoyed, but I can remember a pal of mine, Alf, who just couldn't pick it up at all. He attended backward swimmers every day. Eventually, on the final test before leaving Ganges for sea service, on completion of training, Alf still couldn't pass the test. The P.T.I. with the clipboard said, with resignation: 'I'm going to sign your certificate as a good swimmer, boy. But if your ship ever goes down, my advice to you is to jump over the side, sink to the bottom, and run like f..k!!'

Another of my forte's was rope climbing. We had to climb a rope to music, make fast at the top with our legs, no hands, and then descend to music. Our class was selected to take part in the Festival of Remembrance at the Albert Hall. For months we practised club-swinging and maze-marching in the gyms. As we stood and swung our clubs to music there was always a crash of wood and a cry of pain as one's clubs hit together. We marched to the Can-can song.

At the Albert Hall we were all in our new shorts in the corridor waiting to go in for a practice. Also in the corridor were some W.A.A.F.S. As the tannoy said: 'And now the Boys of H.M.S. Ganges!' which was our cue to run out. One girl, casting an appreciative eye over the hairy legs and flesh on view said: 'Hmmm. They don't look like boys to *me*!'

On the night the Queen was in the box and thousands of people watching, we were dreading hearing the clash of clubs, but luckily it all went smoothly."

THE COLLINGWOOD MUTINY AND THOUGHTS OF MURDER
Bryan R. Tetlow. 66 Class. Collingwood Division. 1953/54.

The whole of the existence at Ganges was harsh, worse for some than for others. One of my worst memories is of the Gymnasium, even now I break into a cold sweat at the thought. My class, 66 class, Collingwood Division, (1953/54) and, of course, other classes sharing the same P.T.Instructor, had a particularly bad time right from the word `go!.`

The Instructor was called Sharkey. At first I thought he was picking on me in particular because I was not a sportsman type, but it later appeared that everyone else had the same dread of him. He was very sarcastic, indeed he lived up to his name, `Sharkey` by having a thin mouth with two rows of teeth top and bottom, and always looked as if he might literally take a bite out of someone.

Every physical training period he seemed to take great satisfaction from finding the slightest fault with the way we were dressed or the way we performed. He was particularly vindictive to anyone who might be struggling to manage the physical side. For instance, if you came last in a race, or climbing a rope, etc., he made you do it again, and if you couldn't, one of his favourite punishments was to make you do bunny-hops, backwards and forwards, across the lower sports field until you dropped, then he would double all the class up and down the concrete steps, Faith, Hope and Charity. Once he got worked up, and got his teeth into you, he wouldn't give up until you either cracked or the end of the session mercifully arrived.

Hit list
This went on week after week until one day we had all had enough, and one of the other classes and our class got to discussing our woes!

We all got together, our class at the end of our session, the other class at the beginning of theirs, and sat cross-legged on the floor of the Gym and refused to move.

Sharkey tried to belittle us and make us move, but nobody moved. After about an hour the Office of the Watch and the Divisional Officer came and accused us of MUTINY. But we still refused to move unless our complaint was made official and something was done about it!

After about another hour a strange P.T.I. turned up and told us he was to take us for physical training in future, and the `Collingwood Mutiny` came to a successful end.

The new P.T.I. was as different again as Sharkey, and almost a pleasure to be with. Obviously, it was all hushed up, for if it had been widely known the whole of Ganges might have done the same. I hated him so much that for a long time Sharkey was top of my imaginary `Hit List,` until one day, several years later, when I had

transferred to the R.A.F. Airsea Rescue, we had some Navy Pilots come aboard our high-speed launch for survival training; and guess who was the Petty Officer Physical Training Instructor? Yes, you`ve guessed it. *SHARKEY!*
At one particular moment I was standing behind him at the stern. The guard-rails had been unshipped; three powerful propellers, at full speed, were churning the sea into a boiling white froth. No one was looking. I paused, thought for a moment, moved stealthily forward, and then......stopped myself. *He will never know how near he came to being food for the fishes!*
The moment passed, and with it my intense feeling of hatred. I had triumphed over Sharkey and proved myself the better man of the two of us. It was at that moment I realised that he was nothing more thaN a big man with a bigger inferiority complex, inasmuch that he once held power over people half his age, and knew he could terrorise them with bullying which surpassed the bounds of human decency. I never saw or heard from him again, but often wondered if he came to the sticky end which he so deservedly earned because of his misdemenours."
Smudger Smith, September, 1945, started naval life in H.M.S. St. George, ex Cunningham`s Holiday camp. "The captain`s name was Harvey," Smudger carries on: "So we called it `Harvey`s Holiday Camp.` In the gym we were being weighed and measured - in the nude. One lad in front of me was very well endowed in the sexual region. A P.T. Instructor asked him: 'Didn`t you have any toys to play with when you were at school?' One of our first tasks was to pass the swimming test. We were doing quite well up to a point. We had to swim two lengths of the pool, breast-stroke, and float for five minutes. It didn`t matter how far or fast you could swim on the front-crawl, if you couldn`t swim two lengths of the breast-stroke you failed. Most of us got through but one boy, a non-swimmer, was having trouble. The P.T.I. was getting worried, he thought he was about to have his first failure. Suddenly he lost his cool. He had this lad on the end of a handy-billy arrangement; webbing under the chest, supporting him as he attempted to swim - like a little kitten about to drown. He hoisted the lad out of the water, four or five feet, and let him go: SPLASH! He did this two or three times, then with a boat hook pushed him under the water. We did not like this of course, I had thought him a good Instructor, but this was different. The boy got over this, did quickly improve and passed his test. At St. George we swam in the nude, there was no swimming trunks and no females on the ship. The Instructors kept a wet lanyard, which was quite painful when applied to the buttocks - those who got

lashed with it were heard to murmer: `Ooh! That smarts!`"

The conclusion is that it would have been impossible to expect all Instructors and P.T.I.`s to be good, and thankfully, not all of them were bad. Most had a sense of humour, even if it was sometimes coarse and misdirected...

"His greatest attribute was his manhood..."

Nick Nicholson, 1960: "We had to sew our names in our kit when we were in the Annexe, but as soon as we left Ganges we unpicked the lot so as to appear to be old salts. While I was in the Annexe there was a Nozzer, like myself, who became quite pally with me, he was from Ireland. He was very, very naive and had some unusual physical characteristics: one being five perfect fingers and a thumb on each hand. His hands measured fourteen inches from the little finger to thumb. It was a wonder how he passed the medical. He was also over six feet three inches tall and still growing. His greatest attribute however, was his `manhood` which defies all normal descriptions. One P.T.I. asked him if his mother used to pull him out of the pram with it. We called him Paddy, and, due to his gigantuan attributes, he was the butt of frequent jokes, some of which reduced him to tears. He was not happy about going naked, especially to swimming classes at which the club-swingers would tease him frequently. The `club-swingers` were Royal Marines and Royal Navy Physical Training Instructors. We had to pass our swimming test by jumping off the top diving-board, swimming two lengths and floating for three minutes. In my case I was quite happy to do this underwater, but I was a poor swimmer on the surface. We were told to jump off the diving-board naked, and told to grasp our private parts firmly lest they became detached as we struck the water. We were then give a white duck-suit to wear. At first the suit was a wonderful bonus as the air entrapped in the suit rises to a point near where Quasimodo`s hump would be, unfortunately, the air disperses and the suit becomes an encumbrance and one sinks. The `club-swingers,` being very supportive, force you off the pool side with long boat-hooks as you try to reach safety. This encouragement was accompanied by: 'Swim, you bleedin` Nozzers! Swim!'

When Paddy came to his test he refused flatly to jump off the top board and they left him until last. With everyone watching, the two `club-swingers` tried to get him off the board`s edge. He easily held both of them away from him on the board. At this they tried using two boat-hooks and still he wouldn`t let go. They had to give up and Paddy never learned to swim at all.

"Urinating in the wash-basin"

I felt a bit sorry for the bad time he was going through until I learned

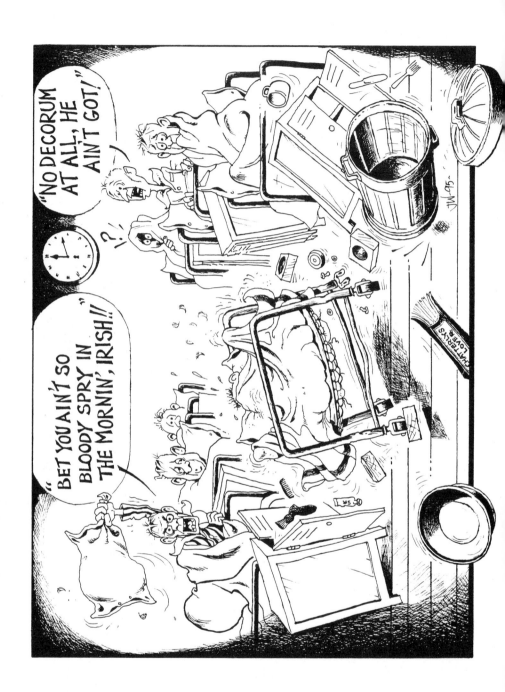

I was against him in a boxing match. My sorrow turned to fear. Everyone in the Annexe was required to go into a boxing ring and try to kill each other for three minutes. Not wanting my mates to think I was a wimp, I decided, as I was built for speed and not endurance, I would go for a quick kill. Paddy was so tall that all my blows hit him very low. I must have hit him a hundred times but he did not seem to be affected. He did hit me a couple of times without any real aggression, but by this time my arms felt like lead. The last thing I remember is his fore-arm hitting my left ear and the lights went out. Paddy had two habits which made us all collapse with laughter, but we had learned not to laugh out loud at Paddy`s antics because there would be repercussions, like being made to double around the nearby football-ground wearing an oilskin and a gas-mask. In our mess, in the Annex, our beds were laid end-to-end with lockers in between, the beds touching lockers and lockers touching beds in a long continuous line. Each night, when Paddy thought everyone was asleep, he would carefully and quietly get up and pull his bed out of the line. Then, having done this, he would creep back into bed and masturbate furiously for about ten minutes, then push his bed back into line. He did this because the first time he masturbated after `lights-out` it caused a most fearful racket, spreading along the line of beds, and lockers, shaking them all and waking everyone up, tin hat-boxes, suit-cases; and anything not lashed-up or battened-down would be leaping about to the rapid rythm of Paddy`s wanking.

His other habit, and it was his downfall, was urinating in the wash-basins; he was caught by the duty Instructor one night and made to double around the parade-ground with a gash-bin over his head until he dropped, exhausted. He was discharged shortly afterwards.

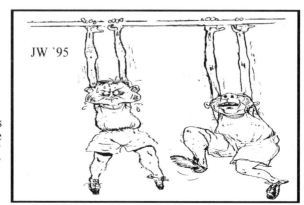

JW `95

They should call us 'Kipling.' We`re always hangin` about in the `Gym!`

77

If you can keep your head when all about you,
　Are losing theirs and blaming it on you;
If you can trust yourself when all men doubt you,
　But make allowances for their doubting too;
If you can wait, and not be tired by waiting,
　Or being lied about, don't deal in lies
　Or being hated, don't give way to hating;
　And yet don't look too good, nor talk too wise.

If you can dream - and not make dreams your master;
If you can think - and not make thoughts your aim;
If you can meet with Triumph and Disaster
　And treat those two imposters just the same;
If you can bear to hear the truth you've spoken
　Twisted by knaves to make a trap for fools,
　Or watch the things you gave your life to, broken,
　And stoop and build 'em up with worn-out tools.

If you can make one heap of all your winnings
　And risk it on one turn of pitch-and-toss,
　And lose, and start again at your beginnings,
　And never breathe a word about your loss
If you can force your heart and nerve and sinew,
　To serve your turn long after they are gone,
　And so hold on when there is nothing in you
　Except the Will which says to them: "Hold on!"

If you can talk with crowds and keep your virtue,
　Or walk with Kings - nor lose the common touch,
If neither foes nor loving friends can hurt you,
If all men count with you, but none too much;
If you can fill the unforgiving minute
　With sixty-seconds worth of distance run,
　Yours is the Earth, and everything that's in it,
　And, which is more, you'll be a Man, my son!

Rudyard Kipling.

Chapter six
General Stories

The following anecdotes are a composite of all the other chapters on humour, humiliation, cruelty, sadism, masochistic tendencies by those who should not have been chosen for the job, mis-fits - likewise, pathos, revenge, horror, and other ingredients, all of which have chapters of their own.

In everything there is a renegade; he is the odd one out in the whole of this book, because his story is the honest admission of an ex-Leading Boy, or Leading Junior, who actually admits to having feelings of elation, borne of power over others which gave him a tremendous sensation of superiority. He commences by saying how well he did in English and maths exams, but later admits to the fault that he had nine weeks extra schooling because his maths were below standard, and his English grammar, spelling, punctuation and layout of writing is lacking; but that is not the point which is being made.

Ninety-percent of the letters in this book have been edited, spelling mistakes corrected, and English grammar correctly observed in most places, but not all so as not to detract from the innocent simplicity and individual presentations of the natural story-tellers. The letter of the ex Leading Junior is printed as received to prove that it was possible for someone of lesser-learning to be placed in charge of those who were probably better equipped for the job, and he, to his credit, admits it.

Nevertheless, it is surprising that someone, who is of inferior literary ability and education than his juniors, should be placed in a position where he could bully them and cause them harm and aggravation to satisfy his personal lust for power. That is what happened in the following case. It should be expected that the person-in-charge should be more experienced than his charges, if only to prove he deserves the title of Leading-Boy.

"The feeling of power was tremendous.."

A.F. Nethercot, Stoker, or M.E.M. the new title for 'Stokers' since the 1950`s, joined 18th April, 1967, writes:

"My mother was very proud of me and kept my joining card and booklet about Ganges She also keep some photo`s of me and my mess mates and instructors. I don`t really know why I enjoyed it at Ganges, maybe it was all the discipline, maybe it was because I was in the Sea Cadets before I joined up or maybe it was because I did well in all the exams. I did have to have nine weeks extra schooling because my maths and english were not good enough to stay in the Navy. It was a great relieve when my mother come to the open day and told me I had passed the exams.

I was made a Leading Junior and took charge of the next lot of Troggs to come across from the Annexe. *The power was tremendous!* Marching them around, making them clean the mess, **pulling their lockers apart** if it wasn't right, making them run up and down Laundry Hill if they spoke after lights out. I won my colours for sports quiet late as I wasn't much for sports but enjoyed Hockey Rowing, shooting, Field Gun. I enjoyed P.T. but didn't like the P.T.I.'s because they thought they were all Mister Universe with their muscles and they used to knuckle you on the head if you did something wrong or wouldn't do anything they told you to do.''

It might have been worse, like pulling your locker apart, marching you about, making you clean the mess when it didn't need it, order you to run up and down Laundry Hill and generally making you uncomfortable!

There is an obvious injustice here; an injustice directed towards the narrator of the story. As a Leading Boy he treated the newcomers, the Nozzers, the would-be T.R.O.G.'s, as dirt, but he expected to be treated with much better respect by those in charge of *him!* There ain't no justice, is there? Well, not at Ganges anyway, if the latter story is an example. Whatever his ambitions or aims, he never made it to final demob. because he says:

"I lost interest and got threw out..."

"Of the 250 that joined when I did, only about 150 completed the training.'' *(With that sort of unfair treatment, who can blame them?)* ''I lost interest in the Navy when I met the wife. All I wanted was to be with her and so I worked my ticket and got threw out in 1971. It was the biggest mistake in my life."

Does that mistake include the unneccessary bullying of the Juniors in his charge? He admits it, although he thinks he was, in his definite opinion, very right and proper to do so. Others, just as guilty, deny it. At least one other letter with the same theme of the mis-use of power was received, but the writer of it declined to provide further information.

Peter Dolphin, August 24th, 1964, knew how to deal with stroppy Instructor Boys who hid behind their stripes. ''After settling in the main establishment, in Duncan thirteen mess, having come over from the Annexe, I had already sorted out who the weak ones were and who to treat with a little respect. Having taken care of myself through two years boys' boxing, I put myself in the middle. Anyway, whenever we entered our mess, the order of the day was `all boots and shoes off in the out-house,` and put on gym shoes. Boots were not allowed on the polished deck. After doing this a few times, I noticed a quiet, ginger-haired lad called Booker, who was always last.. One day Booker came into the mess with misty eyes and a trickle of blood on the lobe of one his ears.

I said, 'What's wrong, Booker?' But he said nothing, looking rather sullen. The following day, the same thing happened. This time, his other ear lobe was bleeding. I approached him again and threatened him, frightening him into answering.

'It's Somerfield,' he said. 'The Junior Instructor. 'Every time I'm in the changing room, he sticks his thumb-nail into my ear and twists it around until it starts to bleed.'

The next time we all had to change foot-wear to enter the mess, I really made sure I was last. Somerfield came in - and smiled. He shut the door and walked slowly over to me. He said:

'I have a method to make you slow bastards hurry up.'

As I was tying my laces, I felt his long thumb-nail being pushed into my earhole. He pushed and wiggled his nail about until it drew blood from my ear. I could feel the warmthness of it trickling down my face. I carried on finishing my laces while he did his best to hurt me, which he did, but I didn't show it.

My laces tied, I stood up and confronted him - smiling! We faced each other and the alarm and fear showed on his face. My ear was stinging now, and it made me even madder to think that young Booker had to suffer this every day without being able to retaliate, but I never showed it.

I said: 'When you've finished, Somerfield, I am going to hit you - and I'm going to hit you bloody hard to teach you not to be a bully!'

I don't think he believed me. He stopped working my ear and let go. As he stepped back I hit him - hard, for Booker.

Well, I got reported and a received a really good telling-off, but we never did see Somerfield again. The rumour was that he got a swift draft chit.''

"Our Instructor Boy was an animal..."

How many Boys hated their Instructor Boys? Quite a few it seems. There are some who crave power over those who are inferior in rank

"THE POWER AND THE GLORY!"

"THE CHOSEN ONE"

or social standing.

Tom Mcgregor, March, 1958, hated his Junior Instructor: "He was an animal. Anyone caught talking after lights-out was made to stand on his locker with his attache-case held straight out at arms length. The Junior Instructor would produce the jolly old pair of semaphore-flags and as soon as the arms started drooping, a vicious upward swing of the flag sticks would batter the knuckles. Everyone of us felt the pain of these flags before we even knew how to use the damn things! A stoker told me it was spanners with them. I didn`t believe him because all Stokers are liars!"

Not all Instructor Boys, Leading Juniors, were `animals,` but they were of the same rank or rating and not all of the same bloody-minded disposition of '*I am superior in rank or rating to you. You will do as I say - or else,*' - attitude.

It is 1937, and Instructor Boy **R. Margerison**, to disprove the theory that all Instructor Boys were animals, has the complacent attitude of the real man of the world who applauds those who are determined to advance themselves and do better than he. "I was chatting to one of the new entries, an ex Training Ship boy, on the subject of observing charts. In his case, I asked about his interest in such a subject, which was normally for the most advanced tuition.

He replied, 'I`m going for a commission as an officer!'

Seven years later I was more than happy to salute him as Officer of the Watch at H.M.S. Excellent!"

"It didn`t take them long to break us in.."

"I joined Ganges in 1924," writes **H. Young** of Leicestershire, now eighty-seven years old, "And, with a few other boys," he says, "We were sent to Shotley via Parkstone Quay very late on the night we joined. The Petty Officer in charge took us across the river Orwell in a pinnace. We passed a Sloop, H.M.S. Tring, and we thought we were going to go onboard that. It was funny to think at the time that we were going to board her, but I soon found out I was wrong. We arrived in Ganges about midnight, and the Petty Officer took us to have a shower. He sat on a chair at the entrance, and called each of us out of the shower for inspection. At that time, being a boy, I felt embarrassed, standing in front of him with my arms above my head with my genitals exposed. How embarrassing! He gave some of us a slap on the backside, and said: 'Go back and have another shower,' whether we were dirty or not. It was awful the way he shouted at us.

Then we went to get the rest of our kit. It must have been one o'clock in the morning, but now I can say, after all these years, discipline never did us any harm, it never took long for them to break us in. For myself and other boys, on that first night, we all shed a tear on the quiet. It was understandable, being away from home for the first time.

"Cane across our backsides.."

We had a Dormitory in the Covered Way, near to the top, by the quarterdeck. Our Instructors were a Chief Gunnery Instructor and a Seamanship Petty Officer. In the morning we could hear the Petty Officer coming up the Covered Way to get us up. He always swung the swinging doors wide open, and we were all out in a flash, as he did a lot of bullying and shouting. By gum! We were all out like a catapult, and he stood at the entrance of the door with something in his hand. We dashed past him to get to the wash-basin, of which there was not sufficient. Nobody wanted to be last. We had to tidy our beds for the Petty Officer to inspect them. As I said, he was very hard to the boys. But we got over it as time went on. *There was a Marine outside the toilets to stop us smoking,* and if ever we got caught we had the cane across our bottoms. I could say more, but it's a thing of the past, very hard discipline at the time. I must thank you for reading my memories, which is my biggest treasure in life.''

No problem there, shipmate, but it could be considered that you are more considerate towards them than they were to you at the time. You give a fine example of `turning the other cheek`, and I don't mean the bare one!

Dave Davies - joined Ganges on March 16th, 1948, transferred later to the New Zealand Navy - and ended his naval career because of an untimely coronary as a two-and-a-half ringer. His story contains all five of the valid and interesting items included in this book: cruelty, pathos, humour, kind consideration and sweet revenge. It was difficult to decide into which category it should be placed, but dividing the story into five parts would spoil the exciting and professional flow of the experienced author in his writing of it. It is therefore told in its entirely in this chapter as it happened according to Dave. His first memory is of a typical one-in-every-mess-type lad who didn't know his arms from his elbows, nor even his left from his right. It is a tale of humour, spoiled later by the Instructor who introduced humiliation into the story:

Humiliation

"This lad insisted on swinging his left arm forward as he stepped out with his left foot. This is almost impossible for the average person to do, even when they try, but this lad couldn't stop doing it. Eventually we began to drill as a team and the mistakes on the parade-ground became less. We were quite capable of carrying out the most intricate movements without making mistakes. When we reached this stage our Instructor, P.O. Spicer, became quite merciless to those who did make mistakes. One boy spent most of one parade-ground session sitting in a dustbin in the middle of the parade-ground with the lid closed on top of him. Every time the class passed the dustbin, P.O. Spicer would bang it with his `Percy,` and at this signal the dustbin occupant had to raise the lid, stand up, and shout at the top of his voice: *'I AM RUBBISH!!'* and immediately retire back into the dustbin and pull the top down again.

Murder

Our Instructor Boy at the Annexe was named Underwood and he was a right young tyrant. I always swore, when I was in the Annexe, that if ever I met him again I'd give him the hiding of his life. There were times when he made us stand on the bed-springs late at night for some idiotic trifle. I would have cheerfully murdered him - and I meant it, too. I met him again when I came to the New Zealand Navy. He was a Warrant Officer TASI. Time is a great healer!

I still look on Shotley as the period in my life which turned me into an adult who had been given the will to be something. I grew away from my mates in the civvy street which I had left only a few months ago. few of whom made anything of themselves, really. As hard as those times were at Ganges, and as diabolical as some of the things

that were inflicted upon us, it was a cross-roads in my life at a time when I could have gone a number of different ways. We were an important part of the history of a great navy with a whole depth of tradition. I wouldn't have missed it for the world."

Dave said he could relate lots of yarns, and, being very short on material about the kindness of Instructors for this book, he was asked for more stories of that kind. Dave replied thus:

"On the subject of Instructors at Shotley I would have to comment that they were a bit of a mixed bunch. Our Instructors in the Main Establishment were a Chief Yeoman Hall and a P.O. Tel. Tarrant. The Chief Yeoman was a really superlative person. He was firm, insisted on discipline without any 'ifs or buts.' At the same time he was a most compassionate and understanding person, as I found out on a number of occasions. He was not much different to my own father in a number of ways, and I really did respect my Dad. I remember we had an orphan in our class who had nowhere to go for his leave. No prizes for guessing where he spent his leave. It was with the Chief and his wife. None of us boys knew about the boy's circumstances, or where he went for his leave. I only found out a long time later, when that same boy and I were P.O.'s in the same ship.

Nobby Hall was a real pearl and taught me - and I'm sure others, too - some very early and valuable lessons that stood me in good stead for many a long year. Even after I was commissioned there was the odd occasion when I was faced with a problem and I asked myself, "What would Nobby do about this?" I seldom went wrong. The man was an institution whose example was of the highest order. When we left Shotley, C.Y.S. Hall became the Chief Yeoman of the 'Gothic,' the ship that served as a temporary Royal Yacht before the Britannia was built. He would have made a really fine job of that draft because he was a pretty special sort of person. I can never, ever remember hearing him swear."

Cruelty

"On the other hand, Ginger Tarrant was an uncompromising tough nut, and his manner and approach was completely the opposite to C.Y.S. Hall. He made regular use of his 'Percy,' and laid it on hard. He was a capable Instructor as far as wireless training was concerned and he got some very good results, but it was largely because of the fear in which the boys held him, rather than the genuine respect which we all had for Nobby. Some other Instructors were even more tyrannical. I recall one of them who was in charge of the Covered

Way cleaning party for Saturday rounds. It was the only time I can remember snow on the ground at Shotley, and the temperature was below freezing. This sadistic P.O. made us take off our shoes and socks, roll up our trousers and scrub down the Covered Way with cold water from a hose-pipe. I, and others, were close to crying with the pain before the job was done.

Sweet revenge

A few years later, when I was an Upper Yardsman (Air), this character appeared at the door of the carriage of a train I was on, coming into Liverpool Street station. The green pusser's suitcase, and a few other bits and pieces, labelled me quite clearly as `Officer-ish,` and this guy offered his services as a porter, which he was, having been demobbed by this time. After struggling with my bags across the station to a taxi rank, I had the greatest of pleasure giving him the princely sum of threepence before reminding him of what he had done to me in Ganges days. Some might think this action unkind, but then I didn't think much of his actions a few years earlier.

Humorous happenings

There were also some humorous happenings at Shotley. One story I recall was quite funny. The story went around that during the leave period one Summer, it was decided to renew some of the rigging on the mast. The two classes who were Retired Leave Party, a description of those who were left behind to take their leave when the others returned, and were used as the motive power to pull a Dockyard-Matey Rigger, sent from Chatham Dockyard, up the mast in a bosun's chair. This was to be a mere five-minute job. When the rigger got to where he wanted to be, the line was secured. Almost immediately, the tannoy sounded off: 'Stand Easy!' and all the boys trooped off to the galley for tea and bun, leaving the Dockyard Matey completely unattended and hanging on for dear life until 'Out Pipes!' sounded, and they all trooped back again and lowered him down.

But there were some bad times at Shotley as well, times when I would have given my eye-teeth to be anywhere other than Ganges, but those memories have faded, and the broader recollections I am left with are of sunny, warm days, lots of sport, good mates and a sense of belonging somewhere, and of being someone whom my `civvy mates could never be. I was never fitter, and if I can quote from my forth-coming book, `Up the Hawse Pipe`: "The day came to leave Ganges. Behind us was Spitfire Boats, early morning rowing in frosts and biting winds, Shotley Routine and everything else. Our

Instructors were coming with us to Londonderry where we were to join our first ships during a break from Flag Officer Submarine's `Summer War.` The Captain gave us a farewell talk and wished us well. Our Divisional Officer, Lieutenant Loftie, suddenly became human and said, 'If we ever meet again - mine's a gin!' I actually bought him that gin years later when we were both in the Wardroom of H.M.S. Ark Royal.

Our kit had already left in lorries, and, for the first time since ceasing to be civilians, we wore shoes. We also wore tailor-made suits, and our `sea-suits` carried gold-wire Sparkers and Buntings badges.

The Royal Marine Band was fallen-in, ready to lead us through the Main Gate and down through Shotley Gate village to the boats which were to take us across to Harwich Station to catch the train. The class was invited by the Bandmaster to select the tune we wanted played for our march. To a man we immediately replied: `Lincolnshire Poacher!,` the Rodney Division `march-past` tune.

We were called to attention by C.Y.S. Hall and the order was given to turn right. I took a last look around. I would miss the security which had grown out of being at this place, the mast, the parade-ground, the Long Covered Way. Suddenly, I did not want to leave this place to face the unknown.

The order came: 'Draft class and band! Quick - march!'

We marched off with swinging arms and the jaunty steps of fully-fledged sailors, passing through those beautiful Ganges gates of gold and black with, for most, the streaming eyes of lost children.

Had I never gone to Shotley I would probably have not got much further than a South Wales steel-works, or something rather very much less than a Lieutenant-Commander with my own command. It was Shotley that did this for me - and I believe that nothing else could have done it."

Last laugh at Licquorice Legs.

Junior Electrician's **Mate Herby Herbert** was one of the few who had the opportunity to make a bullying Instructor look small, and he took full advantage of it, he starts his story back in the Annexe.

"We didn't actually sign on until we had entered the Annexe and been interviewed by an officer who explained that our twelve years started when were eighteen, two and a half years after joining, and that during the first twelve months we had the option to obtain our discharge by purchase for £20 after three months of service. Out of a mess of about fifty boys, only a third were left at the end of the course. The others had bought themselves out at various stages along the way.

In the New Entry Division everyone gets injected time after time against everything and anything that can attack man in a biological way. Unfortunately, this does not cover unclean needles, and, as a consequence, one of my injections turned nasty.

After many weeks of treatment from the ever-friendly, ever-caring sick bay staff it was decided that I would need a small operation. This was carried out in the sick bay and left me with some stitches, plus the Ganges equivalent of an American Express Gold Card...an `excused everything` medical chit! Pity, really, as I loved sport and had to forego that as well. However, whilst in possession of this chit, one was virtually bullet-proof. Quite unintentionally I put this to the test, and, at the same time scored one against the Liquorice Legs, the Parade staff with their black gaiters.

This particular day I set off across the parade-ground from forty-four mess on my way to the galley at a leisurely stroll. I had gone no more than ten paces when the mystery voice from the parade office bellowed: "YOU! BOY! REPORT TO ME!"

I immediately changed course and headed for the parade office at the far corner of Nelson Hall.

"PICK UP THE DOUBLE, BOY!" the voice screamed at top pitch. I proceeded to move a little quicker whilst desperately trying to control my bowel. Eventually I arrived in front of a very red-faced P.O.G.I.

'J.E.M. Herbert, Rodney Division reporting as ordered, sir,' I said, standing as if a long broom handle had been inserted into a certain orifice!

'WHY DIDN`T YOU DOUBLE, LADDIE?' the red-faced one said, with the same vigour and volume as when I was at the other side of the parade-ground, his voice now filled with menace.

'I am excused doubling, sir,' I said, trying to control the contents of my stomach.

His voice became official, sounding as if he was reading aloud from the rule book: 'WHAT IS THE ROUTINE FOR CROSSING THE PARADE-GROUND WHEN EXCUSED DOUBLING LADDIE?' he shouted.

I responded in the same manner. 'If excused doubling you march smartly across the parade-ground as per regulations, sir!' It was at this point I realised what was coming and a feeling of extreme confidence came over me. With a brief look skyward the red-faced

one then pronounced sentence with that smug, self-satisfied look of 'another one bites the dust.'
RIGHT, LADDIE. MARCH YOURSELF AROUND THIS PARA-DE-GROUND TEN TIMES, THEN REPORT BACK TO ME.'
Turning my features into as cherub-like and as innocent-looking as I could, I replied: 'I can't, sir, I'm excused marching as well.'
I thought his head was going to explode as his jugular vein leapt out of his neck and began pulsing.
After a few seconds he regained control and moved his face to within an inch of mine.'"PISS OFF!' was all he said, and went back into his office.
I had triumphed. I turned and made my way across the parade-ground smiling, knowing that whatever happened in the future, this glorious moment could never be taken away from me."
It has to be noted that in the story of Herby, given different cirumstances in a different place at a different time, if both parties were civvies, this particular case high-lights that, without the appropriate authority to back them up, bullies just have to back down and slink away, muttering obscene profanities in a pathetic attempt to save face.

The one who worked his ticket
George Dodsworth was an ex-Ganges Boy who disputed the R.N. system and eventually became captain of his own vessel, but not a Royal Navy ship. He left Ganges in February, 1951 after trying to obtain his release ticket, and was sent to H.M.S. Implacable for three months' sea-training, where he continued his quest. Although his story is not about Ganges, it does start there, and continues into his first months as a Boy Seaman.
"After three months we were all sent to the various Port Divisions for draft to various warships. I was sent to H.M.S. Superb, a cruiser preparing to go to the West Indies, that would be May/June, 1952. The ship was run in a very cosy style for the officers, not a bad style for the C.P.O.'s and P.O.'s, but a pretty off-hand manner for the rest of the crew. Here, I heard about form S.999. 'Application for discharge.' I filled it in and appeared before the Captain, thus bringing myself to his attention. I wouldn't say I was harassed, but I was certainly watched and known by the Petty Officers of the Deck Division. September, 1952, I was sent to Chatham Barracks, two weeks leave and then in October, 1952 I flew to Malta to join H.M.S. Cheviot (D90), a destroyer of the Mediterranean Fleet for a

two-and-a-half-year commission. Out of sight - out of mind. The ship was in re-fit in the Dockyard and to say it was a mess would be an understatement. After four weeks we were presented with a new first-lieutenant, Lt. Cdr. L. (name witheld by author).

"Misuse of power."

Then my experience with bigotry and personal dislike, leading to misuse of power began. As the ship was going to be in dock until January, 1953, Lt. Cdr. L decided that the Boy Seamen should spend a month on H.M.S. Cleopatra, a light-cruiser which was going to sea to Port Said to be the guard ship. So off we went on the Cleopatra. The experience was incredible, the Commander ran the ship on the lines of the navy of the 1920`s. Scrub decks at 0600 every day - everybody, including the Commander and all officers, in bare feet. So out came the old S.999 and again I came to the attention of the Captain. I`d only been there two weeks!

Anyhow, back to Malta and about the middle of January we Boy Seamen were returned to the Cheviot. Then it began. This 1st Lt. really tried to turn things around after the re-fit. The ship was fully manned with the most unsuitable mis-cast people imaginable. The Captain was a nice guy, and the Commander, but he was led by the 1st Lt. The officers were quite remarkable professionally. Only three of them had a bridge watch-keeping certificate - the Captain, 1st Lt. and one other Lieutenant!! When we did station keeping in NATO exercises it was hilarious - the old man was up there continuously. What is hard about station-keeping? I simply don`t know. Most of the Chiefs and P.O.`s were being kept in the Navy against their will in that they had joined in 1940-ish as Boys for twelve years - from age 18. Ha! Ha!, so were very resentful. Thus, they were easy prey for the 1st Lt., Lt. Cdr. L., to manipulate, and I started having a hell of a time. I kept slapping in the jolly old S.999., and then the Cox`n said that I was not to submit any more. I said I was entitled to. He warned me. So I wrote to my M.P. Wow! That provoked a response. I was hauled up in front of the old man. It seemed that the 1st. Lt. had decided on this action of no more S.999`s from me, and the old man was pretty mad at an M.P. being involved. Anyhow, I couldn`t be punished but the screws were really turned.

The ship eventually come home October, 1954 to pay off and go into reserve. I was informed on arrival at Sheerness, I was Oe-yew-tee-OUT! S.N.L.R. Services No Longer Required. Within two weeks I was away on my first merchant ship, s/s Manchester Shipper.

Over the years I watched Lt. Cdr. L`s career with glee through the Navy List in Manchester Central Library. He never rose to command a ship and retired as a Lt. Cdr. So obviously, his subsequent Captains didn`t see command-potential in him."

George would have been described by his lower-deck contempories as a `Lower Deck Lawyer` by those who were probably not as intelligent, `street-wise` or as enterprising and dogmatic as he. He had an aim, and he attacked that aim with fortitude, though controversial to authority, against what he thought was wrong. George has since joined the Ganges Association, probably for the pull of nostalgic remembrance for his youth.

"Quiet sobbing..."

Ken Ross, 8th January, 1952. "The head-lights of the bus picked out the gates of Ganges Annexe with two white life-belts hung either side. Home and Mother seemed a long way off and a long time ago. We were marched into Jellicoe I mess; two rows of beds down either side facing the middle, interspersed with grey lockers. The walls were a pale yellow and the beds pale green.

There was a boy dressed in uniform with white gaiters who came in the mess and started shouting. He said he was an Instructor Boy, called LYNAS. He didn`t seem to like me, said I looked like a rat. After that we went to another hall where a meal was served by boys wearing blue shirts, who kept effing and blinding, and told us we`d get used to it now we were in the Navy. I later learned they had been in only three weeks. At night, back in the mess, we went to bed, the lights didn`t go right off but glowed red - it all felt very, very alien. Through the night there was quiet sobbing from various corners of the room.

Next day we were issued with our kit and told we had to sew in our names with red silk chain-stitch. A name like mine, A. ROSS was OK, but we did have a C.J. EASTERBROOK in the class. The shortest one was J. ELD. He was finished first with me second. In later days whilst on leave, my mother and sister would go into hysterics at my `sewn in` vests and underpants."

Joe Ray, 1958, had a similar `problem.`

"I remember very clearly sitting on my bed sewing away, moaning and groaning about having to do this stupid task, when the Junior Instructor heard me griping away. He did no more than grab me by the ear, take me into another mess, and introduce me to another Junior doing the same task.

He said to this Junior: 'Stand up and tell this Junior here, your name.'
The other Boy stood up and said: 'T.A.R. SCARBOROUGH!'
The the Junior Instructor said to me: 'Tell this Junior your name.'
I said: 'J.A. RAY.'
To this the Junior Instructor said: 'If I ever hear you moan again about sewing your name in your kit, you will not only do your own, but do his as well. Now hoppit!'
Needless to say not another word was uttered about sewing names in kit again. By the way, we all helped 'Scarby' with one item of his kit.'''
Back to Alan Ross.

"Shorn to the bone.."

"Then we learned to march. One day on the parade-ground, learning open-order march and so on, I was called out, ordered to lay down my rifle and see the dentist. I had never been to a dentist in my life. He put me in the chair, opened my mouth and yanked out a bad tooth. No injections. Nothing. I then rejoined my class, swallowing blood and thinking that I definitely didn't like dentists. I had nothing to compare it with and thought that was normal.

Some of the times were good. Someone had worked out a mnemonic for the phrase, H.M.S. GANGES. '*Her Majesty Says Girls Are Not Getting Enough Shag*!' Brilliant!! My mother wrote to say she'd received a post-card from the Navy, printed DEAR MUM, ARRIVED FIT AND WELL - PLEASE SEND MY FOOTBALL BOOTS, YOUR LOVING SON,' which puzzled her because I didn't have any football boots and I never wrote the post-card! Another thing was they wanted my religion. I didn't know because I never went to church - so I said I was a RECHABITE. I knew there was such a religion because they used to meet in the chapel in my village whilst I was bird-nesting in the roof. So, because I had a thick Geordie accent, I had to attend the Church of Scotland parade!

Our hair was shorn to the bone, but I don't think any of us liked it or disliked Ganges. We were just there and stuck with it, although there was great conjecture as to the best way to puncture one's ear-drums with a darning needle and a cork. A couple went on the run and there were rumours of boy's hanging themselves with their lanyards in the night heads, but I cannot substantiate the latter, but believable in the circumstances."

Boy Sig Cooke of 19 Mess Grenville Division hung himself from a gas bracket in his bedroom whilst on Summer Leave, 1948.

Dancing lessons

"My Instructors," continues Alan, "Were PO Charlton and CPO Tomkins. I was terrified of them both, we all were. But I think they were fair! PO Charlton used to carry a fish-slice everywhere for whacking boys who committed any sin."

That was fair?

"We weren't allowed to approach them direct, only through a Badge Boy and had to stand to attention when speaking. One day we were told to report to the small gym for 'dancing' at 1930. Well, the rumours started and eventually it was stated that GIRLS GIRLS GIRLS were there waiting for us. There was such a rush to get ready. Dress was night-clothing and brown canvas shoes. We were marched down in a fever of excitement. The gym was empty except for a huge fat woman in a long green dress with beads plus a gramaphone player. She bellowed for us to fall into a line facing her. We were stunned into silence, hoping she'd hidden the girls next door and they would suddenly appear, but no! This female G.I. proceeded to instruct us in marching.

'Now step off with the left then the right. Now together. One two together, approaching me. One two together.'

Eventually we got so good at this that she allowed us to have music. We endured this for six sessions, learning to turn and then alter the tempo into a waltz. The rumour was now that we would get girls once we'd learned to handle ourselves on the dance floor. But it was not true. The Harwich girls didn't want to know us. We had no money, no hair and, having to be back at Ganges by 2100, they considered us as virtual prisoners."

"Cutting grass with scissors..."

Ken Street of November 1945 was amongst the first boys to enter Ganges at the end of the war, starting the establishment once again as a place for Boy's training. "We were opening the barracks at Shotley, which had been closed down as a boy's training establishment during the war. The training for boys had been moved to the Isle of Man and the boys would be joining the re-opened H.M.S. Ganges after the Christmas leave.

The regime was hard and several of those who had joined straight from 'civvy street took some time to settle down. However, I had been at the Training Ship Mercury on the Hamble river for 15 months, so I found the routine at Shotley easy after that. I was in 33 mess Benbow Division and Lt. P.L. Meryon was our Divisional

Officer and C.P.O. Harvey was the senior Instructor.

One saturday afternoon we had organised games. This consisted of each mess running a relay race. The starting point was in front of the P.O.'s mess at the far end of the parade-ground, and we had to run down one side of the parade ground, climb over the mast via the futtock shrouds, and run along the other side of the parade ground. When we reached our mess line we handed over for the next person to race. Several of us went first to get it over with. This left us at the rear of a line of about forty. We soon got tired of waiting and disappeared. When the P.O.'s became suspicious of our absence they mounted a search and found us in the canteen having a cup of tea and a fag. Suddenly there were R.P.O.'s and Leading Patrolmen at both doors. We were herded out and mustered on the quarter-deck and they sent for our D.O. who gave us a dressing-down and asked if we were prepared to accept his punishment or go on the Officer of the Day's report. We accepted his punishment and for the next three weeks, when the remainder of the Ship's Company were at the cinema, which was held in the Gymnasium, about 60 of us were cutting the grass and bushes on the bank at the rear of Benbow Division's messes with scissors."

"Friendly foes..."

Bob Smith. "Shotley was a place never to be forgotten, in my day, when proceeding on leave, all our belongings were tied up in a blue bundle handkerchief, no suitcases, no attache` cases, like a knight of the road we carried our swag. I remember a Royal Marine telling a yarn about the Adjutant at a certain barracks. This character rode a grey horse at all times, even when inspecting kits. There was no apology given if the horse happened to shit itself all over a Marine's kit, except: 'Just a moment! Clean up this mess.' The articles of kit which were soiled were never able to be washed clean again. But these sort of things did happen.

Anyway, back to joining: The first impression of landing at Shotley Pier and marching to the Annexe was the strong smell of Pusser's soap, our first meal, a large soused-herring was devoured, bones and all, we all came from poor families and food was gratefully accepted.

Two P.O. Boys, Lusty and Jordan, were our friendly foes, beatings were handed out by Jordan, a Geordie, Lusty was a good guy.

I had to enter the hospital for a week due to a vaccination flaring up and causing me to feel ill. Why did they bother putting me in hospital? I spent all my days polishing the floor of the ward. No compassion from staff or others. Real concentration-camp routine. When I was finally discharged I was back-classed a week and that excperience was awful, you would have thought that I had deliberately become ill, the abuse and hassle I received from the Instructor was really frightening for a boy of 16 who had never been away from home before. Eventually I was drafted to 20 mess, Grenville Division.

The following ten months was one period of my life I shall never forget. Our Gunnery Instructor was P.O. Baxter. He took a dislike to me, not apparent at first, but he pulled a few sneaky strokes against me, reporting me for continual skylarking. I and my oppo, a tough Mancunian, Jack Hampson. Actually, Jack was the instigator of our mischieviousness, but Baxter liked him. I was the villian in Baxter's eyes. The first Monday of each month, up to the Commanders table, name of Chad, with the D.O. in attendance. The Divisional Officer was a Lt. Juniper, what his interests in life were, I don't know, but it certainly wasn't the welfare of his boys.

'Boy Smith!'
'Sir!'
'Off cap.'
'Boy Smith, sir.'
Lt. Juniper:'What have you to report?'
'He is improving, sir, so I am informed.'
'Well, Smith?'
'I am improving, sir.'
'Good. See you in a month's time.'
'On cap!' What a farce.

At 0530 on one day of the week we were ordered to march to the Laundry, allocated a sink, strip off all our clothes and commence dhobying each article on the floor. Why on the floor? We were issued with the old-fashioned yellow flannel front. As we washed and rinsed, each article had to be held up for inspection by the P.O. If he wasn't satisfied he would immerse the offending piece of clothing into a sink of ice- cold water, place it around our naked shoulders and wring it out. Sadist.

Another traumatic exercise was the weekly shower. 60 boys undressing in a space built for 20. Good job our clothes were marked. This was the classic concentration camp effort when the Jews and others were conned into believing they were actually going to shower. 60 naked boys to 8 showers, too cold, then scalding hot, no adjustments, wash in the water running to the drains. Hugh, sadistic P.O., his henchmen rigged-up the cold-water hose, switches on full force, my God, it was awful. After five minutes hosing down, in which we all sought to hide. Where? It was one at a time to be hosed down individually, then inspected.

`Aft foresheets!` God help you if you hadn`t removed any debris from behind your foreskin, a whack with a cane on your bum.''

"House of torture..."

''The Gymnasium was a house of torture. Fall in outside, P.T.I. check class-list. Dash into No. 1 Gym, select a pair of smelly, well-worn plimsolls to fit, speed upstairs to the balcony, off jumper etc, then, half-naked speed to the Main Gym to fall in for P.E.

'On the wall-bars, go!' 'Sit down!' 'Stand up!' 'Two ranks facing me, fall in!' Followed by half an hour of exhausting physical training. Our bodies, at the end of the sessions, would be reddened by the huge imprints of the P.T.I`s hands, any error, or failure to comply with a given order was rewarded with a slap from a hand as tough and horny as a turtles flipper. (Thinks) *My God! He`ll kill me one day.*

My Seamanship Instructor, Mickey Dunn, was one of the only two Killick Instructors at Ganges. He was a small, very alert man, understood us boys, in fact, he taught us more gunnery than Baxter the G.I. Being in the opposite watch, Starboard, we were considered untrainable by Baxter. He was totally unsuited for Boy`s training. I can see him now, left shoulder lower than the right, a trade-mark of all G.I.`s, very impatient. We weren`t as daft as he thought, field-gun drill was like a scene from a `Carry On` film. We couldn`t even change numbers. He used to shout and bluster, making matters worse. At the field gun passing-out session even the Warrant Gunner was amazed at our foul-ups, field equipment, drill order, was the only exercise we could perform. Full marching order was a catastrophe. But somehow we passed. `Get rid of the little bastards, they`ll learn soon enough!`

The mess opposite, 19, was blessed with two very strict Instructors P.O. Stair and P.O. Rogers, known as `Fred` and `Ginger.` During the afternoons when all messes were officially out of bounds to the boys, Fred used to sneak along silently, enter the mess and catch bang-to-rights a number of boys lying under their blankets. Arming himself with a broom, he used to burst in like a cyclone, roar in his commanding voice: 'Clear the mess!' As the culprits ran the gauntlet to pass him, he would flay them with his broom, an evil grin on his `orrible face.

They never learned, those 19 mess boys.

Rogers, Ginger, was a big burly man, he once took charge of a cutter manned by myself and class-mates. We had to pull our guts out for two hours on the Orwell. If anyone was unfortunate enough to catch a crab, a spare oar was used to chastise the culprit:

'Ow! Oh!'

'It hurt, did it?'

'Yes, sir.'

Whack! 'Don`t do it again!'

We were scared out of our wits.

Then Ginger Rogers said: 'See that crew over there?' pointing to another cutter.

'Yes, sir.'

'Well, we are going to pull against them in a race back to the pier-head. If they beat us, NO TEA for you, you understand?'

'Yes, sir!'

We won easily, the thought of NO TEA was the spur. We hoped the Instructor who lost the race treated his boys with more kindness.

Another known sadist was Chief Murray. My oppo, Jim Patterson, now deceased, had the misfortune of having him for an Instructor. Jim`s class were among the first to use the four new messes built alongside the parade ground, 1937. They were raised off the ground with a foot or more of space underneath. Chiefie discovered several boys smoking in the space beneath the buildings. He called out the rest of the class, armed them with brooms, squeegees, and other weapons; a hose was switched on and the culprits drenched with water. As they attempted to break out, they were poked back in by their class-mates, encouraged by Chiefie who was present to ensure his wicked orders were obeyed without question.

He also turned the class out at various times during the first watch, 2000 to 2359, either to double until they dropped or climb over the mast.

I believe he finished in charge of Stalag 13!

Joe Fenwick, a huge Geordie, who was slightly mentally retarded, was one of my class-mates. He was one of the unfortunate people who had no natural rythm to his movements, marching behind him was agony. He marched like a Robot. One of his jobs was mess cook, fetching the food from the galley to the mess. On one occasion, Sunday, he conned me into assisting him to carry the tray of cake to

the mess. On our way back to the mess he said: 'Follow me, quick!'
I looked and saw it was the Heads just below the Galley. In I went,
carrying the cake, feeling very perplexed. He then produced a knife
from his pocket and made an attempt to cut the cake in half.
'What are you doing?' says I
'Just let me cut a piece, some for you and some for me.'
I was horrified. Without further ado I fled from the Heads with him in
full pursuit. On reaching the mess I shouted out: 'He was trying to
steal some of the cake!'
He tried to bluff it out, he was too big a chap for anyone to attack. He
was given a verbal slagging which failed to penetrate his thick skull.
My God! He was a monster! When we were having our final Gunnery
exams, Joe and I were seated at a small table with the Gunnery
Officer, a Lt. Cdr., conducting the exam. He asked Joe about the
Vickers range clock. Joe blatantly hissed in my ear, 'What is it?'
I gave him an answer which I knew was wrong. He repeated it to the
Gunnery Officer, who corrected him, informing him that it was the
wrong answer. Joe hissed an obscenity at me, and learning forward
on the table, his huge close-cropped ginger head, shielding me from
the view of the Gunnery Officer, attempted to hit me. Talk about Fred
Karno's navy. I was in stitches and, strange to relate, the Gunnery
Jack never turned a hair or spoke one word in rebuke. I think he was
as puddled as Jo, he was a veteran of the battle of Jutlland and had
lost a leg in that engagement.
Joe was also a bully, and, after lights-out would get out of bed and
use his gym shoe to whack one of the weaker members of the class.
Eventually he was told to stop it or else, and he did. I never saw him
again after leaving Ganges. He went to Portsmouth and the Iron
Duke.

"Vicious and unsociable.."

My eldest sister used to post to me a parcel of chocolates once a
month, like Billy Bunter. I always looked forward to the occasion. A
huge Marine post-man used to open the contents, looking for
contraband fags. Imagine if my sister sent me any fags.
'WHAT'S ALL THIS? FAGS?'
'Don't smoke, sir.'
'We will see about that! Commander's report!' The result was cuts
with a cane and jankers. My bloody sister! I'll kill her when I go
home. It never happened to me, thank God, but it happened to others.
Work ship. Now that was a change. I was allocated the job as a

100

general messenger, all smart and clean in a duck-suit, boots polished, very smigget! I was employed delivering messages to various offices. On one occasion I was sent to the gym. I knocked on the Instructor's door, no answer, I went in. No one there. A full-length mirror fixed to the wall. I preened myself. Did I look smart, wow!

'BOY!' God! What was that?

'What are you doing in the Staff Changing room?'

'Looking for you, sir'

He hit me a savage blow on the face with his hand. I was fuming.

'NEVER enter any Staff Room. You understand?'

'Yes, sir.'

'And don't look at me like that or I will have you on a contempt charge. GO!' And I went. A boy harshly done by, face hurting, ego demolished. May the wrath of the Gods descend on that bastard and do to him what he done to me. But, a lesson well learned. Never enter Staff Rooms without permission. What makes these people so vicious and unsociable?

School was another compulsory rule, the toilet situated outside the building was a favourite venue for the smokers. 'Lobs a Jock!' was the cry when a Marine on patrol was sighted. One warm-hearted boot-neck, a favourite with the boys, always chanted: 'Lob's a Jock!' when he walked around the heads, echoing the familiar cry, much to the delight of the boys.

Ganges made me and other boys obey all orders without question, good training for the rigours of shipboard life. A sense of humour was a must."

That is true. A terrible tale of woe, or a sorry story of sadness or sadism, if told in a jocular manner, can be placed within the confines of 'humour.' **`Pancho` Brett** of 1957 fame, relates his poetic version of life in, or at, Ganges:

"Ganges was about suffering.."

"Long before the phrase, 'wind-chill factor' was invented, it could have been used to describe the east coast winter of 57/58 which blew long and hard. Icy winds from Siberia howled across the parade ground to freeze the noses and hands of poor boys standing to attention on divisions or on pay parade. Although I can remember being issued with gloves and scarf, and laying them out at kit musters, I cannot recall being allowed to wear them, regardless of how foul the weather! Their Lordships, in their wisdom, must have decided that it was unseemly for boys, who were training for the

Royal Navy, to wear such comforts.

Ganges was about suffering!

I wrote home to whinge to Mother about a Ganges boy's lot being a poor one, not enough to eat, taking turns sitting on the drying-room pipes to thaw out, and, because I was not suitably attired, I was suffering with split lips and knuckles due to the frosty weather.

Starters.

You can imagine my excitement when my Instructor, Black Jake Hubbard, presented me with a parcel chit and told me to report to the post office at stand-easy.

Puffing and panting, I arrived at the post-office counter, chit in glove-less hand, to be glared at by a Killick Regulator, who looked like he ate boys for breakfast. With a black scowl he ripped the chitty from my hand and, locating a large parcel on the shelf, threw it on the counter in front of me.

I looked at the package with hungry eyes, thinking of what goodies would be under that brown wrapping. The Regulator saw the enjoyment on my face and decided to put a stop to it. He had been well-trained, and experience had taught him how to make boys miserable.

Example:

Ganges Rule no. 1 for Regulators:

Boy happy - Regulator unhappy.

Solution: Regulator make boy unhappy, then Regulator happy.

He began to open the parcel and when I protested he informed me that it was rules and regulations to check the contents of boy's parcels. What could he hope to find, I thought. Dirty books, drugs or some other contraband?

At this moment he may be sitting reading this, surrounded by a loving family, much respected and admired, but at that precise moment he was degrading and humiliating me, and I wished at that moment that he was dead!

He poked my fruit cake and rattled my box of biscuits and then his eyes widened with triumph and gratitude as he lifted up a pot of skin cream. I'll never forget it, it was called `Smiths Cramola.`

'What's this for, laddie?' he sneered. The words stumbled out as I explained about my split lips and hands. He removed the lid, and, sticking in a grimy finger into the cream, he lifted it to his nose and said with menace, 'Are you sure you're going to use this on your hands and lips? It looks like `starters` to me!'

I didn`t know what a `starter` was until years later when I found out it was a cream of sorts used by homosexuals for various reasons. He was disgusting.''

A `bloody` good lesson.

Tom McGregor, in a previous tale, called his Junior Instructor `an animal.` `Pancho,` of 57/58, had first-hand experience with not only animals, but pigs in particular.

"During the Christmas and Spring terms, visits were arranged to local factories and institutions, the object of which was a break from normal routine and to broaden one`s outlook.

Visits were made, among others, to Churchman`s, Bernard`s, Ransome`s and Trinity House, but Hawke 47 Mess were off to Harris & Co., the bacon factory!

We were all excited, no more being bellowed at by Instructors, nor the the fear of Shotley Routine around every corner; a day to enjoy, or so we thought!

Boarding the bus after breakfast we had the obligatory Pusser`s Bag Meal shoved in our hands - most of which was devoured by the time we passed through the main gate. Entering the factory yard, the first thing that hit us was the smell, and then the noise. The smell was blood and flesh from the previous day`s production, and the noise was coming from the unfortunate porkers being herded into the pens for today`s gruesome ritual. I`m sure that the animals knew what was in store for them, because they became quite agitated when they got a whiff of their oppo`s who had gone before.

I had worked as a butcher`s delivery-boy on Saturday mornings before joining-up, but nothing could have prepared me for what I was about to experience. I became a little frightened and I`m not sure who was more wary of entering the factory - me or the `trotters.`

Inside we became the object of interest as the work-force stood at their battle-stations, sharpening the most fearsome knives and cleavers, looking at us as if they would like to practise on us first.

The first batch of pigs were driven into the premises and set about by men with what I can only describe as electric head-phones which stunned the creatures. Then their back legs were tied together before being hauled over great baths. As they passed across the baths their throats were slashed while they still twitched and were left to drain off over the bath.

Watching the great spectacle of blood was too much for one boy who doubled outside and mustered his kit. I started to feel queasy and, looking around, my class-mates all seemed to be turning green. The butchers, seeing this, set about their tasks with added vigour and one individual grinned at us as he slid his cutlass slowly across the pink throat of a large hog who emitted a final grunt.

The rest of the visit was a nightmare which haunts me still; the squealing of the swine being herded in, the smell and blood as they went down the line, being dissected. Nelson's Jolly Jack Tars would have taken it in their stride, used to `paying the butcher's bill` after a battle at sea, but for boys fresh from their mother's bosoms, I fail to see what benefit it gave us all.

We returned to Shotley in silence, suffering from trauma after what we had witnessed and I vowed never to touch the flesh of the porciner again. But the following day, at breakfast, I tucked into my greasy bacon rasher and rubbery-egg, too famished to resist it. All resolutions forgotten."

What a gruesome story - especially the part about 16-year-old boys being `fresh from their mother's bosoms.` They certainly took a long time to mature!

Invaluable training.

"Athough I agree with comments regarding the harshness of discipline and life generally at Shotley," writes one ex-Ganges boy, **no name given,** "I was to prove that this training was invaluable during war service where I was a three times survivor, and, in particular, was mentioned in dispatches in 1941 after surviving 19 days adrift in the Bay of Biscay. Throughout that paricular experience and in other circumstances, I was able to use the many skills of seamanship and discipline which I had learned at Ganges.

Within minutes of entering Ganges I instantly realised that I was no longer a person and was to become merely a number, and so started my new career. We were introduced to our Instructors who were named Price and Hollinsworth, and, upon forming a ragged two-deep line, we were told by P.O. Price, 'As a child, I lost my wooden soldiers. My mother asssured me that one day I would get them back. And this is that day!' He paused, then said: 'She said I would get them back again, and I have. You have replaced those dirty, unintelligent, wooden soldiers, and it is our job to lick you into shape, and,' he added, 'We have a hopeless, formidable task, because of your slovenly appearance, general outlooks, and levels of intelligence which appears to be of the lowest possible order, and we are amazed that any of you have been allowed to join the Royal Navy!'"

Humiliate them first, make them feel inferior, and they will be putty in your hands.

"We had been in the R.N. less than two hours and this was the greeting extended to all ratings and the feeling was that surely things couldn't get worse. How wrong were we all eventually proven to be!!!!!!" The exclamation marks are not those of the author but those of the writer. But if the remarks of the Instructor are genuine, isn't this the beginning of a brain-washing scheme to make the new entries believe they are less than intelligent so that the Instructor can now treat the recipients of his speech as menials and subordinates?

"Corporal punishment...kept us in fear.."

"Corporal punishment was another salient factor which kept us in fear. Although, in fairness, I never experienced or witnessed any severe blows from Instructors with closed fists. The main, effective deterrents, and regularly applied, were a rope's-end smartly directed at the butt, and it really hurt. Or the use of a cane or nobbly stick which, to this day, is recalled as being called a 'stonnicky.'"

Blows, whether by closed fist, rope's end, nobbly-stick, or stonnicky, are administered, does it make the punishment less severe if the blow is *not* delivered with a closed fist? And can the perpetrator of the blow be excused if he does not actually *punch* his victim?

"Weekly," our writer continues; "all hands were marched to the laundry where each individual washed his kit. Each item, when washed, had to be shown to the duty P.O. who gave minute inspection to underpants and duck-suit trousers. The area scrutinised was the crotch and the rear seams, and, upon observing a stain, no matter how small, the P.O. would scream out, for all to hear: 'Look at this dirty filthy little bastard! His gear is smothered in biscuit dust!!!!'

A spell in the laundry was never to be forgotten. All ratings who failed to launder their gear properly would find the whole item of kit in its soapy and soaking current state, suddenly, and with great force, would be wrapped around the offender's head, or upper torso, and all the lads were always in fear that this painful experience should not be for them." *Fear rules again.* "The laundry was situated on a hill near the foreshore, and all ex-ratings will remember with fear and virtual terror that it was located on an exceptionally steep hill, known as Laundry Hill. It was the penultimate in dishing out physcial punishment where this was in virtual constant use, sometimes by a whole mess of forty lads. We were taught many terms regarding boat-sailing and `aft fore sheets` was, for us seaman, a common term. It was also used on bath days when the Instructor would give the order to all those who had not been circumcised. On command: 'Aft fore-sheets!' that particular lad would have to pull back the fore-skin of his penis so that this vital organ could be inspected for the lodging of any debris within this region. It was embarrassing but accepted as being logical for health reasons."

A helping hand.

On the subject of inspections, **Charlie Kent,** who talks well of his Instructors, P.O. Spriddel and Tiggy Eaves, gives us a story about a certain kit inspection:

"Kit inspection never had me worried for I used to keep most of my kit rolled and taped-up, in fact, I often gave assistance to other lads. We had in our mess one fellow, no name mentioned, but I`ll call him Fred. He was so scruffy in himself and his kit, and it is a fact that he was scrubbed with a nail brush at one time and ordered to lay out his kit for Divisional Officer`s inspection. I am none too sure, but I think the R.N. were considering giving him discharge, not only for his appearance, but for his attitude towards his life in general. Even P.O. Spriddel, or Tiggy Eaves, our kind Instructors, could not have any effect on him. He seemed to all that he was hopeless. It so happened that we were all sitting around on our beds the night before his kit-inspection was due. He went beserk, and started to tear his kit and to throw it about. Several of us went towards him, a bit afraid of what he might do next. Alfie Button, a skinny weed of a fellow, managed to quieten him down, gathered his kit and placed his arms around his shoulder and managed to cool him down. A few of us decided that whatever was torn we would put needle and thread to it, and hide whatever had to be hidden.

To get to the point, the kit passed inspection. The Divisional Officer did not pass comment, nor Spriddel or Tiggy Eaves, but what was noticed in the future, Fred`s attitude began to change slowly for the better towards us, the navy, etc. By the time when it came for us to depart for our allocated ships, Fred, on his `goodbyes` to us, openly thanked us for what we had tried to achieve and succeeded.

In the years to come, I happened to be in Canton, gun-boat country, and who do I run into but Fred: good manners stopped me from making remarks upon his excellent appearance. He was a picture of elegance, a credit to the R.N. and he had made it to Chief Petty Officer, decorated for bravery for some action he had taken part in.

Then, to my amazement, he spoke about the incident at Shotley. 'You know, Charlie,' he said, 'If they had tossed me out I am sure I would have ended my life. Ganges was home for me. I was a boy from the streets and I never had a good home like yourself.'
I replied: 'Fred, I know how you feel.'
'I had no-one to turn to at that young age,' Fred continued. 'I took up the life of a tramp, then, on the spur of the moment, I walked into the R.N. Recruiting Office in Chatham.'
Like myself, he passed the writing exam, English and essay, but on arithmetic we both were duds. It was the same Royal Marine Sergeant who did our arithmetic for us. Whether it was out of kindness or perhaps we were worth a few bob to him, we don't know, but we were grateful to him for it. The last time I saw Fred was about five years ago. I was getting off the train at Chatham, Fred was getting on. I was en route to the Isle of Grain to see Bill, an old shipmate. When I mentioned to Bill that I'd seen Fred, he said: 'Yes, I know him. I served on three ships at different times with Fred. What a lovely fellow, always so smart, never a thing out of place.'
Do you know, even today, I have never seen Fred since, but is one of my thoughts; the only thing I can utter is - 'well done Fred!'"

"Discipline was strict but NEVER harsh..."

"During my time at Greenwich School and in the Training Ships, discipline was strict but NEVER harsh, but of course, by the time I joined the Navy, I had become accustomed to 'discipline,' triced-up on a box-horse, and receiving twelve cuts of a cane to the back-side."
Those are the words of **J.F.W. Norris** who joined Ganges in 1930 via St. Vincent and Greenwich School.
'NEVER harsh,' he says with emphasis on the NEVER, but is there anyone, apart from those who actually enjoy being caned, who can say that receiving twelve strokes of a three-foot long, half-inch diameter bamboo cane, delivered with as much strength and force as possible onto one of the most tender parts of the body, is not in the least harsh? Everyone has their limits, it can be supposed. J.F.W. Norris continues:
"I left Greenwich School in October, 1928 to join St. Vincent at Gosport. Being a native of Pompey I was somewhat chokker to be drafted to Shotley, being a Pompey stalwart. After one month in St. Vincent, to undertake Signal Training, and in January, 1930 I joined the 'Emperor of India,' a flag-ship of the 3rd Battle Squadron as a Signal Boy.

As a Greenwich School Boy I suffered 12 cuts of the cane on two occasions. At Shotley I was awarded 12 cuts of the cane, 14 days 10A, and 30 days leave stopped over the Christmas period for hopping over the fence and buying 300 fags at Ma Butchers, the village shop.

A couple of days before Christmas leave, authority took pity on me and I was allowed to proceed on leave to return on New Year's Day. The Yeoman and P.O. Tel Instructors were in a cold sweat, dreading they might be required to supervise me during the leave period. But they were not required.''

Authority took pity on the Instructors who were in danger of being deprived of their Christmas leave.

That incident took place in 1930; to his credit the writer attained the higher rates: "In January, 1945, I got made Chief Yeoman and, on the same day, I bumped into my old Instructor, by then he was a Pensioned Chief Yeoman in the Recruiting Service. It gave me great pleasure to shake his hand. In 1949, I changed over to the Fleet Air Arm as Chief Airman at Siskin at Gosport. Crossing over on the Gosport Ferry I spotted among the passengers, Vice Admiral Francis M. (Bunny) Austin, retired.

Sidling up alongside him, I whispered in his ear: 'You once gave me 12 cuts of the cane.'

He turned his head to look at me, clearly not remembering me from all the hundreds of boys who had gone before, but with the grace and manners of the true naval tradition of a naval officer, he grunted: 'I expect you deserved it.'

I hold no grudges.''

Is it possible that someone can be so institutionalised, having suffered harsh punishments such as barbaric caning to the extent that he thinks that painful punishment is normal? Does it cause him to be immune to the humiliation of corporal punishment, painful though it must be, and obviously was?

Another Ganges-ex who holds no grudges is **Brian (Taffy) Jones, 1954/55. Benbow Division, 33 Mess.**

"Our Instructors were C.P.O. Basher Bates and P.O. Blossom Bloom. This story isn't in anyway knocking Ganges, in fact, I'm proud to have been a smally boy there. I say 'smally' because I was one of the little ones in my class, and always seemed to dip out. For instance, when we got mid-morning cocoa and buns the tall boys used to collect the cocoa in fannies and buns on a large baker's tray. The big lads would carry the tray on their heads so that us little ones couldn't reach. Nine times out of ten we didn't get one, but we didn't complain for obvious reasons, and if anybody did their life wasn't worth living in the mess. C.P.O. Bates played God, we dare not answer him back, but thinking back he was the salt of the earth and helped many young lads like myself en route to that big wide open sea and the many hang-ups we would come across in our future years. Now P.O. Blossom Bloom was very different, he was laid back and told us many a good sea story when we should have been learning Seamanship.

I made two very good oppo's whilst at Ganges; Doug and George. They come into the story a bit later on. But for the moment let me mention the polished deck and other tortures.

I remember we spent about a week getting ready for Captain's rounds, scrubbing and polishing anything that didn't move. Anyway, the night before the inspection we had strict instructions not to use the night heads so that they would be clean for rounds the next day. We were told to use the outside ones at the bottom of Benbow Lane. Yes, you've guessed it, Blossom caught me having a pee after lights out. I was put on a charge; I think I got three days jankers but we all had a good laugh, it did me no harm and I was beginning to realize that an order was an order and not to be disobeyed.

"Stamping all over his kit..."

"As Ganges boys you will all remember the wooden block floors and how we used to use our boot-brushes to polish them, and, after the brushes, our own bed blankets; one would sit on the blanket and two boys pulled you up and down the mess. Yes, you've guessed the inevitable - splinters in our bums.

Nobody complained because we all strived to have the cleanest Mess in the Division. Cleanliness always came first as boys, and if anybody didn't keep themselves clean they were soon spotted by the Instructors. All their kit was taken out of their lockers, tipped onto the steps at the entrance to the mess. Then all the sixty boys in the mess were ordered to put their boots on and march up and down over the kit until it wasn't worth looking at. After that, his kit was thrown into the wash-room; the offender was given a bar of pusser's-hard soap and told to remain there until he scrubbed it clean. To this day I don't know who was worst, the offender or the ones who dished out the punishment, the Instructors." The `offender` offended no-one but the Instructor. The worst of the two was the Instructor for causing unknown and untold misery and humiliation to the Boy.

"Punishment on Laundry Hill will remain with me forever. The Instructors took extreme delight issuing us with broom-handles, ordering us to place them behind our knees and made us bunny-hop up and down that horrible steep hill. I think many of us went to our bunks and cried ourselves to sleep."

The culmination of these stories of harrassment, unfair and unjustified treatment to Taffy Jones and his oppo`s could have only one natural conclusion. Taffy himself gives it the title of:

Now for the great escape from Alcatraz!!!

"One Sunday afternoon, my oppo`s, Doug, George and myself, started discussing all the injustices we believed we were suffering, and definitely came to the unanimous decision that it was time to go. We even called ourselves the *Great Escape Committee.* (Silly Boys, weren`t we?) We decided the following week-end was going to be IT. On the Wednesday or Thursday of the following week, we started bringing bread, bits of pie and any other tit-bits we could smuggle in our number eight shirts, ready for the big day.

We decided on the Saturday morning that to-night was the night.

Saturday night it was raining cats and dogs but that didn`t deter us, after all, we all started off as simple village folk and didn`t think of the pit-falls.

We waited until night rounds had come and gone, then we made up our beds to look as if we were still in them, went round and said our good-bye`s to our oppo`s, and to this day I don`t know why the Leading Boys didn`t report us; maybe they would have loved to come along but with all that rank and responsibility at the tender age of 15 it stopped them.

At a later stage, the lads in the mess told us how they fell about laughing when Basher came in next morning and tipped our beds over, as we were the only ones supposedly still in them.

Back to Saturday night: out we go through the back window, pitch black outside and pouring down with rain. Then making our way down to the Lower Playing Fields and into the night. We were soaking wet but we were young, healthy, and in very high spirits with no thought of going back. If the truth was known, each one of us was too frightened to tell the other two that it was a damn silly thing to do. Anyway, on we goes, the blind leading the blind over muddy fields, about four in the morning. We had eaten the scraps we had purloined from the Dining Hall hours before and were absolutely knackered, cold, wet, and very, very stiff, so we decided to find shelter.

We came upon this large farm in the middle of nowhere, found an open door and in we go. It turned out to be a cow-shed with mangers for feeding the beasts. Doug found an old Army trench-coat and promptly donned it; I wasn't so lucky, I only got a chaff sack, I can't remember how George managed! We didn't sleep much for the cold, but at least we were out of the driving wind and the rain, and though it was cold, it wasn't as cold in the barn as it was outside.

We had a lot of small talk between us, but by this time we were all very frightened and wished we were back in our warm bunks and waiting for Basher to come and say: 'Get out you lazy lot! Hands off Tiddlers, get moving!'

We did get a caller, but not what we expected. This huge mountain of a man in black wellies, splashed with wet cow-dung, stood at the door and shouted: 'You little buggers you! Ganges boys aren't you? You just get out of here and come with me.'

He took us up to the farm-house and told us to wait outside until he made a 'phone call, then in he went. We were Cold, hungry, and almost dispirited, but we still weren't prepared to give up, so we ran like hell across the fields, never to see that farmer again.

Going across the fields I caught a baby rabbit, and, being a country boy, I knew how to kill the poor wee fellow. I remembered it's small, warm body still twitching as I skinned it. I ripped out the kidneys and offered one to Doug, but he declined, so I ate them. After that I broke the body into portions with my fingers and, yes, we were that hungry, we ate the lot. But it wasn't enough to stem the hunger, so on our weary way we went. Next we came across a field with Brussel sprouts growing and had our fill of them. Remember, we never had any money, we hadn't been bright enough to have the aforethought to save anything from our five shillings a week.

Our next discovery was a field of red-currant bushes, so we had much more than our fill, gorging ourselves until we all had stomach pains and, I might add, the trots too!

We had been on the run for less than twelve hours, and things weren't looking too good, all we wanted was our mothers and a hot drink and something substantial to eat. This came quicker than we expected. By now we had had enough and decided that thirty-three Mess, Benbow Division, was the only place to be. So we walked along the road into this small village. We later found out it was called Manningtree. We hadn't been there three minutes when the local 'bobby' pedalled up to us on his bike. His words! 'You little buggers! I've been up all f......g night looking for you three little bastards! I hope you get what's coming to you!' Then promptly took us to the police-house, let us have a wash and clean up. His good lady, bless her, made us a very welcome hot drink and buttered-toast. After what we had been through we thought we were at the Ritz! By this time, of course, 'Mr. Plod' had phoned Ganges. I think we waited about half-an-hour before the Blood-Wagon arrived!

Getting back, we were placed in cells which were along by the Main Gate. At the time, Ganges was busy changing over Commanders, so we were remanded in cells for six days.

"Death sentence..."

The duty R.P.O. used to march us out daily for exercise and one day called us to a halt on the Quarter-deck and pointed to a window-ledge which had a nest with little birds in, and he said to us: 'Why can't you behave like them and do as Chiefy tells you?'

It raised a laugh at the time, but a very feeble one, and we didn't have the same enthusiasm as our dear R.P.O. because we were waiting to get weighed off and fully expected to receive six cuts apiece. The cuts were usually delivered with a three-foot bamboo cane by a Regulating Petty Officer with large muscles and, according to others who had received them, they really hurt, leaving weals of red and blue, and sometimes drew blood, and most times tears as well.

The time came to meet our new Commander. All three of us, myself, George and Doug, stood in front of him. The charge was read out by the Jaunty and the Commander looked at us and he said:

'The punishment is six cuts for absconding, absent from place of duty without permission, which is punishable by death or any such means as mentioned specified hereafter.' And we wondered what was coming as he continued: 'But as you have been in cells for a week, your punishment will be fourteen day's number 11's.' *Jankers.*

That was a sigh of relief, I can tell you.

Us Ganges boys have a bond that no 'civvy' could understand.''

"God Bless all of you"
Taffy Jones

112

Chapter seven
Amusing Stories

Despite what many ex Ganges boys have written or said in this book, it is inevitable that there must have been some humour in existence at Ganges. Life is never one long slog of misery, but neither is it one continual heaven of mirth. There are mixtures, sometimes the times are good, and sometimes the times are bad. Never at all are they all good, nor are they always bad. Often it depends who you are and what your disposition is, whether it is positive or negative, or whether one has the strength, courage, fortitude and ability to see the humorous side of events. It must be agreed that to go through Ganges, a sense of humour was an asset and a priority; those ingredients were as esssential to Ganges as vanilla is to custard...

The boys cussed 'ard...

L. Webster, 23rd June, 1931, who must be 86 or 87 at the time of writing, remembers that the galley was half-way down the Long Covered Way, and sometimes, he says, any food left over was placed outside for the boys to take and dispose of as they wished - if they wanted it. **Did** they **want** it?

"On one occasion," writes L. Webster, "A large tub, about three to four feet across, and about two and a half feet deep, was placed outside the Galley containing custard left over from the sweet. There was a concerted rush by the boys, **hoping to get a dip of custard.** Unfortunately, rivalry was rife, and

JW. '95

HMS GANGES GALLEY.

HAPPINESS IS····

"GAsh Custard -"

the first two boys to reach it started scrapping and wrestling with each other to be first to have a `dip.` One of them unceremoniously picked up the other one and dumped him in the tub of custard. I recall seeing him dragged out by a Royal Marine Patrolman and escorted to the quarterdeck, dripping custard all up the Long Covered Way towards the quarter-deck for an investigation. I don't recall the outcome but the incident caused quite a lot of amusement." But there cannot be any doubt that the custard-clad victim cussed-hard afterwards!

Charlie Kent, a man of many stories, has a wonderful sense of humour, and calls this story:

'A Foreshore Romance.'

In another story by Charlie in this book, as a seventy-plus-years-still-employed character, he shows the young girls, at the factory where he works, a photograph taken when he was a young man, and they remark: 'Were you really as good looking as that?' Charlie replies that indeed he was, and added: 'Bloody Admirals fought over me!'

Here's his story:

"It was whilst playing a game of hockey at Ipswich that I became involved with a young and lovely girl who lashed me up with chocolate. I fell for her, hook, line, and sinker, making a date for the following Saturday or Sunday at Shotley. I would be on my two-hour Shotley leave. How I looked forward to that. It seemed the week-end would never arrive. It did, so did she. Cor! She looked gorgeous.

'Where shall we go?' I asked.

'Where could one go in Shotley,' she asked the question. 'Where's the best place to go?'

For what? I thought, hoping for the best. 'Foreshore,' I answered.

'What's the foreshore?' Before she could learn the answer, I'd taken her there. The weather was hot and sultry, I was sweating, and, for a while, we sat and conversed, what about escapes me now.

'Phew! Boy, it's hot,' she said. 'Don't you think?' she asked. And in the next breath: 'Why don't you take your top jumper off?' So I did, except for the trousers and pants.

'Oh! Charlie, boy!' she exclaimed. 'What a lovely chest! You have hair on it,' said she, sliding her hands over my chest. Well, I was only sixteen and you can take my word for it, I was a virgin, but I had a feeling this was going to change - and soon.

'Want any more chococolate, Charlie?'

'No thanks,' I said.

After a while, I noticed, she lit up a fag, had a few drags, then she had another go at rubbing my chest, dropping the packet of Gold Flake cigs into my hat, and I didn't really take much notice of that at the time, I was too interested in what she was about to do. Oh, Gawd! I thought, 'ere we go! This is the last day of a respectful life!

Suddenly a shadow was cast over us, and a mighty, deep voice boomed: 'What the bloody hell are you up to, boy! Stand up, you nasty little creature!'

Jesus! Who is he, and where the bloody hell did he come from? There stood the nastiest and meanest Royal Marine, looking down upon us. 'And what's the fags doing in your hat?' he boomed.

I suddenly remembered she had only put the Gold Flake fags in my hat. Smoking was forbidden. The punishment was twelve cuts. In those days one did not use the word, 'pillock,' but it doesn't matter what I called her. It was something worse than 'pillock.'

The Marine spoke again: 'Get dressed, you horrible thing!' I was told, 'What's yer name and number? Your Division? Number of mess?'

I gave him all the answers.

'Right! Make your way back to your mess, lad! Now! At the double! Move!'

I started back and suddenly, about a hundred yards gone, it comes to me: why wasn't he escorting me back to the quarter-deck? I had better ask him. So I returned to the scene to see what I saw. I was about ten yards away and he was lying down by the side of my girl-friend and he was having his chest rubbed!

So I was still a virgin and from what I gathered the Royal Marine was not in a panic. I had taken it for granted that he was. You know those Royal Marines, smart at their drills. Whenever I saw that fellow again, a nod and a smirk came across his face. You never know, she may even be giving him a chest rub to this day! And does she still feed him chocolate, and does she still smoke Gold Flake fags!?"

Smoking, by Boys, was forbidden in Ganges up to the 2nd World War, and the punishment for being caught was six or twelve strokes of the cane.

J.E. Pearce, now 81, joined in July, 1929. His story is a mixture of bullying Instructors and humour with a touch of misery for one boy. He starts with reminiscences of the hard times:

"For small misdemenours, slackness, dirty boots, etc., you could get from one to ten days no. 11's, doubling around the parade-ground, with short rests in between. Some of the sadistic Petty Officers would give you 'exercises' during your rest period - like holding out your rifle at arm's length. There was a rumour that not long before my time at Shotley, a Petty Officer Boy had been discharged for making boys mark-time in bare feet on the wire mattress of their beds while holding a kit-bag on their shoulders. For the major crimes, smoking, or being in possession of a dog-end or a few strands of tobacco in your pocket, or even just a match - six strokes of the birch.

One day we were all assembled on the quarter-deck for evening quarters when the silence was shattered by the sound of hob-nailed boots marching up the covered way.

In full view of the assembled ship's company marched one of the Boys in our mess, Scouser Smith, flanked by two very large Royal Marine sentries. Smith was holding a broom-handle in his hand from which dangled two bootlaces knotted together to make them longer. The lower end of the bootlace was smouldering, giving off smoke. He had been caught poking his pole and boot-laces - like a fishing rod - down the chimney of one of the small boiler-rooms to get a light for his fag. Needless to say, he got six cuts.

My time In Ganges was tough, but looking back, things don't seem too bad, but at the time it seemed like it was Hell!"

Brian Johnson, who says he was 'Interred from 1950 - 52,' has several anecdotes, most of them humorous, and they are included here, although the first one is on a very sad note:

"The outstanding memories of that period were the loss of P.O. Boys Ricketts and Middleton while out exercising on MTB`s. During night manoeuvres two of the boats crashed, cutting off the bows of the one in which the boys were asleep. I don't think they were ever found."

"Cock-a-leaky soup!"

I didn't like much the early morning sailing, cutters and whalers, training for coxswain crews. The Divisional Officer used to toss his dog, Pickwick, over the side with cries of: 'Man overboard!' We had to come about and rescue the mut. This dog was well-known, especially at kit-musters, when, it was said, he had been trained to cock his leg over one's white duck-suits and white-fronts to cries from the rest of the mess of: 'Re-scrub!' It was understood that he was `lost' one morning after falling overboard from a cutter somewhere among the reserve fleet ships!

I'll never forget jankers; doubling up and down Laundry Hill with a .303 rifle, then, as further punishment, we were sent to the cell-block to prepare soup for the Regulating staff. We got our own back by mixing in dead cock-roaches and skinned field-mice into the stock to give it some delicate flavour.

Punishments were hard, even though one was in the right when committing a misdemenour. One morning, after a cross-country run, I returned to find my breakfast had been eaten by the duty-bugler. We had a fight, and, after the scrap on the mess-deck we were given D.O.'s report with option of Captain's report, which meant six cuts or a grudge fight in the gym in front of the full Division. We chose the grudge fight and we fought until one of us, the bugler, fell, but we still received the cuts which were delivered whilst we were strapped down over the back of a chair in duck-suit trousers. We doubled round the parade-ground so no one could see the tears. Neither of us could sit down for a week. As I said, we were sometimes punished for things of which we were not guilty of. Dhobey sessions were a typical example of this.

"Boys whipped with wet towels."

Boys who were backward-swimmers wore life-belts all day, P.T.I.'s whipping boys with wet towels to keep them moving. In the wash-house a Royal Marine would inspect the washing, if the item was not clean enough he would throw it on the floor and stamp on the article; boys who were dirty would be scrubbed in the bath-house with bass-brooms and hand-scrubbers until they bled. We were all green from home, but learning fast - the hard way.

One lad, who was very religious, knelt by his bed every night to say his prayers; he was ridiculed by most of the boys, but he turned out to be tougher than anyone. He was a judo and martial-arts expert, so, religious or not, and, after teaching the boys judo and martial arts, he was soon accepted as one of us. There was an R.C. priest who suffered from a head wound. He would give away £1 notes one day to the boys in the covered roadway, and then asked for them back next day. Then there was a boy in our mess, Rucker, who tried to hang himself one night because he was in love with another boy. A boy called Barnett broke into the D.O.'s office and stole a stop-watch. Maybe these were cries for help. Then there were the girls, 'Sweaty Mary,' who always showed her wet arm-pits when she raised her arms, and 'Penelope Persil' who never seemed to be without a white sweater, showing her boobies. They both sold sex through the chain-link fence on the Lower Playing Fields foreshore every Sunday afternoon by putting their arms through the chain-link fencing and masturbating any Boy who would give them five woodbines.

What memorable events! Young men, all in their prime, starting the great adventure. We left Ganges with tears in our eyes. Don't let anyone tell you that Ganges

---

Truth

When Boys of the "Ganges" shout "Ahoy,"
By no means are they glad.
In fact that savoury mouthwash,
Inclines to make them sad.

But cheer up Boys, remember
That when on leave to say,
You wouldn't leave the Navy,
For all a civvy's pay.

Boy EVANS, Class 257, Drake

117

was different. The only home some of the boys knew for two years. We meet up all over the world, and the community feelings are still there." Brian adds a p.s. "Officer-in-charge Signal School, Lt. Diamond, he took me onto the quarterdeck one day for knocking out a boy called Fairbrace, who had called me `illegitimate.` I got away with it - but enjoyed a week of gargling on the Quarterdeck with a `mouth-wash`:

`Ahoy! Ahoy! Ahoy! I am a foul-mouth boy! This will make me a clean-mouth boy!`"

It is not known for sure what the `mouth-wash` contained, but it has been reported by several contributors of letters to this project that it was a mixture of Teepol - the stuff used to scrub off the polish from the mess-decks - and/or a dreadful-tasting laxative concoction from the Sick Bay, with liquid-bowel-producing symptoms, reminiscent of diarrhoe`a. Bluebell polish has been added by the more adventurous and those of vivid imaginations, together with many other distastful ingredients - some of which may be true. The mouth-wash is often described by Bingo-callers as 'Number nine, doctor`s chum!' A `number nine,` was a potion supposedly prescribed by Army doctors for inducing bowel movements. In the case of the foul-mouthed boys of Ganges, it was a nasty-tasting liquid, introduced by Captain Robson, circa 1948, who believed in the 'eye-for-an-eye' syndrome and which included punishments such as one boy seaman plucking enough hawthorne berries to fill a one-pint glass as punishment for picking just one blackberry from a bramble bush on his way back to the Main Establishment from the Gunnery School; or, for a Signal-boy, made to lie down on the playing fields for an hour every make-and-mend Wednesday afternoon for a month, as punishment for lying down during morse-flashing and semaphore instruction.

This chapter is about humour, but it has to be said that up to this point, including this chapter and the foregoing chapters, they contain stories which are mainly about unfair treatment to the boys, by Instructors and Instructor Boys, and, worst of all, the cruelties of boys to boys. The ex-Instructors should also have a chance to put forward their point of view: the difficulties of trying to knock into shape the boys in their charge- and that is not intended as a pun - tho' it could be taken as one. Instructors had their problems too. There were a few boys who were just impossible.

To examplify: imagine an irate bully of an Instructor chasing a young boy with a rifle, bayonet fixed, screaming obscenities, curses and threats, cheered by a crowd of other Instructors urging him on. This story would then have been placed under the heading of 'cruelty to boys.' But because this story is an example of a situation which is a turnabout of the other way around, it has to placed under the title of 'Humour,'

Fix bayonets! and charge! - the Instructor!

Harry Norman, 1935, is not an ex-Boy who hated Ganges, and he has often had reason to be thankful for the training he received there, so he cannot be accused of being biased against Ganges, either by vindictiveness or by personal qualities. He says: "My memories of Ganges are still quite vivid; one of the Instructors was known as the 'Shotley Terror.' He was a typical P.O. Gunner's Mate, tall, thin and nasty. When he appeared, emerging from the P.O.'s Mess to take any class for a session of Field Training on the parade-ground, a general groan was audible. His favourite punishment for slack drill was to make a boy hold his .303 rifle, weighing about nine and a half pounds, above his head, squat on bent knees and bunny-hop around the parade-ground. The Inquisition would have loved him! He had another nasty habit of walking down the line of boys, and, if he did not like the look of something, he would crack the boy's shins with the butt of his own rifle.

There was one particular boy, who's shin he cracked once too often. This lad, throwing down his rifle and clutching at his wounded shin, yelled at the astonished G.I., calling into question his parental credentials. Then he picked up his rifle, whipped out his bayonet, fixed it, and charged - lunging at his tormentor who, realising the boy was definitely not joking, headed at a high-speed gallop for the drill-shed. Other classes, under similar instruction elsewhere on the parade-ground, were treated to the spectacle of this much-disliked G.I. galloping along with an irate boy a few yards astern with a rifle and fixed bayonet at the horizontal. The 'Shotley Terror' shot into the Drill Shed, slamming the big wooden door behind him as his pursuer lunged at his vanishing rear, the bayonet sticking in the door.

By now, of course, other Instructors had arrived, overpowered the boy with the bayonet, and he was led away to cool off and suffer the consequences of an incident that could have had an unfortunate ending. Unfortunate that is, for the Shotley Terror, but fortunate for a great many of Ganges boys. That particular G.I. received a draft-chit quite soon after that glorious day."

Smoking syndicate

Jock Elder of 1949 recalls the Destroyers Bicester, Bleasdale and Cowdray, which were used for a day's sea-training to selected classes. Jock also recalls that his mess had a 'smoking syndicate.' One of the rules of membership was that they pooled their tobacco resources. One boy, Jimmy Green from Belfast, had the idea of purchasing cheap smokes in the way of naval 'Tickler,' rolling

tobacco, from the crew of one of those ships.

"I have forgotten which ship we were to carry out our days' sea-training," explains Jock, "but Jimmy Green, the instigator of the idea, had conceived a daring smuggling plan. He knew the ropes and was determined to return to Ganges from his sea-going sojourn with a quota of 'tailor-mades' or a tin of 'Tickler,' as they called it, Pusser's tobacco, naval issue. Inevitably, much of our day's training was spent cowering out of the wind behind the after smoke-stack and trying to retain our breakfasts in rather queasy stomachs. A gang of us saw Jimmy in earnest conversation with a stoker mechanic. Contact had been established! We eventually completed our day's sea-going training and returned to harbour later in the day.

Back in Blake House an excited group of smokers gathered around as Jimmy pulled the contraband 'baccy from his stocking. A round, shiny tin of 'Tickler' was produced, it wasn't sealed, but that didn't matter, there was enough to keep Jimmy and the 'syndicate' in 'roll your owns' for several days - and very cheap! The atmosphere was tense as Jimmy prised the lid off the tin and poked about inside.

'Wait a bit,' he said. 'hang about,' his brow furrowed with perplexion. 'What's this?'

'What's up, Jim?' we asked.

'This 'baccy smells a bit strange...'

He lifted the first half-an-inch of tobacco and revealed that beneath it the rest of the tin had been stuffed with cotton-waste. Jim was livid.

'That dirty, rotten bastard!' Jimmy shouted. 'I'll get that bastard, see if I don't! He's seen us off!'

On further investigation it was revealed that even the top layer of tobacco was shredded-up dog-ends. We'd been had, and Jimmy, much to his disgust and frustration, never did see that thieving, son of an-unmarried-parents-stoker again!"

Dwelling upon smoking: **Roy E. Orkney,** Drake 40 Mess, 1951, now of Australia, recalls: "One evening, just prior to 'lights-out,' Boy West, who's bed was opposite mine, sat up in bed smoking a cigarette when the duty Instructor, C.P.O. George Wedges, walked into the mess. West put his hand, the one holding the cigarette, under the bedclothes to try and hide it. We will never know whether the duty Instructor, C.P.O. Hedges, had seen this movement and acted out the charade of being surprised and alarmed, but as he walked into the mess he spotted smoke fumes coming from beneath the bedclothes of West's bed. He rushed over, declaring, 'West! you're on fire!,' and proceeded to pat the bedding as if it was alight.

To the rest of us, this was funny, but another boy, Boy Wisdom, who had not noticed that West had been smoking, grabbed a fire-

extinguisher, rushed down to West's bed and sprayed it all over with foam. Needless to say, one boy spent a very cool night curled up under a damp, smelly sheet, minus blankets and counterpane, and then having to explain to the D.O. the next day why a fire-extinguisher had been discharged. Two lessons were learned that night:
1. Never smoke in bed before 'lights-out' when the Duty Instructor is due, and:
2. Fire-extinguishers sometimes do work!"
It may be obvious that the amount of happy stories which happened at Ganges are on to a losing battle with tales of sadness. I asked originally for humorous stories of or about H.M.S. GANGES: **David Ablitt,** June, '62, Blake, 6 Mess:
"Having served my sentence from June, '62, I have searched my memory for any amusing anecdotes but am saddened to realise that nothing comes to mind, in fact, I'm fairly convinced nothing too amusing ever occurred at Ganges. I was fortunate enough to represent Ganges at cricket, 'away' at St. Vincent. Freedom at last! I remember 'Badge-boys' drunk with power, the likes of which they will never experience again in a free state."
That is all David had to say. At least you tried, Dave.
T.R. Clarke-Irons was a junior Divisional Officer in Hawke Division, 1942-45, and Activity Leadership Testing Officer. His story is from the officers point of view.
"I recall that one of the officers, a non-Executive sub., took a party of WRNS and nurses in a sailing cutter up to the boatyards at Pin Mill. Coming back on the ebb-tide he failed to give enough sea-room out of the Orwell Estuary and, with the wind from the East, the cutter grounded on the 'Spit.' The young officer was in summer whites and, not wanting to soil them, he made the girls get out into the shallow water and the rather sticky, black mud, in order to lighten the load on the boat. He then told them to push it off toward the open water, then to hang on and climb back in-board. Seeing the party return with one immaculate male and a crew of very muddy females caused some considerable comment and amusement."
The man was an officer, but obviously not a gentleman!
Not all of Ganges boy entrants saw the funny side of life at that place. To some it wasn't funny in the least, to most it was just about tolerated, but to any who could see the humorous side of it, it was not only funny, it was hilarious.
C. Adlington of Sheffield, Ganges, early part of 1950. His story: "I was Captain D.C. Hill's chef for about two years. It was a most enjoyable experience and his wife was a joy indeed." (*I'm glad he*

didn't explain that, and I bet he is too, but I wonder what he means?)
"I was on a short leave and the county was blanketed by fog for the whole period. I set off by my usual train but was greatly delayed and arrived very late. As to be expected, I was put on Commander's report and then to the Captain's report.

On the morning I had to appear before the Captain I discovered that there was no public transport available. As I was staying at Erwarton Hall, the Captain's residence, I requested transport. Someone, somewhere, must have thought it was a good idea that, as I was already at the Captain's residence, and on his staff, and I needed a lift, not knowing that I was in the rattle, and there was nothing wrong in supplying one car to transport two people to the same destination from the same starting place. So it was the Captain's own car which arrived to pick me up. I sat in the back of the car and, after a while, Captain Hill came out of the house, took one look at me in the car and his face went scarlet. He wrenched opened the door and said: 'Get in the front! You are the bloody prisoner! Not a bloody V.I.P!'
I never lived it down. The staff were watching through the windows. He gave me seven day's confined to barracks and loss of pay. Afterwards, on his return home for lunch, he popped his head round the door and said: 'We'll have lunch now. O.K. Adlington?' He looked quite sheepish and didn't seem to know where to put himself. Needless to say I didn't 'doctor' the meal or anything, mainly because of his wife's sake! (ha,ha)"

The statement, "I didn't doctor the meal because of his wife's sake," could be taken that if it wasn't for the Captain's wife, who was obviously a 'delight' to Adlington, would he have 'doctored' the meal? And what does he mean by 'doctored?' Like the boys who prepared a meal for the Guard-room staff? With dead field-mice and crushed cock-roach Soup a la Ganges Patrolmen?

"I was a Ganges boy, and was also at several other concentration camps later in the war. I joined the L.D.V. at 17 in 1942 and was O.D. on the Ganges ferry, working on the ferry-boats 'Harricott,' 'Ferry Brice," and 'Brightlingsea," says **Dick Harman** of Clacton-on-sea.

It seems that L.D.V. was something to do with ferry-boats, and Dick was a junior deck-hand, or ordinary seaman. He continues: "I was not sent to Shotley until I was eighteen into General service in 1943. I was not allowed to board the ferry to go on leave because I did not have 'P.P.S.' stamped in my pay-book." P.P.S. is something to do with passing the swimming test, so we can presume that all new-entries had to pass this test/exam before they were allowed ashore, and that included Dick Harman.

"Anyway," continues Dick, "I asked the officer-in-charge if I could go ashore if I had my own boat.

He laughed and said, 'With your own boat? Yes, of course.' I presume he was taking the piss, thinking that a new-entry at Ganges could not afford his own craft.

I rang up my mates on the ferry at Parkstone and they came over and picked me up, much to the surprise of everyone, including the Officer-of-the-Watch. My late brother was also at Ganges and got jankers for standing on the button whilst the flag was flying!

Later, during the floods in 1953 at West Mersea, near Colchester, I assisted an old gentleman named Captain Barnes to refloat his 80-ton sailing vessel, named `Black Fox`. Captain Barnes was, at that time, 92 years old, and had been a midshipman on the `Cordelia,` and assured me that the mast at Shotley was the mizzen-mast from that ship. He was convinced that steam was only a flash in the pan, and sailing ships would soon take over again. He was a very fine old gent and told me that he had been the navigating officer on one of the Antarctic expeditions."

"Concentration camp..."

Back again to the expression: `Ganges was the first, last, and only concentration camp in England,` originator unknown: A letter from **Peter Monks** of Terrace Bay, Canada, passionately denies that Ganges was the first, the last and the only concentration camp in England - H.M.S. St Vincent was, he claims with some pride. So, although he was not a Ganges Boy, we'll give him space to tell us why H.M.S. St. Vincent deserves that dubious, and in his case, coveted title:

"I was not at Ganges, but the **better** of the two establishments, H.M.S. St. VINCENT. I liked the barb about it being the 'First, last and only concentration camp in Britain, second only to the Foreign Legion.' My only connection with GANGES was when I represented H.M.S. St. VINCENT in a sailing competition, back around 1952 or `53, sailing cutters. Due to budget restraints no crew was sent, only the coxswain, myself. I was assigned a Ganges crew on the day, they were not an enthusiastic bunch as I recall, I guess it is hard to race against your fellow mess-mates for another ship. I seem to remember I was doing pretty well, until, rounding one of the buoys I was just able to squeeze in front and had to call for `water.` Shortly thereafter I was on a long tacking leg when everyone else was taking much shorter and more frequent tacks for reasons only known to them, puzzling me at the time, but becoming very clear later when I ran hard-aground jamming the bows of the boat firmly into the sticky black mud of the Orwell.

'Oh, yes,' one of the crew called out, as an after-thought. 'Watch out for the mud flats!'

I guess the honour was served. The Ganges boys were of the opinion that they did not have to crew a winning boat against their own ship, even if it meant a Division other than theirs winning. I received a frustrating day's sailing, and a rich experience of how human nature will react under certain circumstances.

To indulge in a spot of nostalgia: did you have the discipline of being made to eat cigarettes if found discarding them on the parade ground?"

Of course we did, Pete! Not only that, but they made us eat them BEFORE we got chance to drop them on the parade-ground! YOU lot were lucky! But what's the gripe? Did you ever eat one?

"I have never smoked," continues Peter, "I did not think much to that idea. I did, however, eat quite a fair amount of 'pussers hard' soap for swearing. That is something that I was once proud of, and now spend much time trying to avoid. As I recall, one had to eat a one-inch cube of soap for each infraction. I found that I could chew and swallow without a moment's delay, such that I often wound up with another in case I had somehow got rid of it. I also remember luxurious hot showers followed by the cold tank that one had to jump into and completely submerse. This form of torture was combatted by leaping over the side, down into the water, then up again and out in one smooth motion, taking maybe no more than a second or two.

Then there were the P.T. Instructors in their white shirts and shorts with their rope 'starters.' I remember the long vault over the box-horse, one had to get your hands placed at least two-thirds of the length of the box. This was usually marked as the rope starter. If you did not make the required distance and 'walked' with your hands along the vaulting horse top, the starter would be snatched up and laid sharply across your backside whilst you were still in the air and in a bum-up stance. One fellow broke his wrist by not stretching far enough and walking along the top. He was left writhing in agony on the ground while the rest of the class was made to do the job properly before he was carted off to the sick bay for treatment. That was OUR ship, St. Vincent. YOURS, Ganges, I understand, was much softer."

I don't know about that, Pete. Your letter goes on to say that after leaving Ganges you left the navy when you reached 18 because of continual sea-sickness. Ganges Boys were much hardier!

G, White, 1938, signs himself, 'Fellow Internee:' "One cold bleak morning when we were all grouped about the mess square, not at all happy about going down to the pier to hoist and scrub the boats out, we'd all had a stint at this finger-numbing evolution, someone groaned and said: 'ere comes our Gunners Mate!' It was Chief Petty Officer Records, striding across the parade, whistle and chain swinging around his neck, many of the boys who were inclined to be rather sluggish at these early mornings were revitalized by that chain."

This is the same P.O. Records, later promoted to Chief, who returned again as an Instructor in 1946, uncle of Peter Van Der Weele, 1946, who was eventually discharged after being A.W.O.L. from Ganges for six months.

G. White continues: 'Feeling cold this morning, lads?' said the Chief.

'Yes, sir!' from every throat, hoping we would be allowed to light the coal fire. No such luck.

'Fall in outside with your kit-bags,' the Chief shouted. 'Right turn, double march!' Up and down Laundry Hill.

'Who said we were cold?' he shouted.

The mutterings in the ranks were, to say the least, unprintable, and then down to the boats and the jetty we were doubled.''

Hanging

One boy in our mess wangled a week-end compassionate leave and had not returned by `lights out` on Sunday evening, although we had expected him back by then. After everything was quiet, some of the lads thought it would be a good skylark to fill his pyjamas with his blankets, like a dummy, with a bit sticking out of the top like a head, and hang it by the neck with his hammock lashing, dangling over his bed to give him a fright when he returned. We all stayed awake, quietly awaiting his return. Unfortunately for us, before he arrived, two patrolmen turned up in the mess on their rounds. We held our breath and stayed quiet. One of their torches lit up the dummy. The Patrolmen nearly had fits. They took the dummy down after verifying that it was not real. One of them, by this time, had turned on the mess lights and they screamed at us to get up onto the quarter-deck in our pyjamas. They fell us in outside the Quartermaster's office and reported us to the Office of the Watch, who, when he arrived, was doing his damnedest not to laugh.

The one phrase I'll always remember from this episode is the Officer-of-the-Watch saying:'Bring out the body!' He then doubled us around the parade-ground for a while and sent us back to bed. Commander's report the following morning. I believe this was one of the times that we towed the field gun up and down Laundry Hill for a few hours.

I wasn't much good at sport, apart from rowing and shooting, and with a few others of the same mind we formed a card school. One afternoon about six of us were all seated on a bed at the far end of the mess playing brag. There was quite a bit of money in the pot, about three or four shillings. We had got down to three players with just one to drop out before the hand could be called.

A voice spoke and said what we thought was: 'I'll see you!' and one of the players threw his cards down and shouted, 'Ace flush!'

Only then did we realise that the voice which had really said: 'I see!' had two-and-a-half gold rings on his sleeves. Of all people, we had been caught by the Divisional Officer. Nothing could have been worse. We got fourteen days jankers for that.

We left Ganges in October, 1946, and most of our class joined the `Formidable` aircraft-carrier which was being sent out to join the British Pacific Fleet. Although we were considered the lowest-of-the-low as boy seamen on board, our training in seamanship and other skills was highly regarded, in fact, in a way, we were rather an elite group - we were GANGES BOYS. We were professional sailors, trained men, in fact, at eighteen years of age, we were actually rated AB(TM) - Able Seaman, Trained Man."

John Goulder was a Boy in Ganges and later returned as an Instructor and again later as a Divisional Officer. He retired as a Commander and admits, when talking of an old shipmate and fellow-Instructor, George Bishop, who has a story elsewhere in this book: "Neither of us `spared the rod,` but in general we had a `Happy Class.` Those whom we met later at a class reunion said how much it stood them in good stead in later life. They, of course, are now in their 60`s, George and I are some 12 years further on."

John Goulder`s story is a humorous anecdote of the time when he was a Boy. "I should be able to recall many humorous stories, but I always remembered the occasion of the story of the `shaky bread.`

Twenty-three class of 1937, Rodney Division, our mess was a double G.C. class who`s Instructors were Reginald Arthur Stevens and William Maslen. Willy, as he later was known to us, was our Seamanship Instructor, a two-badge Petty Officer, tall, slim and smart with a youthful but weather-beaten complexion and a wry sense of humour.

He was very firm usually, a just disciplinarian who`s stock phrase for anything not up to standard was, `shaky!`

It was the custom that, those who were not involved with plating-up meals at meal-times, assembled in the covered way. When the food was on the table we marched in and took up positions by a meal. If Willy considered some meals were larger than others, and there had been collusion between those who dished them out, he would say, 'Right turn! Quick march!''And we would shuffle round the tables;

then: ` Halt!'Placing us by a different meal.

He would then say, 'Any complaints?'

One supper time all this happened; at the question: 'any complaints?' one member, who obviously did not think his slice of bread was as thick as the others, held up his chunk of bread above his head and, waving it about, said: 'Yes, sir - shaky bread!'

Willy, quick as a flash, turned, looked at the bread closely, and said: 'At the order `one` you will all hold up your bread. At the order `two` you will shake it. At the order `three` you will lower your bread. One!' We all held our bread above our heads. 'Two!' We all shook our bread, waving it all over the place. 'Three!' We lowered our bread again

Willy said: 'Now you ALL have shaky bread,' and disappeared out of the door. We stood there looking at each other in silent disbelief for moments that seemed an age - then, as one, we all laughed, sat down and got on with our supper.

One of the other pleasant things which have occurred was last year, when some dozen members of 12 mess, 1945, located myself and George Bishop, my opposite number Instructor in 1945, and led us to a reunion in Portsmouth."

"Doing a bunk.."

Larry Webster of the thirties recalls two boys in his class who decided to abscond, or, in his words, `do a bunk.` "In order to finance their escape they went round to as many of their friends as possible, and bet each one that they would indeed do a bunk that night. The wager was tuppence a head. They took my money, and that of many others when they went. They didn`t stay away for long, being captured by the local constabulary and returned the next day!

Most of the boys in my class indulged in surreptitious smoking, and one way to achieve this was to light the end of a boot-lace in the fire and keep it glowing by vigorously swinging it around in a circle, then, with the piece of bootlace cupped in the hand until they reached the cover of the bushes near the playing fields, applied the glowing end to the cigarette. I lived at Ipswich during my time at Ganges, and was always asked to bring back cigarettes on Sunday evenings on my return from weekend leave. This was achieved after being passed by the R.P.O. at the gate and told to report to the Regulating Office at the top of the Long Covered Way, I would pause alongside the bushes by the road and, pretending to stoop and do up my bootlace, I would toss a packet of smokes to a class-mate concealed in the bushes. I never got paid for the smokes."

Times was `ard..

Gerry Gray was known as Ginger Gray, but being in the `Andrew`

he was probably called 'Dolly Gray' after the 1st World War song of that title. His recollections of Ganges, January, 1947, are a mixture of humour, hard-times, bordering on the hilarious, so they must, because of that, come under this heading of 'amusing.'

"The first few days were nightmarish; heads shaved to the bone, arms swollen by needles and vaccinations, scabs all over the body from the shock, and washing with Pusser's Hard. Standing naked at those huge sinks, scrubbing at brand-new kit which would never be cleaner and didn't need it, and the continuous roaring of the Instructor's voices. The snow was several feet deep by now and the temperatures were well below zero, but we were in Sports rig with punishment given if we wore anything underneath. We all had 'flu and bronchitis, but there was no 'sick call' unless you wanted extra work shovelling snow.

We had cross-country runs over endless dunes of frozen snow which sliced chunks out of our legs as we fell through them. Several of us had to be hauled out of seven-foot drifts - don't think we lost anyone, the roll-call was invincible." The humorous bit is yet to come! He continues:

"Mast classes: I was never frightened of heights until I worked my six-stone frame round the half-moon, finger-nails scrabbling at the ice-coated ropes. A chap from Birmingham dropped his blue handkerchief deliberately, and said, as it slowly wafted downwards, 'It's a long way down. We'll get shredded into chips in that net if we fell from here.'

Next time we climbed the mast I tried dodging through the Lubber's Hole and got caught so I had to attend a week of Mast Classes. I was petrified. And guess what the first job I was given onboard my first ship, the old 'Boxer?' Painting the mast! They never missed a trick!''

''Blonde W.R.N. stripping naked in the galley.''

One lad in our mess escaped three times from Ganges and they caught him at Ipswich railway station twice. The third time he was on the run for several months and gave himself up a few weeks before the rest of us had finished our year's sentence.'' *That boy was Dave van der Weele who tells the story of his 'escape' in another chapter.*

''Best times were Sunday afternoons with spuds baked on the mess coal fire; and the three a.m. call when a certain blonde WRN used to do a strip in the Galley changing-room prior to reporting for early duty. The line-up, to peek through a hole in the bricks, ran into hundreds; was she aware of all those lust-full teenage-eyes? She took about an hour to change into overalls, so it's possible. Then we decided to become religiously Confirmed to get an afternoon's leave in Ipswich. Doughnuts and tea in the Church hall. The food-fight on

129

leaving-night, lobbing peas and mash all over that holy of holies, the polished deck. A dozen trips up and down Faith, Hope and Charity in full kit, followed by three kit-musters and mess inspections didn`t put us down, we were Boy Seaman 1st Class with a career in front of us.

Sports could be avoided by volunteering then quickly nipping through the iron railings with the missing bars, by-passing Patrols, using skills that Red Indians would have envied. Then to shin up into the mess attic where we had a stock of fags and studied yellowing copies of Naturist and spoke in whispers of what we were going to do to the local ladies on leave. This back-fired on one occasion. Time was important and only one lad possesed a watch. We were in the Inter-Divisional qualifying cross-country. Two Divisions at a time went out at intervals, each with red or blue sashes. The best-timed to go into the final.

We had raced ahead, taking the foreshore path, hid in the bushes, then made it to the calm and warmth of the attic. Our time-keeper became absorbed in a swallow`s nest with it`s young, and allowed his arm to trail in the water cistern. Time stood still, literally, and we hadn`t a clue how long we had to go so we made it back to the bushes. Strange! No stragglers, or even the gasping and panting of the `triers` bringing up the rear. After deliberation we raced, very tiredly, to the Main Gates where we were met by a clip-board-and-stop-watch officer.

'Names?'`he demanded excitedly. Adding, 'You have broken the best time by several minutes.' Discarding our red bunting sashes, we bathed briefly in the glory of the moment.

'Just a minute,' he said, concerned. 'Which Division are you?'

'Collingwood, sir,' I said.

'Collingwood? Collingwood?' he repeated. 'They`ve been back hours ago. Benbow and Rodney are out now. Master-at-Arms!!'

We did quite a bit of running over the next few weeks on jankers up and down Faith, Hope and Charity.

Mess scrub....even the bad times were good.

Worst thing I saw was a lad who hadn`t washed his neck properly. It was smudged with the dye from the blue serge of his suit. It wasn`t his fault, it could have happened to anyone of us under the circumstances, but he was ordered to be cold-scrubbed.

Stripped and crying, the poor little blighter was hosed against the tiles and attacked by his mess-mates with long-handled brushes until he was red raw. I later saw him in RNB Portsmouth when I was due for demob; he was a C.P.O. and had signed on for the full whack, so no harm done?

I progressed slowly, saw the world, made some good mates; even the bad times were good. Would I do it again? Of course I would. It tempered me into a human being."

A similar story is told in another chapter by another person in more detail. But what was a `mess-scrub?`

A `mess-scrub` takes place when several boys, armed with long-handled, hard-bristled deck-scrubbers, like brooms with bristles as stiff as nails, wait for several other boys to throw buckets of cold water over the naked, cringing and whimpering boy, cowering in a corner of the wash-room, then they set upon him with vigorous up-and-down scrubbing movements over every part of his body. The result is red-raw, bleeding flesh on the wretched victim. Everyone has enemies, and if the wretch has several of them in the mess, perhaps bearing some trivial grudge, human nature decrees that permission to attack the victim gives them the right to venge their wrath without recourse to punishment for doing so, and they `lay-to` with unjustified enthusiasm. However, it is unlikely that an Instructor would order this torture; or, should it not be unlikely, it would be against the rules and any Instructor doing so could rightfully be accused of bullying sadism. Other similar stories reveal that a mess-scrubbing was ordered by an Instructor, but it is more likely that, in most cases, as in one case the author had actual knowledge of, the boy was a victim of a vendetta by another boy or boys, who would incite others to join in the mess-scrub.

A mess-scrub took place in 19 Mess, Grenville Division in 1948. The victim suffered from acne; he was mature in advance of his age; there were red pimples and blackheads on his face; a natural happening for most teenagers. The perpetrators and instigators of his torment shaved only once every three or four months; later, they suffered the same inflictions of pimples and black-heads, and probably thought nothing of it. He had started to shave earlier, too, and shaving high-lighted his condition by making his pimples bleed. He was as clean in his habits as the rest, but the loud-mouthed bully-boy of the mess, a know-it-all-Londoner, didn`t like him, and used the feeble excuse of a `scabby, pimpled, black-headed face` as an excuse to suggesttoa few other cowardly bullies, that he deserved a mess-scrub. It was pre-meditated. There was no Instructor to witness or stop this barbaric, humiliating treatment, and it was carried out in the wash-room where the victim was forcibly stripped, flung cowering into a corner and had bowls of cold water flung over him whilst the rest of the cowardly gang dabbed and poked at him with hard, long-handled scrubbers as he cried out in fear for mercy which was not forthcoming until he lay upon the cold stone floor, a shivering, trembling sobbing wretch.

Whatever the poor boy's inner thoughts were as all this was happening, can only be imagined. If any of the Leading- Boys or Instructor Boys were aware of this, or were watching, no-one made a move to stop it. The mess scrubbing made not one iota of difference to his pimples and black-heads.

Although several of the boys accused some of the Instructors for being cruel and sadistic - the boys' own punishments were most times unjustified and sometimes much worse.

"They had to knock us into shape..."

Emma Hall's father was born in 1896 and ran away from home at 14 to join the Royal Navy. She says, "I think he joined the Ganges in 1911, and from all accounts, life was very strict and discipline severe."

It is thought that because she refers to port-holes, and indicates, in another tale, reference to preparing meals to be taken to the Galley to be cooked, that he may, at the age of 14, have joined a Training ship such as Arethusa. However, we shall assume he was at Ganges, the regime being similar - one way or another.

"I remember saying, as a small child, 'The navy training was very cruel, daddy, wasn't it?' His reply was, *'No, they had to knock us into shape to make us real fighting men; men who instantly obeyed an order without question as soon as it was given.'* These were the men of the bull-dog breed who made Old England's name. The rigging had to be climbed every morning at day-break whatever the weather; sometimes with six to nine inch icicles hanging from the ropes which lacerated our legs and arms as we attempted to shin upwards. Woe betide anyone who slipped, for the P.O. Instructors were behind with a sharpened bamboo cane! First-aid was a bucket of brine chucked over the wound!"

Kitten stew and dumplings

Emma's memory recall serves her well as she remembers the stories of jokes played on the raw recruits; who were told to stuff the macaroni with currants, using a darning needle, and putting Epsom salts in the plum duff.

"One day," she continues, "A boy smuggled a kitten on board, pets were forbidden, and they were playing with it on the mess table when they heard the Duty Officer approaching. One of the boys took the kitten and, to hide it from the Duty Officer, put it into the stew-pot which was hanging under the mess-table, not knowing that the cook-boy had already filled it with raw vegetables and water, ready to be taken to the galley to be boiled for the following day's dinner.

When the inspection was over, there was no sign of the kitten, or stew-pot. The cook-boy had already taken it to the Galley.

Next day the stew-pot was returned, steaming hot, from the galley - need I say more?"

Double injustice..

Another story by **Emma Hall** tells of gross injustice, not once; twice; but it is so spiced with humour that it belongs in this section of humour rather than any other. It must be said that the incident, though amusing to Emma, and perhaps the reader of it, it could not have been funny to her father when it happened.

Emma again: "My father was a P.O. Boy, and one night a row broke out between two lads, one of whom threw his boot at the other and broke the glass in the port-hole. When the Duty Officer made his rounds he noticed the broken glass and said to my father: 'Who's broken the glass?'

My father replied: 'I don't know, sir.' Three times the same question was asked, and each time my father answered: 'I don't know, sir.'

'Report to the quarter-deck in the morning,' the officer said, and walked away. Next morning, on the quarterdeck, in front of the Captain: the Captain asked: 'Who broke the glass in the porthole?'

'I don't know, sir.' Three times he was asked and the answer was, 'I don't know, sir.'

'Very well,' the Captain said. 'Six lashes.'

My father was tied to a vaulting horse and three lashes were administered on one buttock, and three on the other, then a bucket of brine was thrown over his backside. He couldn't sit down for days! He was just getting over this punishment when the same officer was making the rounds again. He looked at my dad and said: 'You know you were foolish not to tell me who broke the glass? Don't you?'

'Yes, sir. I know, sir, but I couldn't sneak on a mess-mate, could I, sir?'

'Oh, so you did know who the culprit was, did you? Well report to the quarter- deck in the morning.'

After doing so he was given another six lashes for telling a lie.

He was not at all resentful of the punishment meted out to him as it was all part of the training. My father was a T.I., T.G.M. and served on M.T.B.'s under Beatty at the battle of Jutland. He left the R.N. at the end of 1936 and was back in uniform again in 1938.

He was killed in action on the 27th May, 1941."

The Instructor's story:

Dick McBurney joined as a boy in 1948 - *his joining story is in the joining chapter* - and returned as a Petty Officer Instructor in 1962:

"I had classes 49 and 50 and was pretty keen in those days and, being unmarried and living in the P.O.'s Mess, I did frequent duties at week-ends. It was a difficult task to occupy the boys, or Juniors as they were called by then, on Sundays. I devised a scheme based on a kind of paper-chase where the boys were each given a list of questions to answer. They had to get the answers by running out of the camp and looking in various places. The questions were listed in such a way that each boy started with a different question. So they scattered in all directions at the Main Gate. The questions took the shape of: 'What is the oldest grave in the local churchyard?' 'What is the name of the local pub?' 'etc.etc.

Well, they all eventually came back and I marked the answers and told them that they had done well. The next day I was sent for by the Captain, whom I had never actually met before. He commended me on my initiative in devising the scheme for the boys the day before, but did suggest that some more care should be taken in making-up the questions. I queried the reason for that suggestion and he told me that on the Sunday afternoon his door-bell had been rung forty times, and each time he answered, a different boy asked him if he was the Vicar of Shotley!

When I asked my boys about it, they all gave, more or less, the same answer: 'One of the questions, sir, was: 'Who is the vicar of Shotley?' So we called at the biggest house around the village because we thought that would be the Vicarage, but there was this old man, in slippers and dressing-gown, who opened the door and said he certainly was not!'

I also remember one shy, quiet boy who had been missing for a short while and eventually turned up. When the class was fallen-in I demanded to know where he had been.

'Please, sir,' he said: 'I was trying to sort out the Padre's Surplice.' I don't think he ever lived that comment down during the rest of his whole time at Ganges!"

"I enjoyed every minute of it.."

"Times were good *and* bad," says **G. Palmer,** April, 1965. "On the whole I think most of us enjoyed every minute of it. I know I did. I truly believe it made us better people. The discipline was hard, but it taught us all to work as a team and to rely on each other, as well as building up great friendships. I had specialised as a Radar Plotter but my dream was to become a Clearance Diver, which I did later. Anyway, one of my Instructors had a bet one day with one of his colleagues from another Division that we could beat his lads in a pulling-race. They both wanted to win, so the crews were pushed, threatened and even tortured during the practices. Both teams were told by their respective Instructors: 'YOU WILL WIN THIS

134

RACE...OR ELSE!!'
As the day for the race got nearer, four members of our team went ill, but our Instructor wasn't going to lose face by backing down.
He told me: 'You want to be a Clearance Diver?'
'Yes, sir!' I said eagerly, wondering what was coming.
'Right, then,' he said. 'I've got a job for you, a type of test. Follow me.'
I couldn't wait to see what it was as I followed him down to the foreshore and jetty where the boats were moored.
'Now then,' he said, 'I want you to fix six buckets to the bilge rails under the boat of the opposition. Get on with it.'
I couldn't believe it! An Instructor, who was supposed to be teaching us fair-play, ordering me to cheat. I didn't want to face the prospect of running up and down Laundry Hill for the rest of my stay at Ganges, so I did as he asked. It was a tough job, but I managed it, and awaited the big day, next day in fact.
As the race got underway, people watching must have thought we were marvellous, or that the other team had burned themselves out as they were the favourites to win. Anyway, we did win, and it was several days before the other Instructor discovered the buckets.
I heard him, and our Instructor, discussing it and, lucky for me, the question: 'Who fixed the buckets?' didn't arise!"

"Not impressed with Ganges..."

Alan Pitcher: "My first day at Ganges didn't impress me very much. I arrived at the Annexe about 11.30 a.m. on the 4th Jan, 1955. We were taken there by bus from Ipswich, having come down from Norwich where I had enlisted. We were led into the dining-hall to queue for dinner which consisted of luke-warm meat and gravy, roast potatoes and boiled leeks, which I never did get to eat. The boy in the queue in front of me was tapping his knife and fork. One of the Instructors came up and said: 'If you reckon you are so musical, you can spend your dinner-time practising on the parade-ground.' Unfortunately, he overhead me say to another boy: 'What the f.....g hell have we let ourselves in for?'
I was jumped on from a great height, and, consequently, the 'musician' was sat in the middle of the parade-ground, beating out time on a dust-bin lid with his knife and fork whilst I was doubling around the perimeter shouting: 'Ahoy! Ahoy! Ahoy! I'm a foul-mouthed boy!'
Such was my introduction to naval life. Over at the main establishment one time, for making excesssive noise after lights-out, the whole mess had to wear gas-masks, helmets, oilskins buttoned up back-to-front, and bunny-hopped round the parade-ground 'til we

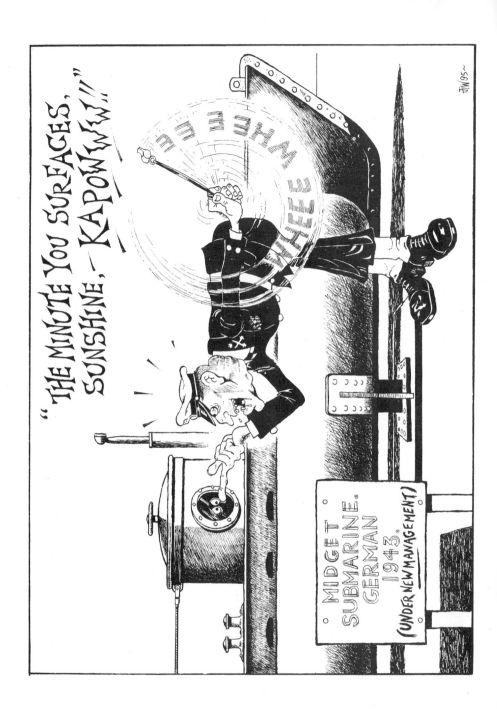

dropped. Needless to say, I was more than glad when my time at Ganges was over."

Alan Ross, 1952. "We had Evening Quarters in Nelson Hall every night at 1700. Near the part where my class used to muster was a Midget German Submarine. Well, as a 15 year-old boy I weaved fantasies around that sub. I could even imagine myself taking it to sea: 'DIVE! DIVE! DIVE! etc.' Well, one day, whilst we were waiting for the G.I. to muster us, I was in the rear rank and I just couldn't resist it. I turned around and I climbed up, opened the hatch and got in, whilst the remainder of the class laughed. And then of course! I should have guessed! Some-one crept up and clipped the hatch shut. I watched with fear as the G.I. approached.

'Class! Atten-shun! By the right - dress!' The class came to attention, dressed, then: 'Class! Stand at ease! Stand easy, answer your names.' He produced a pad and pencil and began calling out the names. When he got to 'Ross' there was no answer.

'Ross!' he shouted again. By this time the class were giggling and glancing at the submarine. The G.I. ploughed his way through the ranks, strode over to the sub., and there I was, peering through the conning-tower port-hole window in an eye- ball to eye-ball confrontation with God himself.

'Get out of there, you cunt!' he roared, which I did, once the hatch was undone.

'Go and draw a f.....g rifle, put it on your f.....g shoulder, and start doubling around that f.....g parade-ground, you stupid little bastard!' Several laps later, with a very sore shoulder, I was reprieved from punishment and allowed to go to supper - but he always singled me out for special attention after that.

I saw that same mini-sub quite recently where it had been relegated as a museum piece at H.M.S. Dolphin Museum. We had quite a re-union, that sub and I, forty-two years later."

Alan Ross relates another story which, if you were not the victim, could have been very funny. It was, at least, very funny to a Divisional Officer who should have known better than to force his superiority as an officer on someone who could not argue or strike back. Alan tells the story with great humour.

"The main topic in Ganges was the kit muster. everything had to be rolled with cardboard and string-stops to a certain pattern. It took hours to prepare and occupied part of our lives almost every day. On kit-muster day the Divisional Officer did the inspecting. He approached with his aides - our Instructors; fixed me with steely eyes, I sprang to attention.

'Boy Seaman Ross, sir, 183 class, kit ready for inspection, sir.'

'Sports shorts?'

'Sir!''handing them to him.

He tore off the string stops, shaking out the cardboard and snapping off the belt-beckets one by one, followed by the buttons, pinging all over the floor: 'Not very good is it, Ross?'

'No, sir.'

'Give me one of your socks,' holding out his hand.

'Yes, sir, handing him a sock.

He held out the sock at arm`s length, bending forward, his face near mine. 'Can you hear little silvery voices crying out for water, Ross?'

'Yes, sir.'

'Yes sir, you say? Give me the socks you`re wearing, boy!'

I took off my boots, then my socks and handed them to him.

'Get me your gask-mask.' I gave him the gas-mask and he rammed my socks into it.

'Steel hat.' I gave him the steel hat and he ripped out the webbing.

'Right! Put on your boots, gas-mask, leave the socks inside. Now the steel hat and start doubling around the parade-ground.'

So around I went, followed by other miscreants doubling with a steamed-up gas-mask, and a steel hat bouncing about on my head.

I don`t think my socks were dirty - I think it was sadism."

So do I. It`s not such a funny story after all, was it? But excuse me , and lots of others, and yourself, from laughing! Good story.

Peter Senter, 1954, begins his humorous tale with reminiscences of hardship:

"Climbing the mast in mid-winter when the hand-ropes were frozen and we were not allowed to wear gloves. Staying up all night before leave to sew illegal badges on our uniform tops. Boys unable to swim had to wear a cork upper-body life-belt all day, and every day, until they passed their swimming test. For serious offences we were marched to the Captain`s Day Room and given six strokes of the cane on the bare backside with a medical rating as witness.

On one rare occasion in the Dining Hall it was announced there were some left-over steak-and- kidney pies. Almost being trampled in the rush I managed to obtain one, but as food was not allowed in the mess-rooms, I put the pie in my cap to smuggle it inside the mess. The cap, with the pie in it, would not sit properly upon my head so I tucked it under my arm, pie and all. Thinking back I do not know why I did this because it was not illegal or against the rules to take food from the Dining Hall, and I could have eaten it on the way to the mess. But, on reaching the Dining Hall outer door, I was stopped by a Marine corporal who ordered me to put my cap on. The only way to make the cap, and the pie, fit my head under these circumstances,was to pull down hard on my cap and squash the pie so that it did not look suspicious and obvious. This I did, taking care to ensure that the pie in the hat was not seen by the Marine corporal. I arrived back at my mess-room with the cap two inches higher off my head than it should have been, with rich brown gravy running down my face. After I had scraped the gooey mess from my hair and face, it just wasn't worth eating!"

Nick Nicholls, 'joined some 40 years ago,' recalls good Instructors, bad Instructors and a Mr. Barraclough clone of 'Porridge' fame:

"I was eventually to be sent over the 'Main' into Collingwood Division, 44 mess. It was situated next to Mr. Fisk, the photographers. Just after we arrived a nearby mess was nearing the end of their time at Ganges, and, as we subsequently found out, it was the custom that the seasoned matelots leaving would carry out a raid on suitable Nozzers - like us!

They came into our mess tipped up all the beds they could with us still in them, kicked all the spit-kids and highly-polished dustbins all over the place and, worst of all, pulled all the burberry's off the coat-hooks, ripping the beckets. The burberry's had been folded in perfect cylinders and secured above and below with white tape in perfect alignment as you entered the mess. To cap this off we were punished for having a mess looking like a scran-bag, the punishment was bunny-hopping around the main parade-ground holding a .303 rifle over our heads. To do this we had to get down on our haunches and hopped around the parade-ground; after a while we had a break but our legs would not work due to impaired blood-circulation. This punishment was frequently used and was dreaded even more than being on number 9 punishment, doubling up and down Laundry Hill. I had the dubious honour of running up and down that hill with a mess-mate for sword-fencing in the drill-shed. We were playing, as youngsters do, with two naval drill-cutlasses, they were quite heavy, and, whilst we were skylarking around one of the swords touched one of the electric fires which were fitted in the drill-hall walls. This unfortunately removed part of the chromed sword point. We were lucky not to have been electrocuted. The ultimatum punishment was 'cuts' which one received whilst laying over a lectern. This was severe and reserved for serious crimes or going 'on the run.' We did hear of of one boy who, whilst on punishment working in the P.O.'s mess, urinated in a rum tub.

This brings to mind an incident on a ship later; I was bosun's mate on the gangway and off shore came an obviously drunken sailor. He saluted as he came aboard but almost fell over the side as he stepped down onto the deck. Knowing he had a reputation for doing crazy things, the Cox'n told me to follow the sailor down to the mess-deck. As he passed alongside the highly-polished rum-tub he urinated therein. Needless to say, I refused my rum issue at 'up spirits' the following day, leaving it in the mess-fanny for 'queens.' 'Queens' is the left-overs which is the difference between the measured tot with the measuring vessel overflowing and what the mess rum bosun gives you in your glass.

Tattoos were the 'in' thing when I was at Ganges, and which we obtained from an 'artist' near Colchester prison. We would do anything to appear as 'old salts,' but some of the tattoos turned septic and we ended up in the rattle for what the Crushers called, 'self-inflicted wounds.' This also applied to sunburn.

"Boy molested by Instructor.."

Another good time was going to the Holbrook School for a camping expedition with big tents and the inevitable cuisine of corned-dog sandwiches - corned-beef. The entire naval victualling system would collapse if it had to do without Fray Bentos delights.

It was at one of these camps that a boy got molested in an Instructor's tent. Our term for it was, 'being trunked.' The Instructor gave the boy some 'blue liners,' duty-free cigarettes, presumably to keep his mouth shut. His days were numbered, however, and his other antics drew attention to our plight. He made us do our dhobying naked. After we had finished, this Instructor would line us up and made us pull our fore-skins back. He called this 'check fore - aft main,' and if he thought you were unclean he would tap your penis with his stick. Someone went to the 'sin bosun' about this and complained. Within two days the small, red-faced P.O. G.I. disappeared. Some said he had got seven years at a prison in Shepton Mallett. We were chuffed that he had gone as he was a bit of a tyrant. He had delighted in coming into the mess at 'call-the-hands' and kicking the spit-kid down the mess, or putting his stick inside the dust-bin and clanging it about. He would also turn over the first dozen or so beds with us still in them, either side of the mess. Tipping over our kit lockers was also a much-hated trick that he would perform. When he was in a good mood his punishments were just as bad as when he was in a bad one. He would make us scrub the polished deck with boot-brushes or sometimes tooth-brushes. On reflection, apart from his strange behaviour, he was typical of most Instructors at Ganges. We called them 'brainwashed.'

Fred Barraclough...

Our replacement Instructor was exactly the opposite of the former. He was a dead-ringer for Mr. Barraclough in 'Porridge.' It was absolutely incredible, we thought we had been delivered into the

Promised land. Fred would come into the mess at `call the hands` and he would actually *ask* us, timidly, almost apologetically: 'Would you like to get out of bed now, boys?'

We took advantage of him and this question was greeted with a general: '*F... off, Fred! Come back later!!*'

His partner Instructor, however, did not stand for this and he made sure that we were soon back under the boot-heel, with intensified spells of gun-drill. The gun-drill area has, like Laundry Hill, a special place in my memory. The G.I.`s would drown us with fire-hoses, with relish, to simulate gunnery in foul weather.

They would also throw thunder-flashes at our feet to simulate incoming projectiles. While this was going on we had to be nimble enough to avoid the rear-ward ejecting ammunition.

Our careers in the navy were decided by educational tests and by personal preferences. At the top end, the Communications Branch were considered to be elite, of superior intelligence, with the Stokers requiring minimum brains at the lower end. The Radar Plotters were supposed to be the most clever of the Seaman Branch, with TAS, Torpedo, Asdic and Sonar ratings, next. Despite passing Educational Test 1 and Educational Test 2, I ended up as a gunnery rate. How did this happen?''

The longest serving?

From Nicky to Dicky: Nicky completed his training and has nothing to complain about regarding his 12 months in Ganges, but Dickie Doyle - **John Henry Lionel Doyle** - from September 6th, 1948 to November 15th, 1950, is a contender for the above title of `longest serving.` Dickie is a stanchion of the Ganges Association, and his motto is: `If you want a job done - ask a busy man.` He should know because he`s always too busy to say `no,` and got his nick-name, Dickie, because his height was three inches short of the five-two minimum, hence his bottom was nearer to the ground than most, earning him the tag, `Duck-arse Doyle,` corrupted fairly swiftly to `Dickie,` and he`s been a little Dickie ever since.

"Shortly after going over to the Main," he writes, "I was resident in 41 mess, Collingwood Division. Our Instructors were P.O. Tel. Raven and Yeoman German, both very strict, harsh men, handy with their stonnickies, not of the rope variety, but lengths of rubber hose. Their first task was to elect possible leaders. The first Boy they chose lasted only a few minutes. He was told to go out in front of us lads, who were fell in outside the mess, and call us to attention. He gave the order: 'Mess! *Alert!*' whereupon both Instructors charged at him and beat him, their stonnickies, flailing like mad from all directions at various parts of his anatomy. It turned out he had been a Scout

Leader. I felt the full force of one of their stonnickies myself one day when, as `postie,` fetching the mail from the mail office which, in turn, I should have handed over to the duty Instructor in the bedding store to be distributed over dinner, I was overheard by the duty Instructor telling one of the lads that he had a parcel from home when suddenly, from behind - the Instructor had crept up behind me - he hit me with the full force of his stonnicky across the top of my head. My hat was driven several inches over my forehead, past my eyes - I thought I had gone blind - and, needless to say, I lost the job of `postie.`

Towards the end of my stay, having risen to the heights of Leading Boy of 46 mess, my special duty was in charge of the Fire Escape, a cumbersome contraption of a ladder on two large wheels which we exercised every Saturday forenoon after Divisions. One Saturday evening, after cinema in the gymnasium, the bugle call for fire sounded, followed by the pipe: *'Fire! Fire! Fire!* Fire in the incinerator!'* Being well-trained and keen, we mustered by our `Escape` and trundled off at the double in the direction of the incinerator. Half way there we stopped our progress and held a conference. We realised that the *only* place that there *should* be a fire was the incinerator, so we returned our machine to it`s parking place. No one every queried our non-arrival, and we never discovered if there was a fire which required extinguishing, or whether it was the QM having had too many tots - or perhaps he just forgot to add the `For exercise` bit.

One of the lads in our mess stole some `blue-liners,` cigs, from the Chief`s Mess. He was routed out later and received six cuts for theft, and all the smokers in the mess, who had taken part in getting rid of them, were awarded cuts for receiving the stolen cigs. I was about the only one, a non-smoker, to avoid that punishment.

I left Ganges after two years and two months, probably a record I think, the lengthy period being due to long stays in the sick bay. My wife still maintains that it was because I had a crush on one of the nurses! I tell her that I didn`t. That`s *my* story - *and I`m sticking to it!* Best wishes to all you ex-Ganges lads. I`m in the `Ganges Association,` we meet once a year and have great fun reminiscing about the good old days! There`s a Divisional Branch in most areas!

Entrance to Annexe

143

Sunday Divisions
in the Annexe

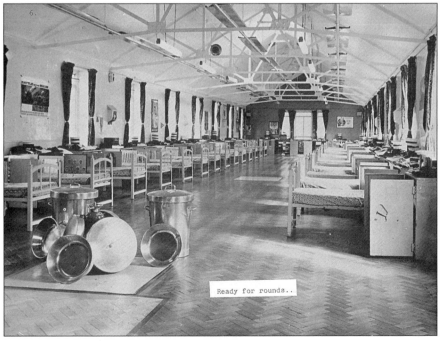

Ready for rounds..

Kit musters

Nozzer's Lane

145

Boxing finals

H.M.S. GANGES

Chapter eight

Cruelty...

"There is no greater sorrow than to recall
a time of happiness in misery.." Dante.

It is unfortunate, and sad, that only a small portion of stories received in response to a request for humorous tales actually portrayed humour. What was intended to be a book based entirely upon humorous happenings during the Ganges hey-day of Boys Training, is reduced to just one chapter, and the rest is made up of various themes. One theme, on the cruel doings of some Ganges occupants to other Ganges occupants, is three times longer than the `humorous` section.

There must be a reason; perhaps the reason is that the ratio of humour to cruelty/humility/sadism is three to one?

Ship-mates became whip-mates...

Was H.M.S. Ganges the only establishment in the Royal Navy where **ship-mates became whip-mates**? H.M.S. Bruce in Scotland, H.M.S. St. Vincent in England, and several more, including the Training ships of Arethusa at Greenhithe, the Royal Naval Hospital School Holborn etc., all claim that Ganges was a holiday camp in comparison. They had their reports of extremely harsh treatment for very small misdemenours as trivial as a single button missing, which warranted six cuts of the cane, and the same treatment for a badly-tied bootlace which had worked loose. Even so, the Boys seemed to laugh with outrageous bravado at the strict discipline, pretending with false bombast in their new-found manliness, that punishment was a joke.

Tom Robson hoped to join Ganges in May, 1947 but was diverted to H.M.S. Bruce because Ganges was overflowing with eager Nozzers.

"I arrived in Bruce as a small, timid, frightened boy from a tiny mining village in County Durham," says Tom, and one has to agree with him when he says that Ganges wasn't the only boys` training establishment to attain the infamy of being accused of such nasties as `barbaric,` `cruel,` and other derogatory adjectives. "*Bruce* was the old Fleet Air Arm station, *Jackdaw,* and had lots of facilities for punishment: long runways, large hangars and, of course, a mast, same style as Ganges but smaller. Bruce was only opened for three years, but had a bad reputation for cruelty, desertions and even a suicide. The captain, T.W. Marsh, had been an ex-boy seaman and wrote the questions and answers book for Leading Seamen and Petty Officer candidates.

Our `Faith, Hope and Charity` equivalents were air-raid shelters which we had to run up, over, across and down, forwards and backwards, rifles above the head etc. The equivalent of the `Shotley Shuffle` was the `Crail Crawl.` The Chief G.I. of the Gunnery School was the infamous Harry Hoskins who had already terrorised the young officers of Dartmouth College. However, I won't dwell upon the training, but I emerged as a more confident and grown-up person, although I would never say I liked it! My standard of education, which had been poor, improved a lot at Bruce and helped me in my naval career, passing for P.O. when I was 21.''

Tom has already had his autobiography published, and has almost completed another book on boys' naval training from 1790 to 1976, the year when Ganges closed down, and, because he first joined Ganges as a boy, he was able to join the *Ganges Association.*

An example that Ganges Boys looked upon their punishments with some humour is obvious by this extract taken from the newsletter of the **Ganges Association,** the **Ganges Gazette,** Winter, 1994. It was taken from a **Shotley Magazine**, no date given, written by **A. Non:**

"The Instructors run H.M.S. Ganges. This is a fact well-known to all Instructors. The Divisional Officers think THEY do, and the Badge Boys have the audacity to think THEY do, but it is definitely the Instructors. Let us examine these paragons of all the virtues. To look at, they are suspiciously like lesser-mortals, coming in all sizes and nearly all shapes. It is their inner-selves that differ. Spiritually far-advanced of the remainder, they treat the numerous problems and complications of service life with absolute confidence, tact, and usually a swift swipe to the left lug-hole. Amongst other virtues which these intellectual giants possess, is patience. It is a touching sight to see a wizened old Chief, listening to a long rigmarole about 'Why I wasn't there, Chief,' from a Boy who is obviously a juvenile delinquent of the worst order; and it is only the more sceptical amongst us who construe the look on the Chief's face as `disbeliev-ing` or `malicious.` Being possessors of such fine natures, Instructors lead their boys gently along the steep, narrow and winding paths towards the highest standard, both technically and domestically. So do not believe those amongst us who, in an endeavour to decry the Instructor's efforts, bear false-witness and talk of blows, kicks and, as I once heard, making Boys stand in the offal-bin and shouting: `I am rubbish!`"

The writer of the above wished to remain anonymous because it was obviously written by a boy who regarded his anonimity as an intentional joke - he could have been discovered and unearthed at any time, and it is a credit to the Ganges staff that they let the letter be printed in the Shotley Magazine, believing it to have not much, if any, truth in it, but the writer of the following letter meant to be derisory - and anonymous. No name, no address, no signature, and no common-sense. There is no preamble, no `Dear Sir,` or even a mere `Dear John.` Obviously written by the single-track mind of one who enjoyed the humiliation and pain which was inflicted upon some boys, he pretends that he read it in my local newspaper, `The West Briton,` which, to hide his whereabouts, `travels` to other parts of the country. My standard letter - which was not always printed exactly as I presented it - asked for humorous stories from ex-Ganges boys who attended *'what was once described as `first, the last and the only concentration camp in Britain,'* etc. It did not say: "John Douglas described it as..."

"Ref. GANGES MEMORIES.

John Douglas, The West Country newspapers certainly do travel the country and I was amazed to read in your article" - *it was a letter, not an article* - "requesting interesting items about H.M.S. GANGES that you came up with this innane piece `Inmates who suffered the harsh discipline`. Tut Tut.

Come on John, dont act the `Jack Shalloo` I spent some prewars years as a boy at Shotley and let me just tell you that it was a well regulated course of discipline and instruction that the boys then received. NO ropes ends   NO stonikies   NO broomhandles.

The instructors had to undergo a rigorous vetting before being selected for instructors at HMS Ganges to be in charge of young boys.

I, like hundreds of others, cannot understand why ex-boys like you come up with all this "Beaten up" rubbish.

I am just one of those living in a small village, Just a good ex Ganges lad. Proud of it Grateful for the training Cheers Aye."

In my letter there was no mention of `stonnickies, broom-handles or rope`s ends.`

At least one person agrees with the `concentration camp` tag: **G.W. Bowkett**, ''I joined Ganges in November 1945 and escaped in November 1946.''

E.G. Farrell, : '' I was a very naive young Irishman from Dublin when I joined on the 15th October, 1952, and believed the slogan: 'join the navy - see the world!' What they didn`t say was you had to suffer 12 months of Ganges. I read a book about Ganges several years ago entitled: 'The last concentration camp in England.' It made very good reading.''

A large amount of letters commence by criticising the Ganges regime, and end by saying that it did them no harm. A variation on this opinion, where the statement of cruel treatment was made first - then later, in the same letter - alleviated the theme by almost denying what he had already written. The variation on this point was a letter from a Gangers-ex who signed himself "Councillor `Smudger` Smith" of Humberside. Smudger wrote to me initially of various atrocities which he had personally experienced, and then, curiously, publicly denied them in a letter to his local newspaper. His letter is printed, again, as with the anonymous one, without the graciousness of his grammar, punctuation and spelling being edited:

"That first time over the mast - I came down and my hands were frozen into hooks - the 5 a.m. awakenings for a cold shower before cocoa and biscuits then followed by the cleaning of our mess decks before Breakfast. I well recall P.O. Patterson (Scarface) finding a Toffee Paper on the deck Hence our journey with loaded Kit Bags up and down Laundry Hill and Faith Hope and Charity and just to satisfy his sadistic pleasure we were also denied our Wednesday Night Cinema Show. We Questioned His Mothers marriage Lines many times. Then there was the Lad in the Mess across the Way who didn`t reach the acceptable Level of Personel Hygeine, (hygiene) I realy (really) felt for Him whilst They Stripped and Scrubbed Him with deck Scrubbers. His Body finished up Red Raw and of Course the Instructor conveniantly (conveniently) turned Blind. They were hard times given by hard disciplinarians but in the Long term it never did me any harm - indeed I feel I benifitted (benefitted) from those Days."

"Hardest school in the world.."

Well, Vic, as for doing you no harm, in your own words:-

"I like to believe my time at the Hardest School in the World, Namely Ganges, has served Me Well...most Certainly straighten`d Me out."

If `harsh treatment by sadistic Instructors, the horror of frozen fingers and the barbaric ill-treatment to a boy by his own mates whilst the Instructor turns `blind,' is the solution needed to straighten anyone out, the obvious conclusion is that they must have been in a bit of a sorry state to start with! He is, of course, entitled to air his own experiences.

"Experience? Yes, it was a great experience!" says **Tom McGregor,** ex-Bunting. He begins by saying he couldn't remember much and couldn't write a book about it. Then the memories return in a rush,

''I hated Ganges, but now, at aged 50, having served 12 years in the R.N., I am proud to have been a Ganges Boy. A great experience. Most memories are now getting vague, but can anyone ever forget

Faith, Hope and Charity? Standing on the button, perhaps a relief after getting round the Devil's Elbow, early-morning boats, Divisions in a Shotley winter, rifle drill when the fingers were so numb **you couldn't feel the .303, and when you could certainly feel it above the head,** doubling around the parade-ground. Was the P.T.I. <u>really</u> human when putting boys through a shake-up in the Gym?

JW '95

" **KIT, SIR?**
BURIED THE BUGGER, SIR,
SIRS ORDERS, SIR, "

It was easier at night, resplendent in pyjamas, on all fours polishing the mess square. I pitied the poor guys who, having failed a kit-muster had to deposit their kit in a dust-bin and fill it with water, or worse, **bury it in the garden.** Work-ship in the galley where an ordinary cook was a god and a badgeman a demi-god, they treated us well. Almost made us forget the prowling G.I''s and Instructors.

I was 15, joined Ganges on March 18th, 1958, a date that will go down in infamy. Three of us on a train from Scotland, singing and happy, off to sail the seven seas, though we were in a 3rd class carriage eating Mum's sandwichs and furtively-bought bottles of beer. We were sailors now, but Shotley was a shock to a young innocent system. We had only left school last week, a few wet pillows were soon to be the norm at night in the seemingly massive messes.

What sadist dreamed up the Annexe? Thrown back to Nelson's time. After meals, having to scrub a wooden table and two benches, then the deck, were we press-ganged or did we actually volunteer? Perhaps if we had known the consequences we would not have volunteered. Still, better than laundry afternoons, fall-in outside on a freezing and windy square, wearing nowt but a jock-strap-type thing, and leather slippers, carrying our laundry bags. Dozens of, 'As you were's!' and 'Left turns!' even 'tho those manoeuvres were already spot-on. Then the skinned, bleeding knuckles doing our dhobeying. Present your white front to the P.O. for inspection, collar and cuffs not quite right, or bright, or white enough, so, onto the deck into all the dirty water it went, and then the P.O. man would stamp all over it and back to the sink you`d go.

Our Chief Yeoman was a nice guy, but he seemed to have a pair of semaphore flags super-glued to his hand, and, if you fell foul of him, any part of the anatomy was a legitimate target for those hand-flags! He was a hard task-master, but when I met him years later in some far-flung place we got on famously. I have a lot of memories of Ganges, but I wouldn't have a clue about writing a book of it. When you tell people about `cuts` and Shotley Routine they don't believe you. Never lived!"

Several letters mentioned Shotley winters; the sharp-edged biting east winds from Russia, bound for the east coast of England from frozen Siberia to deliberately add more misery to the lives of young lads already suffering the frugalities of cold-comfort Ganges. The ideal time to join Ganges, we know by hindsight, was mid-Summer as a Boy Seaman, who`s term of training was only 12 months. They would have the benefit of a couple of month`s sunshine, one Winter, a complete Spring, another two month`s of sunshine again before departing for all the ports of the World, mostly sunshine-laden as opposed to Shotley`s snow-ridden clime. The Communicators, Sparks or Bunting, whichever way it is looked at with their term being three or four month`s longer, the chances are odds-on that they would experience two winters.

Again the 'concentration camp' tag: **Streaky Bacon** from Norfolk writes: "I would just like to say that I never found Ganges as severe as you have stated. When I went to school in the 30's, discipline was often brought about with the aid of the cane, or a smack around the ear! So going to Ganges was not as formidable as it might have seemed to some."

He is right - thousands of children were chastised at school in the thirties, but schools did not have a regime wherein they were punished with Shotley Routine, nor any punishment or anything close to it, nor did they have to double for at least an hour up and down an equivalent of Laundry Hill or a Faith, Hope and Charity at two o`clock in the morning, with bed-chocks down their pyjama trousers whilst carrying a full kit-bag, for some frivolous and silly reason like a toffee-paper being left on the deck; or receive up to 12 cuts of a cane for finding a half-penny stamp and forgetting to report it! But others, who were not treated as well as Streaky Bacon, and were unfortunate enough *not* to have had similar kindly Instructors, P.T.I.`s etc. as Streaky, tell a different story. In fact, Streaky has nothing more to say, other than to deny statements which others have said.

Most times our own experiences can be, and are very often, different to those of others, even though those experiences occurred in the same place at the same time.

The stories speak for themselves of the happenings in H.M.S. Ganges, whether they were tales of the humorous, pathetically pathos, or downright atrocious. In whichever category they were finally placed, the tales eventually found their way back into civvy street where, in the family of **Dorothy Keightley,** mother of **Edwin Keightley**, 1963, recalls a story still told and retold in the Keightley household today. Dorothy describes the the scene as she unfolds her tale, assuming with motherly-love that her teenage pseudo-macho son, Edwin, was really only a *'little sailor-boy'* at heart, and the incident, which occurred long enough ago to be placed in the category of 'We'll laugh about this one day,' not realising that an offence against decency was being perpetrated. It is likely that Edwin saw himself much more manly and macho than the *'little sailor-boy'* which he was at the worldly-wise age of sixteen. Dorothy writes in the vein of humour, but the following really belongs in tales of the atrocious. It wasn't funny at the time, but....

"This happened in the very severe winter of 1963 when Edwin Keightley, Anson Division, Engineering Mechanic, was there. The order was 'No speaking' in the mess after 'lights out,' and all the little sailor boys were tucked up for the night. Poor Edwin let off some very loud wind. Result - noisy titters from mess-mates.

Enter furious C.P.O. Instructor, shouting: 'Who did that?'

Eddie admits it, is ordered to don plimsolls and to run round the block, including parade-ground and Nelson Hall, clad only in pyjamas, in deep snow and freezing temperatures! He laughs about it now, but it does seem a severe punishment for doing or letting forth a natural function. No hard feelings though. Many happy memories of Ganges, as well as the other sort."

Initially, Edwin probably related the story, not to complain, but to take the opportunity to laugh about it and to show how he was easily able to cope with that sort of treatment. That understandable attitude is taken by many others who went through the rigours of Ganges. They deny it was tough so they could prove they *were* tough by indicating that, to them, it was easy. By 'other sort' Dorothy means the spiteful stupidity of a so-called responsible Instructor making a boy double around the parade-ground several times, in the depths of winter, in grossly unsuitable clothing, just for farting, as she puts it. It is fairly certain that anyone experiencing a similar fate, having learned the dubious rewards of honesty and 'owning up,' never owned up to anything ever again. Could it be said then that, amongst other things, Ganges taught boys to lie to keep themselves out of such harsh trouble? No wonder! The laughable part is an Instructor with a massive inferiority-complex, looking for the slightest excuse to prove he is superior. Mrs. Keightley makes light fun of it, but there is no light fun in the following story of **S.A. Hirons,** Ganges 1963, also about the same bleak, snow-bound Shotley. Before that story, let us examine the reasons for such spiteful behaviour on the part of an Instructor who is supposed to be the mentor, teacher and father-figure to the very young boys passing through the very vulnerable, influential awareness stage, of boy into youth into man.

What causes a person to ill-treat those beneath him? Perhaps because in his boyhood days he was badly bullied by other boys, or his parents, a strict father, harsh mother? Had he previouslyy been subjected to authority without the opportunity to strike or answer back? Bullying causes one to adopt the attitude : 'I must be inferior because I am being *treated* as inferior, and I must bully others to show them (and prove to myself) that I am really *superior.*' Demeaning others is the most inefficient way to teach or to obtain the respect of the pupils. A bully is usually the victim of bullying himself, and does not know how to treat others of lesser-standing in any other way but force, threats, humiliation and, sometimes, pain. It is no more, or less, than a pathological need to demonstrate his power over others to make himself look and feel good, an attitude that will never, ever solve his problem, causes resentment, fear and distrust in his menials - certainly not respect, except out of sheer fear. The sad thing about it is that, having been used to being bullied, he thinks it is natural that he should, in turn, bully those beneath him. Bullying, which means shouting, threatening, cajoling, causing actual bodily harm and injury with the infliction of pain, be it by broomstick, stonnicky, rope's-end, wet towel, swagger-stick, billiard-cue and/or any other implement, etc., was dismissed as trivial and actually recommended as a means to be just ordinary, commonplace and necessary to teach young boys how to become men, especially in the Royal Navy, although fear and humiliation seems to be the basis of most military training schedules.

"The most sadistic person I've ever met.."

S.A. Hirons had no respect for his Instructor: "Our Instructor in the Annexe was Chief Petty Officer B....... (Ordnance), probably the most sadistic person I've ever met. Once a week we had to do our washing, and during the middle of Winter (snow on the ground) we had to strip off, put towels round our midriff, then we were double-marched over the parade-ground to the wash-rooms. Silence was the order of the day, and if he caught anybody talking, he would lash them with a length of rubber hosing, if he caught them talking again, they were immersed in a large bath of bleach water, which we had used to bleach our whites in. For not shaving on the first week, at divisions on Sunday an officer proceeded to pull little tufts of hair from my chin, told me to get a shave and I had ten minutes for lunch every day for the next week, while the remaining time was spent doubling round the parade-ground, you know the routine, 'rear man to the front' on command. But I learned fast, and over at the main camp I was only ever in trouble once, and that was for shinning down the ropes on the mast instead of coming down the rigging, but punishment was the order of the day everywhere.

One lad in our mess, which we had to polish with boot brushes, was a bit crabby, so when we had a kit muster, the officer doing it picked up on it straight away. Told him to gather his whole kit up, which was laid out on a blanket, instructed us to draw shovels from the bosun, then made us dig a hole in the Divisional garden, bury his kit, and made us double-march on the spot to flatten the earth. Then he said he would be back within two hours for a re-muster. **So we all dug it up,** and worked like fanatics to get it all washed and ironed and folded into seamanship-manual size for the re-muster, which thankfully he passed. Also, when we used to march to and from tuition, we used to mess about a bit, and one day an officer saw us and that was it. Our feet didn't touch the deck. We were double-marched to the mess, had to don gas-masks and oil-skins, double up to the main parade-ground and we had to bunny-hop and crouch-march for an hour for our insolence."

'Bunny-hopping' and 'crouch-marching' is an extremely agonizing punishment. Doing either for just one-minute is painful; being ordered to do it for an hour is no less than legalised torture. 'Bunny-hopping' requires the victims to squat, holding their rifles above their heads and hop along the parade ground. 'Crouch-marching' is also performed in the squat position, and the unfortunates have to try to walk, waddle is a better description, in that mode, still with rifles above their heads. Both are very, very painful; the calf muscles and thigh muscles, front and rear, go into excruciating spasms of pain leading to eventual total cramp or seizure of all the leg muscles. It has to be admitted though, that this method of punishment did not cause the Instructor any discomfort at all. Indeed, it may have given him lots of pleasure. After that treatment, who would blame anyone for hating Ganges, as so many did because of similar incidents? All is forgiven and the story ends with absolvence of any crimes:

"At the time it was barbaric and there was no escape for anyone, but looking back, it stood me in good stead and certainly didn't do me any harm. I was a Junior Naval Aircraft Mechanic in Grenville Division, and our Instructor was C.P.O. A.E. Stevens. Our Divisional

Officer was Lt. Commander Phillips who was six feet eight inches tall. We called him `Fresh-air Fred.`"

Surely, some would say, thinking logically, would it not have been more to the benefit of those boys to have had extra lessons pertaining to their respective training to enable them to attain greater marks in their final exams? In their future years, how many of them would be called upon to bunny-hop or crouch-march when performing their job, fighting the enemy or even to save their lives?

There are several stories about boys having their **kit buried,** and it is of some significance that, with few exceptions, all the boys helped the victim of this unfair treatment to recover his kit, wash it, iron it, and lay it out for the next inspection. Painful non-productive punishment was also a dead-end exercise. So all's well that ends well, as **S.A. Hirons** indicates in his final words, despite the ungentlemanly behaviour of the Annexe Instructor and harsh punishment of a so-called 'officer and gentleman,' his Divisional Officer.

However, by another Instructor's own admission the word *'gentleman'* does not apply to anyone serving in the R.N., even that of officer, according to the revelations of **Evan Cattanach,** February, 1952:

"On my first leave I lost my paybook, imagine the fear of what awaited me on my return. I received two week's jankers, early morning laundry, square-bashing including Faith, Hope and Charity etc. On the first muster the Master-at-Arms instructed me, the raw recruit, to take the party through the Main Gate to the Officer's Mess. No problem. 'Squad!' I shouted: 'Shun! Right turn, double march!' (It always seemed to be `double-march`). Everything went well `til I arrived at the Main Gate. I reported the punishment detail for the Officer's Mess.

'Who told you to come here?'"was the shouted response. At that time I didn't know a leading-hand from a Petty Officer, or, for that matter, a Commander. To play on the safe side, and, as always, polite, I said: 'A gentleman at the office told me, sir.'

'Gentleman!?' he shouted. 'A gentleman? A gentleman? There's no such beast in the Royal Navy!`'he screamed.

Oh, the embarrassment."

The (only) one who got away

Dave Van Dee Weele, 1946, Benbow Division, the only boy who absconded and got away with it.

"Things were quite cruel at times, inhuman treatment by the Instructors. Our Instructors were Paddy Boyle and C.Y.S. Hall. Chief Yeoman Hall wasn't too bad. Many times I saw the rope's end and broom-stick being used on the lads, and the square inch of soap which had to be eaten for using foul language. The worst beating I ever saw was on a lad named Horton. At that time I was an acting Leading Boy and the lad was caught swearing and refused to eat soap. So, at supper-time, Paddy Boyle, P.O. Telegraphist, thrashed him with a broom-stick so hard the broom-stick broke. Myself and another Leading Boy reported him to the Padre who, in turn, reported the incident to the Commander. Boyle was hauled up before the Old Man and given a rollicking. When Boyle came back to the mess he wanted to know who had reported the deed. Every one kept quiet, so the sadist Boyle put us all on Shotley Routine for seven days.

A favourite trick of his, whilst in the wireless room, was to sneak up behind you, pull back one of your earphones and let it twang back on your ear - very painful. I also was a witness to a lad being hit with an oar in one of the whalers. We were pulling against the tide to get back to shore and Paddy was in a hurry to get back for his rum ration and, in a foul mood, decided we were not pulling hard enough. So hence the beating with the oar.

There was the lad who drowned in the swimming bath, caused by a P.T.I. The lad couldn't swim and if you couldn't swim you had early morning swimming lessons and the P.T.I. had a long pole to keep you away from the side of the baths. This lad was pushed on the head with the pole and went under, the P.T.I. walked away and left him, thinking he would surface, but, as I said, he drowned.

I think one of the most humiliating thing was early morning showers, when, after showering the P.O. in charge made you pull back your fore-skin to see if it was clean.

I was lucky never to get cuts, but knew one or two of the boys that did and saw **the marks on their back-sides.** I think the tight duck-trousers they had to wear made the cuts more sharper and then having to double round the parade ground to get a bit of circulation going. Then there was jankers, first thing in the morning, standing to attention on the quarterdeck and reading the Seamanship Manual for an hour, and then in the afternoon doubling up and down Laundry Hill with the rifle held out in front, and boy, did that make your arms ache! I don`t know if anyone can remember a Chief G.I. named Ted Records. He was my uncle. One day he was taking jankers. I told the rest of the lads we would have an easy time of it, but no! It was the worst day we had, you can imagine what the lads thought of me. Another Petty Officer, O'Grady, short, five feet six inches or so, I'll never forget, I'd got a tiddly bow-wave on my cap and what did O'Grady do? Placed the cap on the bridge of my nose and then with his fist knocked the bow-wave down, causing the cap to work it's way down my forehead onto my nose. Talk about tears in my eyes!

I also remember a lad, Gentiles, or something like that. He did a runner and the next thing he was in the daily papers having killed a girl in Coventry.

"I had it away with Tessie McKay..."

Every Sunday, on Shotley shore leave, a walk down the Ipswich road in Shotley. I was very lucky, I met a little W.R.N. named Tessie McKay and used to have it away with her in a haystack. When I was inside after my long run ashore - when I deserted, I'll tell you about that later - she visited me, bringing chocolate, nutty-bars and so forth. I had joined Ganges on the 7th January 1947 and was discharged in December same year after my 'long run ashore.' The day I left on my long run was visiting day. Myself and a lad from Hull, named Bogey Knight, walked down to the foreshore and along the side of the river until we came to a foot-path leading to the Ipswich road. There we met two girls on bicycles. We chatted them up and told them we needed a lift to Ipswich. They agreed to lend us their bikes and, as they sat on the seats, Knight and I stood on the pedals and peddled like mad to Ipswich. On arriving at Ipswich we caught a bus to Colchester and from there hitched-hiked to Hull. We went to Knight's home and his parents talked him into going back to Ganges. I went to my home town, Grimsby, and joined a travelling fair and stayed with them until the end of the season. I then went back to Grimsby, and, after two or three weeks, gave myself up to the police. I was put in cells to await an escort to Ganges. Chief Petty Officer Fanny Fields, collected me. On arriving back at Ganges, after a night in cells, I went before the Old Man and was told I would be held in custody until they decided what to do with me. It was 28 days before I went up again and during that time I got to know the Crushers and Patrolmen very well and was treated better than being on the mess. I was sentenced to 12 cuts and a discharge, but having been under arrest for so long, the cuts were quashed. I was given a rail ticket to Grimsby for that day, but no bus fare to Ipswich. The mess-men and Crushers had a whip-round for me and I think I got about three pounds, which was more than enough to pay for the fare to Ipswich."

That was not the end of Dave's navy days; he had a liking for the sea and it was natural for him to return to it; so he did, and he did well.

"I was deep-water trawling before I joined Ganges," continues Dave, "And I went back to fishing until I joined the Army in 1949. I became a S/Sgt. Navigator with the R.A.S.C. Water Transport, and came out in 1956. I then went back to sea and got my Skipper's ticket, sailing to Iceland, Greenland, Bear Island and the Wight. So I didn't do too bad."

Note by the author: I was in the Communications Mess, 33 Mess,

Benbow Division in late '47, and knew of a senior Comms Mess further down Benbow Lane, the same one in which Dave Van Der Weele was situated. I recall the boy drowning in the swimming baths. I also remember C.Y.S. Hall, a tall, kindly man: and Paddy Boyle, smaller of stature with quick, hurried movements, who had been pointed out as a man to beware of. When he was duty Instructor, e.g. waking the whole Division, his angry blustering and bullying nature did not endear him to the boys.

Recalling the boy who drowned; I remember the horror that was felt all around the Ganges camp at the time. It is puzzling why non-swimmers, knowing they are afraid of water, want to go to sea. **Petty Officer Burnet** was afraid of water; his story is told by his wife, Mrs. C. Burnet, now aged seventy, of Glasgow. She has many memories of 'the other sort,' as she describes them, told to her by her now deceased husband.

"My husband joined up in 1933 and he used to tell me about the very harsh treatment he got and they tried to break his spirit. He had a fear of water and were going to stop his leave if he didn't learn to swim, but he made it. He had lots of hard times and some of the officers were just pigs, and it was very daunting for a wee Glasgow boy to the first time away from home."

Ex-Instructor **George Bishop** almost agrees: "I joined in 1938, finished training just in time for the beginning of the war. It was tough at Ganges pre-war, especially if you upset your Instructors, and I did, because I got dipped from a W/T and V/S class to a seaman class. I returned as a Leading Seaman in 1946 to take over the first class of boys in January. My opposite number was P.O. Goulder who went on to be a Commander. The impression I had of what the boys thought of us was that they preferred me to be duty-weekend, until one Wednesday I did not mention what was going to happen later. I had already reported that the Petty Officer Boys and Leading Boys could not keep the mess under control, so, instead of carrying on to the Gym on the Saturday evening for pictures, we went for a stroll: Laundry Hill, Faith, Hope and Charity, all on the double, back to the mess, scrubbed it out thoroughly, gave them a pep-talk, and after that we achieved satisfaction all round. One boy, Clark, flaked out."

Eric Ball says they dressed him like Charlie Chaplin in his earlier days, but the humour was lacking: "I was a Boy Seaman in June, 1934. Sergeant Brown King, Royal Marines, was the recruiting officer at the time in York street, Sheffield. From there to Shotley, arriving on a picket boat. A young lad of 15 years and 10 months, homesick and facing a Petty Officer Instructor, who was a real sadist, P.O. Beckenham. Our mess was number 27 at the end of the Long

Covered Way. I'll never forget the first meal that night which was pea soup, one chunk of cheese and a square of bread. I was terribly homesick, and before they could check on me I went out of the mess and made my way to the Quarter-Deck where the Officer-of-the-Watch was pacing. I went across to him.

He said: 'What's all this then?'

I said: 'Please sir, I don't like it here, I want to go home.'

Can you imagine what consternation that caused? The officer, a Lieutenant, saw the funny side and said: 'Do you want to go before supper, or after?'

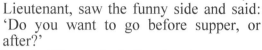

I said: 'Please sir, before.'

My Instructor was sent for and he got a rollicking for letting me get to the Quarter Deck, and when Beckenham got me in the mess **I received a pasting from a stonnicky, which was a rubber cosh. I cried nearly all night.** Then the next day we had the ordeal of climbing the mast, it looked about 500 feet high to us lads, and the last one down received more lashes from the stonnicky.

We were kitted out in uniform; there was no measuring, they just threw a pair of old bell-bottoms and a jumper at you, whether it fitted or not. I was only four foot eleven as I was a special entry, and the uniform would have fitted someone much bigger. We all looked as if were in a Charlie Chaplin film, but when I settled down, I enjoyed it, plenty of sport, it certainly made a man of me."

Ex P.O. Tel. Armstrong, '36 - '37, says: "Discipline was harsh but not unfair."

Discipline is discipline. It is either fair or unfair. If it is labelled harsh then it means that it is more unfair that it should be.

P.O. Tel. Armstrong: "I shall never forget my days at Shotley, discipline was harsh but not unfair. If one did not rebel. I joined Shotley just in time for supper. What a welcome! Steamed cod, parsley sauce, potatoes full of eyes, staring at us as we devoured them. It appeared as if someone had vomited all over the plate." *Some welcome.*

"Then they sorted us out, the bright boys for W/T and V/S, the rest seamen. Unfortunately, two boys missed the liberty boat back, Stringer and Whitfield, the outcome was Shotley Routine for a week for all the mess."

Punishing the whole mess for the dubious misdemeanours of two of

the boys? That was harsh but fair?
"Everywhere at the double, over the mast in bare feet, up and down Laundry Hill, pyjama legs tied at the ankle, two bed chocks in each leg." *This is fair discipline we are talking about here, remember.* "Yeoman Dance, he was a Londoner, disliked Geordies, Scousers, Brummies, Welshmen, Scotsmen, Presbyterians, Methodists and Plymouth Brethren. Unless one was a C of E Cockney, one was on his hit-list. He used to walk round the dormitory dropping odd woodbines here and there, but if one was caught retrieving them, out came that piece of tarred hemp.
We used to place the clips from our pyjamas at the end of the mess table just before 21 hours. One night he was duty Instructor, someone seeking revenge tied black thread to the two bottom outside clips, trailed it out to the Long Covered Way, attached a piece of paper to the end. The Instructor came marching down just before rounds, picked up this piece of paper and the clips clattered all over the mess-deck floor. Was he livid! Next morning at Wakey-Wakey he had that look in his eyes. He was staring out the window at the grass between the messes. Suddenly he shouted: 'You four! Come here! Follow me and clean up those lawns.' It appeared some of the chaps had been clearing their lungs and noses and expectorating through the windows. Those four lads had to pick up all the spit and snot. As it happened, they were the only four smokers in the mess."
It can be agreed that the latter was fair; the culprits had to clean up their own mess; but all of the former is suspect of `harsh,` yes, but `fair?`
Frank Baker was there in '48: "I was in Duncan Division, our Instructor was C.P.O. Mortice. He was known to all as 'Rigor Mortice,' but was far from dead, as many will testify, especially after a session on Faith, Hope and Charity in full pack.
'Cruelty to boys by Instructor boys...'
Other features I recall during my time were mouth-washing in soapy water for bad language, the 24-hour a day wearing of cork life-jackets for failing the swimming test and wearing of tin helmets and gas masks for other mis-demenours. It seems that in this world there are antagonists and victims, and a place like Ganges was very quick to sort out one from the other. The only cruelty I ever saw at Shotley was imposed on boys by other boys. The worst of these was instigated by Instructor Boys from other messes but I wouldnt have missed my time for anything."
'Streaky' Bacon is a man of few words, some of them controversial. He says: "Ganges was the first, the last, and the only concentration camp in England. I joined in 1935 as a lad of fourteen and a half

161

years old. I was in Grenville Division and spent eighteen months there. It was tough, but done you good. Can you imagine these yobs of today being there? They wouldn't last a week! They were the best years of my life in the Andrew. Left there, went to Chatham, and went on the Cumberland to the Far East in 1936."

Most ex-boys will admit Ganges did them some good, even to the point of contradicting themselves. Commander C.F. Bryant, RNZN (Retd.) says: "I didn't really think it was harsh, but the discipline was certainly severe. We were the first Comms class to learn touch-typing, and, in the sparkers' case the first class to learn the morse code using a typewriter.

The thing I disliked the most was boats. I was very small, could hardly lift the oars of those big 32ft cutters, let alone row. The Instructor used to walk down the centre-board and hit us with the tiller, and when we got back to the pier, tired, wet and sore, we had to hoist those damn great boats onto the davits. In the sailing-rowing races, where we were towed a bit, sailed a bit, rowed with the mast up, then dropped mast and rowed some more, our Instructor for this was an Irishman, a G.I. I think. He used to order 'Down mast!' and when the forestay was slipped he would catch the mast in the crook of his arm. This same man gave us a 'Shotley Shake-up' one afternoon - Saturday, I think, because we had been giving Yeoman Jones a hard time. It was on the parade-ground, and the order, 'Over the mast, turn sharp by the Chief's and P.O.'s Mess, across the parade ground. Go!'

Getting over the mast was an effort, and the threat: 'Last six will go again,' spurred us on. I cannot remember his name, but I think he left for putting his hand in various boys' beds'' (*Further elucidation upon this was asked for, but the writer said that he had heard it from someone else and that it may have been a current 'buzz,' and could have been a statement which may or may not have any truth in it.*)

'We also had one G.I. who, during rifle-drill, in the summer, when wearing white fronts and half blues, would hit us across the neck with a bit of black flex. Playing rugby I can remember catching and tackling the Commander who was the champion naval hurdler and he came down with a horrible thump and had to leave the field. I worried a bit for a few days after that. Later in life, I was doing around 10.1 seconds for the 100 yards, how fast I was then, at Ganges, I don't know. We had fun, too. Tying a bit of cotton through the tea mugs which were neatly stacked in a pyramid, so that when the patrol came in they would all come crashing down.

Bed-chock fights, where we would raid opposition messes and slide the wooden bed chocks across the polished floor at great speed. What

I can't remember is how we got the bed-chocks back! A night-time punishment for such antics when we were usually in pyjamas, was to turn our mattresses back, collect our kit-bags from the rack - we didn't have lockers - and with our kit-bags on our shoulders, double on the spot on the bed-springs. I could just about lift my kit bag as I recall.

But the thing which sticks in my mind above all is the Saturday night when supper was a cold meal: bread, shallots, some cheese and something else. We had a fine old time throwing these things at each other across the dining-room, when in walked Yeoman Jones. We were fallen in outside, leading boys, P.O. Boys, and the Instructor Boy - who was living in our mess, and we were doubled from then until quite late. First of all up and down Laundry Hill, and so that the first three couldn't keep a comfortable jog, 'Rear man to the front!' was a frequent order. Then up and down Faith Hope and Charity, sixty-three steps in all. After that down to the foreshore onto the running track which had steep sides leading down to it and we doubled up and down these.

It was then that one boy, Gawley, flaked out, and we were told to leave him there. What happened to him that night I don't know. I do remember that we boys were so pleased later to see the Leading and P.O. Boys had to take the punishment which they were normally excused. They were really 'stuffed' that night!

I can remember one period when we were fallen-in on the parade, after lunch I think, when the parade officer gave a short lecture about various subjects, and on the occasion was talking about Royal Marine officers. He said: 'Royal Marine officers are not recruited, they are quarried.'

I think I was too young to realise the statement had two interpretations. However, having spent some time with the Royal Marines at Ghain Tuffieha in Malta as a Yeoman of Signals, and later at Bickleith, I always had a very high regard for them, and get very cross when they are referred to as 'Marines,' or anything less than 'Royal Marines.'

Despite all of that I look back on Ganges with pleasure. Some of that discipline could do a lot of good to today's youths. Perhaps the parents could do with some discipline, too."

R. Bensley, 1961, was disgusted at having to knock seven bells out of his best oppo when in the Annexe. But although he wasn't afraid of fisti-cuffs, he suffered from vertigo: "As I am frightened of heights I was dreading climbing the mast. I knew as soon as I saw it that they would make me climb it. I finally got over the top after the fourth attempt, with a P.T.I. ahead of me and a P.T.I. behind me, and another couple screaming blue murder at me from below - I've never forgiven them. The other bad memory was that awful swimming test, jumping from the top board with overalls and boots on, swimming two lengths then the agonising swim in the deep-end for two minutes with P.T.I.`s prodding you with poles to stop you touching the sides. It was strict, and the stupid things they got you doing, like polishing the mess floor with your shoe brush or scrubbing the parade-ground with your toothbrush. I was glad when my time was up and I became a real sailor."

Bill Campbell, recalls another Instructor who ill-treated the Boys: " I joined Ganges in 1947, and was standing at-ease on the parade-ground one day, when suddenly I felt a sharp, burning stinging pain in my hands which were behind my back. A voice said: 'Stand still! Face your front! And put your hands in the proper position while standing at-ease!'
This little C.P.O. Gunnery, about five feet three inches high, in the old-style gaiters and webbing belt, was walking up and down the ranks and if anyone was not at the correct position as regards the hands, he would whack them with a length of silver chain - and did it sting! We called him, **'The Mighty Atom!'**

Len Braithwaite, 13th Jan, 1938, didn't think much of Ganges. He writes: "I was an ex-internee of Ganges, Britain's number one concentration camp, and the worst thing I remember was in the heavy gun battery on the foreshore when I was whipped with a firing lanyard whilst in a duck suit. It started on the parade-ground during rifle drill. I was 15 years old and five feet three in height. A .303 rifle with bayonet fixed was nearly as big as I was. I dropped the rifle by accident. The Gunner's Mate, Petty Office Palmer, came rushing across to me, frothing at the

THE MIGHTY ATOM.
Shotley magazine - 1949   Anon, 45

164

corners of his mouth, calling me names that I had never heard of. I started grinning at him, I was always laughing and grinning, it was second nature. Petty Officer Palmer then said: "When I get you in the Heavy gun battery on the foreshore, I'm going to wipe that grin off your face. And he did.

'Whipped with a firing lanyard...'

In the gun battery I was 'loading number,' which meant when the shell was on the tray it was rammed up the barrel of the gun with a ram-rod. Then the cordite was placed on the tray and pushed behind the shell by your fist. I rammed the cordite behind the shell with the ramrod. With that, Petty Officer Palmer picked up the firing lanyard and and started to whip me across the back. I was wearing a duck suit. The Chief of the battery came running across and stopped him, and then asked me if I wanted to take the Instructor's punishment or have him reported to the Officer-in-charge. Of course, the answer to that was to take the Instructor's punishment or my life would have been isolated if it had gone on report. So the Instructor carried on with his punishment. I cried all night long. By the way, a firing lanyard is a knotted rope with a steel hook on the end, the hook was placed on the firing position of the breech of the gun, and when the order to fire was given you pulled the lanyard and, so your hands didn't slip, there were knots all down it.

The mast was not too bad, but scrubbing the Long Covered Way on my hands and knees was awful. Leave was two hours a week, walking around Shotley with an Instructor. My Instructors were Gunners Mate 'Chop- chop' Palmer, and seamanship Instructor Captain Bligh - Petty Officer Findlater." Then, as is usual with the foregoing type of statements, Len ends it with: "It didn't do any harm. There ought to be places like Ganges for the youth of today, it would be a better country." *Firing lanyards an' all?*

Ron Bennett didn't like Ganges; he refers to it as 'that place,' as if mentioning the word, 'Ganges,' brings back memories which he does not wish to recall. His recollections of 'that place' do not lend themselves to any type or form of endearment. Ganges was a necessary evil to be got out of the way as quickly as possible. But analysing the following story, would he have had a different tale to tell, in a more endearing fashion, and a different view, if the presence of just one Instructor, Petty Officer Nobby Clarke, who made his life at Ganges an ordeal, and probably that of others, was replaced by a more understanding person?

"My history at that place commenced on the 26th April, 1934. My account of life at Ganges includes the discipline: jankers, Shotley Routine, the mast, and six cuts with the cane across the arse, *'For*

sucking his teeth when given an order by his seamanship Instructor.'
That was the charge as read out by the Master-at-Arms at the
Commander's defaulters, but it was converted into *'silent contempt'*
towards 'one Petty Officer Nobby Clarke,' a one-hundred-percent
Geordie sadist.

I can remember arriving at Harwich station and getting the launch
across to Shotley where, after a spell in the Annexe, we were
marched to the Long Covered Way to Rodney Division and
introduced to our Instructors; P.O. Nobby Clarke, seamanship, from
Newcastle and a right bastard. Battered features and a permanent
snarl. Petty Officer Denmark, G.I., much more humane, but a
martinet on or off the parade-ground. It was a pleasure to find he was
duty P.O. if you were on jankers. We had wooden poles in lieu of
rifles for a more lenient form of punishment. Normally held over the
head or out front at arm's length. But with a sadist like Nobby Clarke,
it was held behind the knees, squat and frog-hop around the
parade-ground. Busted tendons were not uncommon. Some years
later I was reading a book about Japanese-held prisoners-of-war, and
their experience of some of the forms of punishment they were
subjected to for minor offences. The poles, bamboo in their case, and
were mentioned at the court's martial of former prison guards of
Changi Gaol. They classed that sort of treatment as 'war crimes!'

I remember down on the pier at boat drill, mast and sails rigging, as I
recall, the cutters were sitting on the mud, and on being given the
order to 'Man the boat!' It was, of course, a 'hurry-up' job, assisted
by P.O. Clarke with his stonnicky, an eighteen-inch length of
two-inch rope, with a Turks Head, or Manrope knot on the end, and
the rest covered in blue and white drill cloth braiding, similar to a bell
rope. This happened one morning on the pier at boar drill.

'Palace of varieties...'

At the order, 'Man the boat!' I thought it quickest to go down the side
of the jetty structure. It was winter-time, my hands were frozen, my
feet likewise, and on reaching the first horizontal beam, my boots
slipped on the slimy sea-weed and oil and I fell about twelve feet. I
made contact with the gunwhale of the cutter with my chest, and
splashed down into about two feet of water on top of thick, black
mud. I was hauled out - which was very painful; my mouth was
bleeding and I was ordered up to the pier top by our friend Nobby,
who, after calling me all kinds of idiot, told me to report to the Sick
Bay. The walk up to that 'palace of varieties' I shall never forget. My
chest was on fire and I was covered in mud from head to toe. I was
intercepted by a Sick Bay Petty Officer and a Sick Berth Attendant at
the door-way and, on being told of the events, I was ordered to

strip-off in the door-way. A bucket of hot water was brought out by a junior S.B.A. who assisted removing the mud and blood. A towel and a blanket arrived, and, after being inspected by the P.O. S.B.A. I was allowed to proceed to see the Medical Officer.

He discovered I had bitten my tongue, skinned my forehead, sustained three cracked ribs and decided I should be allocated a bed. The luxury of getting between sheets was pure bliss, except that I could hardly breathe, unable to eat anything except Windsor Soup, and both my eyes had turned black. After four days I was returned to duty, but excused rifle-drill and climbing the mast.

After three more days I went back to the Sick Bay to have my plaster removed. The plaster-tape encircled my body from lower ribs to arm-pits, and it was removed in one fierce, swift rotating spin. I thought I had no skin left, but after a rub down with white spirits I was classified as A1 and returned to full duty.

We were always hungry, and one of the boys in my class frequently received a parcel from home which contained a home-made sparrow-pie. The lad had to report to the mail office, open the parcel, then stand by while a Regulating Petty Officer poked and prodded the pie with a metal spike to make sure no packets of cigarettes were hidden inside. Then it was back to the mess-deck and share it with favoured mates. It was a wonder to me that the Regulating P.O. wasn't looking for hidden files in case we tried to escape! My time at that place ended on 26th April when I left with 150 other assorted Boy Seamen en route for the 'Renown.' It was a case of 'out of the frying-pan into the fire,' the discipline was just as tight, but of a different calibre.

The only person I ever met again, apart from my mess-mates at Ganges, was Big Bill Underwood, the Master-at-Arms, who joined me on the 'Kent,' in 1938. He held the title of 'Strongest man in the Navy,' and his speciality was lying on his back beneath a platform upon which was a grand piano, and raising the whole lot in one lift."

There were many Instructors who treated the boys with kindness; and it may be a fact that their numbers outweighed the bullies. But those that were bullies or sadists, suffering from inferiority complexes, or any other excuse, are guilty of getting other, innocent Instructors as bad a name as themselves. Fortunately, most are, or were, given the benefit of the doubt, the innocent-until-proved-guilty theme. But, despite extensively trying to disprove that stigma, a request for stories of kind Instructors, had a response that is equal to a mere one-and-a-half-percent of those received giving detrimental details of cruelties. The positive news is that there are those who will speak up in favour of good and kindly Instructors. All stories sound good, or bad, until the other side is heard, and there are some who are determined to reveal that other side.

George Bromley, Ganges, 1940-ish, gives an admirable account of the 'other side,' having joined as a boy and returned later as an Instructor. He applied the same principles to his class of boys which his Instructor had applied in his day. He defends the merits of the 'good-guy' Instructors to the point of admiration, and, although this story belongs in the 'Good Instructors' category, it is reproduced here because George admits that there were bad 'uns as well as good 'uns.

George: "Having read various correspondence on the subject of bullying Instructors: I had already reached the conclusion that not all Instructors were sadistic bullies etc. Obviously, Instructors such as Gunner's Mates and Gunnery Instructors only seemed to be stricter, probably because of the intense training and ingrained instinct and tradition that: 'We have got to be seen to be tough.' ''

(Acting `tough` is a superficial indication that the person doing so wants it to be known that **he** *is tough, or* **thinks** *he is, or* **would like others to think that he is.** *It is, invariably, a false front. That type of attitude prevailed mainly in those who had, themselves, suffered at the hands of a bad or over-strict Instructor:* **"I suffered, why shouldn't they?'** *Letters were received from men who joined Ganges as a boy, became Petty Officers and returned to Ganges as Instructors. Their attitude was,* **'It didn't do me any harm, so I gave them what I received and got my own back.'** *Own back? On whom? Innocent boys? It didn't do you any harm? It poisoned and brain-washed your mind to ill-treat your underlings equally as harsh as you had been ill-treated.)*

George continues with an admission that there **were** renegade Instructors: "Personally I came across only two vicious Instructors who seemed to delight in punishment. Mostly I think the clip round the ear and the stonnicky were used to emphasise orders to 'chop-chop,' for example, by P.T.I's in the Gym. However, I have occasion to be grateful to officers and one Instructor in particular. When I joined Ganges in January, 1940, I was a backward swimmer. I was absolutely scared of water and can remember going down the `chute in the deep-end, spluttering and gasping as I surfaced, groping for the offered pole; not letting go, so it ended up in the drink with me - more gasping and going under. A Lt. Commander Havers, whom I believe was a breast-stroke champion, persuaded the P.T.I. to allow me to go in the shallow end. By his encouragement, he urged me to pick up coins from the bottom. This gave me confidence and gradually I lost my fear. The man was kindness himself. But the constant early morning visits to the baths gave me a cold and eventually ear-ache, one of my ears developed a discharge. In the Sick Bay I was placed on the 'detained list.' The work was harder there, washing bed pans, bumping and polishing the wards and so on. My ear did not appear to be improving. It wasn't helped by having six teeth filled at that time. One Sunday morning, I was discharged fit by a Surgeon Lieutenant. I did not feel too good and returned to 14 Mess, Rodney Division, changed into number ones for Divisions and Church. I lay on my bunk and fell asleep. I was woken by Petty Officer Ellis, Gunner's Mate. He said softly: 'You don't look well, lad.'

'I don't feel too good, sir. I've just come out of hospital with an ear infection.'

Then, in a very calm, soothing voice, he said: 'Go to the Sick Bay, lad. Tell the duty 'tiffy' I sent you.' Then, more forcefully: 'And stay there!'

I don't remember any more except waking up in hospital with the Matron and Captain Surgeon at the bedside; even the Ward Master looked human. I had an acute mastoid and was pretty ill.

I don't know what action P.O. Ellis had taken, but I was grateful for his kindly and concerned intervention. Petty Office Ellis was, in my opinion, a professional Instructor, exacting discipline, staying aloof but never shouted or swore, he always seemed to know what was needed. He was responsible for taking to task our Leading Boys for allocating themselves bigger portions at meal times. Knowing this, Petty Officer Ellis appeared on the mess- square, cleared the mess, telling the Leading Boys to stand-fast in the covered way until we had trooped in and sat in their places. He never said a word, and they never tried the 'big-eats' trick again.

This was during the second world war. Later, we were evacuated to St. George and had to clean up one of the hotels, the 'Majestic,' for occupation. When we fell in to march back a young R.N.V.R. Sub. Lieutenant was in charge and tried to turn us into a column of fours to march back. He didn't know how to give the correct command. The Gunner's Mate saved the situation; he told the Sub there was a 'phone call for him, he then quietly marched us back. I have never forgotten Petty Officer Ellis, Lt. Commanders Havers or Cameron. They showed compassion in quiet and orderly ways. There must be many more Officers and Instructors who can be remembered in such a manner; not as bullies, but persons who made life a little lighter for those when it was needed most. Like many others I had seen how various Instructors reacted to their charges and responsibilities.

I returned later to Ganges as a Gunnery Instructor. I remember wanting to see my class excel in gunnery exams and thought I was doing a good job. I remembered Petty Officer Ellis, and tried to emulate him. Sadly, I received a shock! I was taking my class in twin, 4-inch gun drill, and one poor little sod just couldn`t get out the responses, he stood there silent. I thought he was winding me up. I berated him, but only received silence.

At `stand easy,` the Leading Boy came up to me.

"Can I speak to you, sir?"

"What is it?"

"Do you know why `X` cannot answer you, sir?"

"Tell me."

"He`s shit-scared of you, sir!"

I stood for a minute, looking the lad straight in the eyes. I said nothing but I thought: this lad has got style!

At the next session I tried a calm approach, just like Ellis would have done. It worked with this little lad. He spoke to me, and eventually he became quite cocky - great! I had won! I don't know the tale that must have gone round the class, but I had learned something which I have never forgotten. After I finished my twelve years I was demobbed and eventually reached a senior position in a national company as the Training Controller.

Going back to Ganges: I recall that most Instructors `dripped` in the mess about their charges; and what `blocks of wood they were,` etc., etc. *But except for the few radical Instructors who should never have been there,* most of us wanted to do the best we could for them, for the future, and learn from our own past. I never forgot my experiences at Ganges, they stood me in good stead. Ganges was an experience I was priviliged to receive."

The next story doesn't really come under the heading of 'cruelty to boys,' more like cruelty to Instructors - and an Instructor Boy - if the boys could have got their hands on him. It is really more humour than cruel, if you can call chucking half a loaf at an Instructor humorous!

Ginger Cooper, Jan., 1949, says his was the only mess ever to be charged with mutiny. He starts by praising one of the Instructors.

"Our Chief on the Tels course was a bluff old Devonshire man who's name I forget, but he was a real gentleman, as of course were all the Comms Instructors. When we had them for Jankers they always seemed to let us off rather lightly. When we were supposed to be doing the Shotley Shuffle, they usually halted us down on the foreshore for a rest. Not so the Gunners. They kept us hard at it all the time. One Instructor Boy I recall was named Ellis. He and Leading Seaman Freddie Sales got me put on seven days jankers for answering Ellis back. Sales said at the Commander's report that I had called Ellis a bastard. I didn't, he was lying to get his own way, but he was a bastard anyhow, in the sense that he was a bullying bastard. He thought he was a little tin god. I vowed if I ever met up with him we would sort it out there and then, but I never did have the opportunity.

Mutiny!!

Ours was the only mess to ever be charged with mutiny. Instructor C.P.O. (G.I.) Page, a right so-and-so if ever there was one. I had always been told that all G.I.'s were of unknown parentage, well, he certainly was, always threatening to put five lace-holes up your rear end. Anyhow, one night we were having supper in the mess and in walked C.P.O. Page, muttering his usual oaths, etc., slavering at the mouth and the like. I think that by this time we were really chocker with him, and as he turned round to leave, someone, and I do not know who to this day, threw half a loaf of bread at him. It hit him right smack on the back of the head. Talk about the air being blue! No-one would own up to the act, with the result that the Divisional Officer was called out, and again no one would own up, so we were all marched up to the quarterdeck where the Commander came out and read the riot act to us, informing us that what had happened was an act of mutiny, which still held the death penalty in the Andrew at that time. Still no one would own up, despite the death-threats, and the whole of the mess were put on seven days `Shotley Routine.`

That entailed getting up an hour earlier than usual, stoppage of pay, jankers in the dog-watches, working all week-end, but all in all it was well worth it."

The initial exhuberation and excitement of joining the Royal Navy is much-too-soon replaced with feelings of despair, uncertainty and dismay with the shock of short hair-cuts, painful jabs, bawling P.O.G.I.'s, plus the general despair of the introduction of strict discipline, strange, seemingly illogically-contrived rules and regulations and, most disturbing of all, fear of the unknown, especially if previously pampered boys had to learn to operate and survive without Mother.

Ex C.P.O. Telegraphist **Syd Whiting** has one vivid memory which he finds impossible to erase from the normal warm recollections which he has of Ganges. It is January 1940, and, as a Nozzer of only two weeks, the following is firmly burned into his memory:

"A boy who had deserted from the hard discipline of Ganges had been dragged back after two weeks of glorious freedom. It was just after `Stand Easy` on a forenoon, somewhere in mid-week. We were not looking forward to our next training session - boat party, `way down on the windswept wintry foreshore, which meant painfully

171

frozen fingers and all the other cosy niceties which Boat Party training brought with it. So we experienced some pleasure when a stay of execution of this dubious delight was given with the order: 'Clear lower deck, Divisions to muster in the Drill Hall.' The reason was to hear a warrant being read out to the luckless escapee, to determine his fate or punishment. Any warrant for a serious misdemeanour is read out by the Master-at-Arms in front of the Commanding Officer and the entire ships' company. I was 'way back in the rear of the assembly and heard, rather than saw, what was happening, but I knew that the prisoner was being escorted by two Marines and the Master-at-Arms. The latter was, by now, uttering the time-honoured phrases: 'Contrary to King's Regulations and Admiralty Instructions, any person who shall absent himself from his place of duty in time of war shall suffer death or some such other punishment as is hereinafter mentioned.'

Then came the deep, booming stentorious command: 'Prisoner! Two paces forward - MARCH!! Off - cap!'

'My God!' I thought, 'He`s going to be shot here and now!' My mind was so confused I missed the next part of the proceedings, but to my great relief I learned that he'd got the *'hereinafter'* punishment of 6 weeks detention and severe sessions of that healthy excercise known as 'Jankers.' I heard warrants read out on many occasions since then, but never one so memorable!"

There are stalwart defenders of Ganges who are oblivious, blind and deaf to detrimental stories which accuse that establishment of unfair dealing or atrocious treatment of any kind. Why is that? It could be that they were treated well by all of the Instructors - be they P.T.I.`s, their own Instructors, 'Schoolies,' officers, or anyone in authority which they came into contact when they did their training. By previous experience it is expected that there will be those who will claim that the stories in this book are far-fetched, figments of imagination, and never happened. It could also be that those who make those statements have forgotten the bad times and remember only the good. It happens continuously throughout our lives. We want the memory part of the brain to remember the happy times, and put to one side the unhappy times, tho` we are able to recall them - when we are forced to do so! The example is, all of our school holidays were blessed with brilliant sunshine, but it always rained when we journeyed back to school on the first day.

The Instructors at Ganges, and other boys' Training Establishments, were Chief Petty Officers and Petty Officers, sometimes Leading Seamen/Communicators. If the stories of atrocities and injustices, related by ex-boys, are suspect in the truth of them, then perhaps the story of an ex Chief Petty Officer, Gunnery, who related certain horrific tales, how could we, by the same rule, not give some credulity to the story as told by the ex-boy, ex-Instructor, C.P.O. Dorney?

Ex Chief Petty Officer **Norman Dorney, D.S.M. and bar**, Ganges, 1936, commences his recollections as a boy:

"The conditions at Ganges were really horrific and unbelievable, and, on looking back, I wonder how any boy coped. Some, of course, didn't."

He mentions 5.30 reveille's, scrubbing out the mess-deck each morning, cocoa and hard-tack biscuits, 'which had to be beaten against a brick wall to break them up,' steel plates and cups, and standing outside in all weathers waiting for breakfast to be fetched from the Galley and dished up by the boys who had been designated as 'cooks.' He also mentions wearing white duck-suits and the problem of keeping them white.

"Conditions were very bad, during the winter. In a dormitory with concrete floor we had only two smoky stoves, and we were allocated half a bucket of coal per day - we were freezing! No hot water, remove the ice in winter, and aluminium bowls to wash in.

I remember one time we were doing rifle drill and it was snowing heavy. We were in a blue working suit, no gloves, rifle in hand. We had to stand perfectly still for 15 - 20 minutes, getting colder and colder. Any boy who was shivering, or his rifle was not in correct position, would be struck with the butt of a rifle by the Gunner's mate - this caused one to drop the rifle because we were so cold and when this happened we were ordered to pick it up and march to the end of the line, we then had to hold the rifle in two hands above our head and double march for up to half an hour until the Gunner's mate decided we could stop. This was to teach us 'a bloody good lesson.'

'One boy ate four tins of boot polish...'

Each morning for one week at 6 a.m. we had to climb the mast. One boy was ordered to do so and along with three other boys started to climb. When this one boy reached the lower fighting platform he was so frightened he froze, and couldn't move; another boy and myself were ordered to climb up and try to rescue him. We went up but the boy was so frightened we couldn't release his hands from the mast. We returned down and another boy was told to go and alert the Sick Bay and the P.T.I.'s. The P.T.I's went up the mast, managed to get him into a Robinsons stretcher, and he was taken to hospital and eventually discharged.

Just before I joined the R.N. there was another boy who actually climbed to the top of the mast - about 150 feet - and jumped off, killing himself. The safety net, by the way, was made of steel mesh, this of course had no 'give' in it.

Field-gun training was very dangerous and very hard. Accidents happened frequently, fingers wrenched off, and many broken bones. Discipline was horrendous.

In the morning if any boy was slack in getting out of bed, which often occured, they were instructed to put on a duck suit and tuck the bottom of the trousers in their socks, then they had to stuff wooden bed-chocks, around eight to ten of these, down their trousers and were made to double-march to Laundry Hill. An Instructor would be present and as they reached the top they had to turn round and go back down to the bottom, about 150 yards, and this was repeated up and down for about an hour. By the end of it their legs and thighs were all skinned and extremely painful. Sometimes an Instructor would make us wear an oilskin back to front while running, and so the collar would rub the skin off our necks. This was to make it a little more interesting.

One boy, I recall, actually ate four tins of Cherry Blossom boot-polish so he would be sent to Sick Bay. This boy nearly died.

H.M.S. Ganges was a horrific and brutal establishment, and apart from the odd good ones, the Instructors were a sadistic lot. They were there to train you into a good sailor and a man who would not be afraid to tackle anything and who would be absolutely obedient. They were highly successful up to a point. The one thing they did not consider was that these were very young boys, most of them were away from home for the first time and the little affection and understanding which they sometimes needed was absent.

My time spent there did make me into a darn good sailor and, although it was dreadful, I have never regretted my training. I went through three wars, was mined on H.M.S. Fury, was awarded the D.S.M. and Bar, was mentioned in dispatches and only left the R.N. on medical grounds. I, like many others, went through a great deal in those wars, and I am sure that the training I received at H.M.S. Ganges held me in good stead.

I end by quoting a column from an old newspaper which is written under a photo of the mast at Ganges, which will, I am sure, be of interest:

H.M.S. GANGES. By John Douglas (Roundwood Press) 1978.

'Ganges was the concrete ship east of Ipswich aboard which scores of thousands of boys were beaten and cursed into manhood. Every year 2,000 of them aged from 15 to 17, were turned into fully-trained sailors, capable of manning warships. The discipline of Ganges was sadistic but its products were good for the Royal Navy and good for

174

Britain. The raising of the school-leaving age killed the establishment, but its last march-past, on June 6th, 1976, drew back most of it's Old Boys, more than it's 150 acres could hold. **John Douglas was a Ganges boy and his photographic recall** *of those great days* **makes this a book to be treasured by all who served in the Royal Navy."** The author of that book, and this book, writes: "Thanks for the plug but I did not write the above, although I would claim to be the author of some of those words. What I *did* write was condensed into the limited space allowed for reviewing, and re-written by a journalist who, having read the book, added his own interpretations of it. However, his interpretations are not too far from the real truth."

"Ganges was an exception.."

Ex Boy Signalman **Les Wilson** joined May, 1949:

"I thought I knew it all, coming from an area of Newcastle which was decidedly rough and used to finding myself in trouble, but Ganges was an exception to the rule. The comments regarding its likeness to a concentration camp were rather apt and it was, as most are aware, a tough environment under a very strict regime.

I remember vividly at one stage of my career at Ganges I was given 14 days no. **8** drill, which meant **running up and down the covered ways with a Lee-Enfield .303 rifle above my head.** I had absconded with another boy and caught outside March in Cambridgeshire. We were brought back to the Ganges and made to parade in front of all the other Boys. On top of that we were told we had been awarded 12 cuts of the cane. **Awarding,** as if they were doing us a big favour, having already been subjected to unneccessary harsh treatment by the Instructors, which treatment made me abscond in the first place. The punishment was carried out in front of

Shotley Magazine, 1928

175

everyone, possibly 2,000 boys, and it made me bitter and sore.
Another experience in the Summer of '49 saw me wearing a life-jacket (cork) because I had not learned to swim fast enough. A tin-helmet for wearing my hat on the back of my head and a gas-mask for being caught swearing. Prior to having the gas-mask issued I had to stand in front of everyone with a cup, tin mug containing salty water, and say 'Ahoy! Ahoy! Ahoy! This will make me a clean-mouthed Boy!' And gargle with it. Yes! I had every reason to take off, but I was good at my job, and eventually became a Leading Boy and finished my regular Naval service. It was strict and it was harsh, and it did produce some fine seaman. I was proud to be a Matelot. It instilled in me a discipline which I still maintain to this day. I've been Bolshie most of my life but I think when you have suffered the likes of H.M.S. Ganges for a full year or more, and seen and heard some of the suffering, it gives you a streak which enables one to do most things and put up with a hell of a lot." *'Humiliation, degradation, cruel, painful punishment for retaliating, equals discipline?'* That theme is prevalent in most stories about Ganges.

"Discipline was harsh..."

Tony Worthington, 1949, and currently with the Foreign Office in Bombay: "...then there was the ex Marine civilian in charge of the laundry. He used to wander behind the line of naked boys, checking to see if they were doing their dhobeying correctly. Woe-betide anyone who was not, because he got a swipe across the buttocks with a cut-down broom-handle which was carried by this man. Discipline was harsh, and I remember a spell on jankers for some minor offence. We were all made to wear oilskins and carry kit-bags above our heads, up and down the steps, Faith, Hope and Charity, leading down to the foreshore. One of the boys passed out but that did not put a stop to the rest of us continuing to double. He was propped up against a tree whilst we carried on."

A few Instructors enjoyed inflicting their superiority, their power over their menials, exercising an indulgement in satisfying what could be described as an obvious uplift of their own feelings. It has, by now, also been established by some of the stories, that some boys who refuse to acknowledge that their treatment was harsh, must have enjoyed being punished, humiliated and beaten. One wonders if they were the types who later visited Madam Cynthia Payne and paid for painful, but enjoyable, for them, continuances of the Ganges Regime?

"Ganges made men out of boys..."

Is it therefore possible that some boys *enjoyed* the sort of treatment exacted by the Instructors of Denis Preece?

Denis Preece, now in his seventies, joined in 1936 and he says: "Oh, yes, Ganges was hell, but I would not have changed it for anything. It certainly helped me through the war, it made me a good and expert seaman. I finished my time as a coxswain on M.T.B.'s, so you see, it did me no harm."

It should be wondered, again, if being **well-trained in Ganges** is the result of learning by fear. The story Denis tells is that of a sadistic Instructor, who had delighted in prolonging the punishment, and therefore inflicting mental anguish by delaying the moment of carrying out his proposed chastisement. Denis indicates that he was an inmate of Borstal, and continues his own story in his particular way of writing:

"What a pity Ganges had to close, it made men out of boys. I remember the words of our Instructor: 'You may have broken your mother's heart, you little bastards, but you won't break mine!' Borstal was home from home compared with Ganges. I was in Collingwood, I would not say we were the best mess because we had one or two 'scabs' in the class, so we was always in trouble. We got Shotley Routine twice. Oh, yes, how I remember that. My mate and I were sky-larking around throwing soap at one another one saturday morning while we were supposed to be scrubbing out the mess. We were caught by the Gunnery Instructor. Believe me he turned the air blue. We thought that was the end of it, but oh, no! About four days later as we were all about to turn in, he called us both out into the middle of the mess.

'You thought I had forgotten,' said he. I'm sure he was a sadist. He loved dishing out punishment for the least little thing.

He said to us: 'Kneel down on the deck,' which we did. He then produced two hard peas from his pocket, placing them in front of us. 'Right!' he said: 'Now push them the length of the mess-deck with your noses.'

I hadn't gone far when my pea split in half. I started to push one half towards the end of the mess.

'I said the **whole** pea!' he shouted.

I finished up doing two journeys. We both finished up with very sore noses."

That *'finish'* should have been the **'finish,'** but there was much more to this example of man's inhumanity to man:

"From his pocket," Denis explains, "He produced a short rope with a knot at the end. He called it his 'Percy.' It was a stonnicky. He said: 'Bend over the bed.'

He laid it into us and we both had three hard strokes across our backsides. It stung like hell. Oh, yes, Ganges was hell, but I would not have changed it for anything." *Not even the lashing with the stonnicky?* Another who tolerated the harshness of Ganges, says:

"Ganges was a holiday camp!"

It makes one wonder where he spent his holidays to voice that preference, but he says: *"H.M.S. Arethusa,* based on the River Medway in Kent, made Ganges look like a holiday camp," says **Ted Pinder** who joined in 1949. "Discipline in the 'Arry was much more harsh and regimented than Ganges ever was. Because of that, Ganges holds fond memories for me. Although they say it was very hard, I do, when talking about it, forget the bad bits and talk for ages on all the good things that happened there. It produced the finest sailors in the world. I was part of the Field Gun crew at Earls Court. Ganges taught me how to cope with life at it`s worst!"

Les Payter does not agree:

"I don`t know why I joined the navy in May, 1938," says Les. "I think it was because I wasn't getting on too well with my father at the time, and the promise of travel to foreign shores seemed to do the trick. However, I arrived at Harwich one evening and was met by a Petty Officer who made me feel thoroughly down-hearted by cursing all the so-and-so time about so-and-so well having to make a special so-and-so journey across the so-and-so river from so-and-so Ganges just to so-and-so pick me up!

The first few weeks at the Annexe, visiting the barber to get scalped, kitted up and learning to march and do squad drill were bad enough. Homesickness was a thing most of us suffered from but we were warned not to think of trying to run away because it was the boast of Ganges that it had been tried a few times but no one had ever been successful. Eventually we went to the main barracks, mess 22 in the Long Collonade, as it was called. Our Gunnery Petty Officer wasn't human, he hit out at us at the slightest thing and with anything near at hand. Like the day we were slow leaving the mess; he stood at the door with a broom-handle and we all got it across the back or the shoulders. Another time I was feeling ill during rifle-drill on the parade-ground and because my fingers were not in the correct position on my rifle he gave me an almighty crack with his bayonet scabbard. Later that day I collapsed with scarlet fever and he was convinced I had gone sick deliberately.

Punishment was cruel. A boy was given twenty-eight cuts with the cane for stealing two shillings from a mess-mate. Six cuts was a common punishment as was jankers. The pay was five shillings and ninepence of which we received one shilling. Two shillings and sixpence was the most we were ever allowed in our possession at any one time. We told our parents not to send us any money-orders or

178

parcels because everything had to be inspected by the Marine Sergeant in the post office. He confiscated all books and magazines and he was quite partial to cakes. One of our boys got his mother to fill and ice a cake with a chocolate laxative. We never did find out what happened to it! I'll say one thing for Ganges, it made men out of us and I found later in life that no matter what ship you served on, if you mentioned you were a Ganges boy you were given jobs that you were capable of doing and which other seamen would find difficult. It stood me in good stead throughout my 15 years in the navy. But there were always the cruel times."

It would seem then that he's not sure. Ganges was cruel - Ganges stood him in good stead. Another example of remembering the good and forgetting the bad. Where Ganges is concerned it seems that the bad times were so bad that, however much diminished is the memory, the bad times still linger. However, there is no doubt that the training was thorough and professional, and it was that which helped the boys grow into men, *not* the beatings, cruelty and humiliation.

Vengeance....

Harry Smith of St. George, Isle of Man, (Ganges war-time substitution) 1945, was a keen boxer and won the featherweight title, gained weight and became a welter-weight. The Instructors, he claims, were alright to him whilst he was actively boxing, but not alright when he gave it up. His view of Instructors: "There were good, bad and indifferent. We of 279W class had a Chief Tel., Wiggy Bennett. Don't remember him in detail, but I remember him as a decent chap and a good Instructor. The other, Yeoman Tye, Instructor of 278W was a cruel Bar Steward. I remember his long finger-nails to my chagrin. We were having supper, with Tye in attendance, when the next thing I know my neck is being attacked by a bunch of long finger-nails. My neck was bare and, with only a white-front on, nothing to protect it. I leaned to my right on the long bench, trying to avoid those stupid nails. My right hand was in a cocked position to strike whoever it was who was doing this; it was Yeoman Tye, he knew about my boxing reputation, and he must have visualised my fist crashing between his eyes. Next thing I know is I am doubling around the parade ground, and shortly after the whole class suffered because of my misdemeanour. The Chinese-style verdict, punish all and you also punish the culprit. No, I never won with Tye, but wish I could see him again now. He once threatened me with court-martial. How infantile, as an Instructor, can one get? One of my ship-mates, Lt. Commander Pete Wailes went back as a Chief Telegraphist Instructor and later as a Divisional Officer, another, Pete Shotbolt, a Chief Telegraphist also went back as an Instructor - I like to think and hope they were decent to the lads.

Ps. We had just joined up and arrived at St. George. Within the first week this lad was caught 'sleep-walking' between chalets by the Officer-in-charge of 'rounds.' The lad was out of the R.N. within 24 hours. Was it a perfect way of 'working your ticket?' Or was he genuinely sleep-walking? If he did a similar thing on a Destroyer he would be over the side - gone!"

Jolly Jack riding a camel?

J. Roberts had never been out of his Welsh valley when he joined Ganges in 1937. "I had walked into the post office in the village and there inside was a large poster of a sailor sitting astride a camel. I was hooked line and sinker."

J. Roberts never did ride a camel, but he did have an encounter with the Commander's Labrador dog.

"My first introduction to naval life when on arrival this man in uniform arrived on the scene, shouting: 'My name is Petty Officer Goode. I am a Chatham Gunner's Mate!' The other half of the act was Petty Officer Haslim. If one was good-looking you were in with a chance, if not, it was the fist and the boot if you forgot your seamanship. He enjoyed two things, one, entering the mess in the middle of the night shouting: 'Blanket and polish. Move the beds!' Then it was up and down with the blankets and polish the mess floor on our knees. The order, again in the middle of the night, shouting, 'Everybody outside,' in our night-shirts, up to the parade ground, 'Up and over the mast!' with him goading us on with his whistle-chain lashed harshly upon on our buttocks. Then it was Shotley Routine. That was tough, day or night, out of the mess, everywhere at the double, meal-times grab what you could from the mess-table, up and down Laundry Hill with gun and limber.

Kit inspections were frequent; the Commander and his black Labrador following, inspected the laid-out kit. Occasionally the dog would cock its leg up and piss all over our kit. Unable to complain, it was always our fault when that happened. So it was back to the wash-house and get prepared for another kit inspection."

ROLL ON MY DOZEN!

"I have a copy of your book, 'Roll on my dozen!' and have read it many times, but have always thought you had it soft at Ganges compared with what it was like in 1935 when I joined that brutal and sadistic establishment," says **S.W. Smith** of 25 Mess, Anson. "I am now seventy four and will never forget my days there. After it was closed down about five years ago, when the bulldozers were demolishing it to make way for a sports complex, it was closed to visitors, but as I had some of my family with me I was really

determined to get into that place, and we did so by going along the foreshore and walking up the steps known as Faith, Hope and Charity. My mess had been situated at the end of the Long Covered way and was now just a heap of rubble. I felt a little sad, but I still hated the place and always will. When I joined I was standing on the jetty at Harwich, awaiting the boat to take me over to Ganges and was puffing away on one of my new packet of fags and noticed an old man sitting on a box, so I walked over to him and said: 'What's it like at Ganges?'

Concentration Camp...

He said: 'Son, you are going to enter a concentration camp, and you'll never forget it as long as you live.' How right he was.

We sat talking and then he said, 'Here comes your boat, and your escort, and he is Instructor Boy Taylor, a real mean little sod, and if you have any money or fags or food on you he will take it from you when you land the other side.'

He was right. When we landed and were walking along the foreshore, the Instructor Boy asked me for fags, money and food. I refused to hand them over. He then started to knock hell out of me and I had to give in. All this happened on Monday, February 1935.

There is no doubt that life there was very brutal indeed and all the Instructors were sadistic and were given a free hand to do as they wished as the Officers just did not want to know, and all they were concerned with was to turn boys into men - and as soon as possible. I was flogged at Ganges for stealing a ship's biscuit as we were always so very hungry and I was dished out with six of the best by a Crusher who enjoyed every stroke of it.

There were times when we had a few laughs. We were one of the first messes to be issued with pyjamas and the first night wearing these was great fun, so much so that our mess was reported for making a noise after lights out. So, at three a.m. we were ordered to get out of bed and fall-in under the mast, still in our pyjamas and ordered to start climbing. We spent three hours up that mast and the month of March can be very cold. Not funny at the time, but in later years we can laugh at these things, but all in all there was not a lot to laugh about."

Perhaps not, but it has been said that other training places were even worse than Ganges. The Hospital School, Holborn, for example, just along the road from Ganges. Mr. **P.G. Thorpe,** 'remembers it as if it were yesterday.' "I joined as a Boy Entrant on the 9th June, 1954, after spending four and a half years at the Royal Hospital School, Holbrook, near Ipswich. I had heard many stories of Ganges reputation before I had even joined up. We were at the new entry training centre, a short distance from the main complex, listening to the raucous and obscene voices of the British Navy, which, as a teenager, seemed like the Gestapo. The Gunnery Instructors were shouting things like: 'Everything you do here is done at the double and you lot are a shower of bastards!' As if we had no mothers.

I passed out as a 'sparker' in the Communication Branch, we were supposed to be the *Intelligence Unit* of the R.N. as it was somewhat a more extensive term of training on the technical side, as opposed to the Seaman Branch who did only a year's training. There wasn't a class that passed through Ganges that didn't go through the agony and torture of the punishment which became known as the Shotley Routine. If someone did something wrong the whole class were punished. After so many days of this gruelling and degrading punishment, consisting of **frog-hopping with a .303 rifle above your head for hours** around the parade-ground, it often crossed my mind as to what the hell did I join this mob for, and what did we do to deserve this form of punishment? As I recall, if anybody fell down whilst on this punishment routine you were struck somewhere on the anatomy with a stonnicky, a form of wet towel with a knot tied in, which, if inflicted on any part of the body would leave some very nasty bruises, and you dare not complain otherwise the punishment was extended. I can remember one such Gunnery Instructor named Banjo West, who was a somewhat rotund figure of a man and seemed like something out of hell to fifteen-year-old boys like us. Near to Shotley Pier were three flights of stone steps, Faith, Hope and Charity. His gruelling task was to make the whole class frog-hop down the steps **with rifles above the head** and once you reached the bottom, the whole lot had to double up to the top again. We asked ourselves that there must be a better way of making a living. However, I was to learn that in years to come, Banjo West came to a rather horrendous ending whilst serving aboard a ship in the Med. Fleet. I served with the R.N. for nine years before taking up my post as a Police Officer in Edinburgh."

K. J. Callow, 1952/53, neatly condenses the *'Forgetting the bad times and remembering the good'* syndrome, by stating: "I was a Ganges boy and actually had fond memories of the time spent there." Then a rememb`rance that it wasn't so good after all when he recalls: "Probably the worst memory was that of being turfed out of bed at one a.m. for making too much noise. The whole hut, up the mast, round the Devil`s Elbow, and back again. A real nightmare."

The `fond memories` turned out to be a *nightmare* of a *day-dream*!

"I remember watching your video, 'H.M.S. GANGES, The Final Farewell,' and it really took me back to 1933 - 34 when I suffered as

184

Big Bill Underwood

Big Bill Underwood. Regulating Petty Officer. Mr. Ganges & formerly Mr. Hong Kong.

a Sparker boy, living in number one mess, top of the Long Covered Way,'' writes **Garry Owen** of Birmingham. "We were next to the quarter-deck and the wardroom. Many nights, when the wardroom had a party, we were woken up by the officers playing bowls with the cannon-balls taken from the cannons on the Quarter-deck. Sometimes they used to roll them down the Long Covered Way and they made a loud, rumbling noise. At the time I was there, there was a strong man, they called him Big Bill Underwood, the strongest man in the navy. He used to be known as Mr. Hong Kong. He was a Regulating Petty Officer in my time at Ganges. I remember at one of the annual shows he did a strong-man act on the stage, bending iron bars and lifting weights and, finally, holding up a grand piano with a number of boys sat upon it. It was his job to dish out the cuts with a thick bamboo cane, and it was rumoured that he really did lay them on, and if he drew blood when delivering the cuts he was put on the Commander's report and questioned. Then he was given two shillings and sixpence for `*doing his duty properly,*` by causing the blood to flow. The money was paid out from the Commander's own pocket.
I am now 73 years old, and must be one of the earlier Ganges Boys.''

Chapter nine
Stories of Good Instructors.....
.....and those who enjoyed Ganges..

Not all of Ganges boys were angels on temporary leave from
Heaven, some were yobbo's: at least one boy had been a street-wise
tramp who, as a Boy in Ganges, had experienced the unfortunate
situation of being the wretched victim of a mess-scrub, ordered by his
P.O. Instructor. The victim later became a Chief G.I. and gives
thanks to Ganges for directing him on the road to a success which he
would not have achieved if he had taken another path. It does not
follow logically that ordering the Boy to be mess-scrubbed was the
right treatment - or punishment, even though he overcame that
situation and triumphed in the end. It could have gone entirely the
other way and made a failure of him because of the humiliation. The
fact that he overcame that situation, and made good, is all to his own
credit and efforts, and not the result of the harsh decisions of a stupid,
callous Instructor. Some Instructors ill-treated their charges because
they liked doing so, like-wise, excusing their deplorable methods
with the time-honoured Chinese excuse/rule:

'**Confucius, he say: Punish all - and you punish the guilty one.**'

"I joined the Annexe on July 13th, 1948," writes **Peter Medhurst** of
July, 1948. "Our Instructor was Petty Officer Paddy Boyle. I had
been there three weeks when some friends from home were
holidaying at Felixtowe; they came at ten o'clock one morning and
asked if they could see me. I went to the C.O.'s office and he told me
that he had given my friends permission to take me to Felixtowe for
the day but I had to be back by 1800. It was a great thrill for me to
dress up in uniform and go out.

"Our D.O. was a gentleman.."

In the Main Establishment I went to Exmouth Division, number 3
mess. Our Instructors were Seamanship P.O. Mummery and our
Gunnery Instructor was P.O. Fred Flowers. They were two very fair
Instructors with a good sense of humour. They told us to address
them as 'Sir,' but we often referred to them by their first names.
When we had our two week's coal-ship they joined in with us and
enjoyed the change from normal routine. Our Divisional Officer was
Lt. Cdr. Asquith who played rugby for the R.N. He was a gentleman,
and every Sunday afternoon would invite up to six boys to his house
to tea with his wife. That was a good treat with a real feast of cakes.

One of the boys, Boy Seaman Pearse, had a lump develop on his wrist and was told he would have to leave the navy; this was six months after he had joined, and he sat down and cried his heart out. We all enjoyed our stay, I don`t know of any of us who wanted to get out, although we looked forward to joining our first ship. Also, our P.T.I., Petty Officer Walsh was great, so it was not all bad, the Instructors were doing their jobs without any fuss - strict but fair."

What is the meaning of `strict but fair?` Opinions differ greatly on the meaning. `Strict but fair` to one, is harsh and unfair to another. It depends wholly upon the upbringing and outlook on life of the perceiver. One man`s delight is another`s despair. Those of an exuberant nature would make the best of, and probably enjoy, the fires of hell itself, but their opposite numbers, the pessimists, would complain vociforously of being a few bob short of winning a million pounds on the lottery. H.M.S. Ganges was different things to many different people; very few would have regarded it as a blessing in disguise.

"It made a man out of me..."

To be sure, to be sure, can you not almost hear the poetic lilt of the Irish brogue as J. McCarthy tells of his first day at Ganges:

"I joined Ganges on St. Patrick`s Day in 1936, which is a very apt date for a 16-year-old boy from County Cork to be joining the Royal Navy. Joining the R.N. was one of the best things that I ever did, and being sent to GANGES for my initial training was a blessing in disguise. The nine months I spent in GANGES will remain in my mind forever. There were times when the going was very tough, but at the end of the stay, I felt that it had made a man out of me. I could write a lot more about GANGES."

It`s a pity that he did not write more about Ganges, or a book about the positive side. Those who wrote letters saying, "I could write a book about Ganges," did neither write a book or a letter longer than a page and a half! Most of the writings about Ganges gave the impression of the bad and negative side, which is contained elsewhere in this book, and taken from the letters received. It is a national characteristic trait that when the English peoples are asked to give an opinion, they take it as an invitation to complain rather than to praise. Such is human nature, but it does not detract from the fact that atrocities were actually committed, and the unlikely defender of the Boys in the following story, and the Boy`s Champion, was no less than someone who, because of his position, would normally have been the natural arch-enemy of Boy Seamen:-

George Johnston, Master-at-Arms.

GEORGE JOHNSTON, B.E.M., joined H.M.S. Arethusa as a boy of eleven in 1921. George's widow, Eileen, who spent some time in Shotley when George was M.A.A. of Ganges, tells his story:

"It does seem a pity that stories from Ganges reveal so much brutality and unhappiness and George certainly learned the hard way that no good came of it. He never forgot his experiences on the Arethusa, based in Greenhithe, prior to joining Ganges. He was an orphan, joining Arethusa in 1921 where he stayed for five years before being sent to Ganges in 1926."

Arethusa *had a bad reputation for harshness and ill-treatment, although, human nature being what it is, there will be those who will refute that statement. But all of the ex `Arry` boys I have known tell the same story: Ganges was a holiday camp compared with* H.M.S. Arethusa. H.M.S. St. Vincent *ex-boys say the same!*

"It was on the `Arry when George sat down to his first meal, stretched out to take a slice of bread, and the senior boy present stabbed George's hand with a fork, and he was told, in typical naval-type terms: 'You're last in the so-and-so queue and you got to so-and-so wait 'til all the rest have had their so-and-so turn!' Substitute foul language for `so-and-so` and the scene becomes clear.

Eileen Johnston relates the stories as told to her over the years by George:

"He went without that time, but it made him determined that it would be the last time he would be bullied."

Being an orphan, and suffering five years on the `Arry, would make or break anyone. It was the making of George Johnston.

"The stories he told," says Eileen, "Were truly unbelievable and, being a rebel, he was regularly caned and punished for the slightest misbehaviour. He had his fair share of punishment and was hardened to the cane at Ganges."

That statement belies the denials and theories of the Ganges stalwarts who insist that such harsh treatment never took place in any of the training establishments for Boy Seamen. There were some who stood up to the bullies, sadists and masochists which included some Ganges Instructors, Physical Training Instructors and Naval Police - known as the Regulating Branch - or, as individuals, rather than the run-of-the-mill sheep, rebelled, not against authority or discipline, but the stupidity of a regime which punished a boy with twelve vicious cuts of the cane for smoking a cigarette, delivered by a person who probably smoked forty a day. And wasn't it stupid to be made to scrub twenty square yards of the concrete-based Long Covered Way with a tooth-brush for talking whilst fell-in, waiting for dinner?

Back to George Johnston's wife:

"In 1941 he did a spell at Ganges when he passed out as an R.P.O. He then returned in 1956, his last posting, and I was lucky enough to accompany him. He always said he had had the hardest apprenticeship to life at Ganges that any lad could have, and, on returning as Master-at-Arms, was determined to treat the lads as human beings. The boys had great respect for him, but it was a healthy respect born out of his kindness to them; they thought the world of him, he was a fair and just fatherly figure to them. I'll give you an instance of how that respect was won:

A boy was caught stealing food and was dutifully reported. George decided to deal with the matter in his own way. He asked the lad why he stole and the reply was, "I'm hungry," so George took him to the galley and obtained a tray of plum pudding. These were large rectangular metal trays. Then they obtained a very large pitcher of water and proceeded to the guard-house. George sat him in the cell and ordered him to eat. The boy commenced to eat the pudding and drink the water. Of course, to eat all of the pudding was impossible, and when the lad had forced down as much as he could, George told him to go back to his mess. Had he been placed on Commander's report, he woud have received a caning, six cuts, and possibly a sacking and also had a very salutory lesson. He went on to become a Leading Boy, and George was sure that his way of discipline paid off in most cases, as he never forgot the extreme punishments he suffered when he was a boy at Ganges, even for crimes he was guilty of, but decided that sport was the answer.

He excelled at everything he did, such as athletics, boxing - he never lost a fight - rugby, hockey, swimming, field gun and tug-of-war at Olympia, winning all the medals.''

It is not surprising that a man who is competent at sports, especially boxing, and has confidence in himself, can treat others with the compassion which George Johnston did. It is those who suffer with inferiority complexes, lack of confidence in themselves, who have to prove they are superior by making others seem to be inferior. That is so easy when their 'inferiors' cannot retaliate because of fear of retribution.

Eileen: "George's youngest son now has all his trophies; both his sons followed his sports, especially swimming and rugby. George always said that fair play was the rule to a lad's good behaviour.

"R.P.O's shall not brutalise the boys...."

When George returned to Ganges in 1956 for his last two years of service, he said he would do his best to see that no lad was brutalised by any of his staff. **There were three of his R.P.O.'s that he described as sadists** and he made a point of keeping them off the list for caning the boys. George's one aim was to talk to the boys and to get to know how they were thinking and why they found themselves in trouble. Nine times out of ten he said it was teenage defiance and high-spirits which they would grow out of, and **punishment by brutality only made the boys more cussed and truculent.**

On parent's day George would see that when the Captain met a boy's mother or father, he would know all about the lad as an individual, George first having got to know the boys, and through him, George then passed this information on to the captain who was able to talk to the parent on a personal basis. An early form of public relations?

"Sorting out the `Teds.`"

"George enjoyed his time at Ganges in 1956/58, and many times he would come home with stories of the boys and their escapades. George was always on the side of the boys and he tried in his way to redress the balance of his treatment in his earlier years. The following is a typical example of how George would handle a situation. In the 50's there was a craze among teenagers of that time called `Teddy Boys.` They wore their hair in a distinctive quiff, their smart jackets were loose with velvet collars and the trousers were called `drain-pipes.` This attire was finished off with heavy, clumsy boots or shoes known as `beetle-crushers.` These youngsters, girls as well as boys, had spent their childhood rebelling about school uniform, and yet here they were all dressing alike. The girls wore very tight short skirts. It was really the beginning of the `Teddy-Boys.` They had found an identity, had money to spend, were spurred on by their new idols, Elvis, Buddy Holly, Bill Haley and the rising British Rock `n` Rollers. To add to the image of the draped jackets etc, they were armed with flick-knives and bicycle chains etc., and were generally found in gangs, specially where there was trouble. One of their favourite haunts were the sea-side resorts and Felixtowe was one of them. As you probably remember, at Ganges, Sunday, for the boys was, after divisions, and lunch, free time, and the majority went across on the ferry to Felixtowe. This crowd of uniformed lads, with their short hair and squeaky-clean image, presented a threat to the `Teds.` They saw them as an invasion of their territory and used to wait for the boys to land from the ferry. The result was that the Ganges boys were attacked by the mob, who made good use of their weapons. The boys had no defence except their fists, and, on return to Ganges, represented sorry pictures with various damage to uniform and their anatomies, and, of course were answerable to authority as to the cause of their predicament. This was where George came into the picture, and by talking to the lads and drawing the stories from them as to what had been taking place, he was able to act upon it. It was obvious from their battered and bedraggled state that something was wrong. So George gave up his Sunday off-duty and, with a pep-talk

"*Lookout! They've brought their farver wiv 'em*!"

to his lads, organized a trip of his own. It took him very little time to sort out the `Teddy-Boys,` and his lads never had any further trouble. The cartoon enclosed tells the story; it`s a very good likeness of George. He enjoyed his life but when he was on duty he was every inch a thoroughly loyal sailor. The navy came first in his life and even in retirement, never left it. He was a great judge of men and was

192

always very cheerful - nothing ever got him down. He always said it was important to be able to laugh at oneself, and when in later life, his girth grew even more rounder, and people would say he was fat, he would say, 'It`s relaxed muscle from my earlier sporting days!!'

He was universally liked and I recall in 1952 when on the Abercrombie at Chatham, we were staying with him at the N.A.A.F.I. Club and went to Canterbury for the day. In the train carriage with us was a sailor in uniform. George was in civvies and there was no sign of recognition between the men. George left the carriage first with the three children, but as I got up to leave the sailor put his hand on my arm and said, 'Look after him lady - he`s the best there is.'

When I asked George who the sailor was, and told him of the remarks, George said: 'Oh, I expect I came down on his side when he was in trouble sometime - I don`t remember.'

This was the man - he wasn`t easily fooled, but was a very generous person. On duty he went through the ranks like a ship in full sail. He was a great husband, father and `gramps`, and after being married 49 years I still miss him very much. He died of a heart attack in March 1986 at the age of 75. I miss him terribly even to this day."

George Johnston was awarded the British Empire Medal in 1952 '..for his interpretation of his duties and specially his interest in, and care, for the junior ratings.' The phrase 'For interpretation of his duties pertained to his unearthing a Communist ring - a real threat in those days - in the Reserve Fleet in 1951."

The above proves that not all Ganges personell were the unloved-sons of a female one-parent family.

Charlie Kent is one of many who actually loved his Instructors, or at least, one of them, and his feelings for the other was also one of affection: here`s his story in his own words.

"I joined Ganges on Armistice Day, November 11th, 1930. On the train to Harwich I became friendly with Billy Webster, a friendship which was to last throughout our time at Ganges. We arrived in Harwich at 7.30 p.m. It was dark and raining, but we were not too downhearted. We were young, we were tough and adventurous, and weren`t we joining the Royal Navy and going aboard a ship called `Ganges?`

We could see lights in the harbour. 'Which of those belonged to Ganges?' We asked the Old Salt on the picket boat which was taking us across the light-dappled waters of the harbour.

He said: 'No, lads. Ganges is not a ship. It's a Naval Barracks. A school for boys joining the Navy.'

We've been duped! Still, we thought with optimism, never mind, life will be a doddle, if it's a school. We were so wrong! We were met on the dockside by a Petty Officer who made us double up Faith, Hope and Charity, a flight of concrete steps which led from the foreshore to grounds of the Signal School. Thank God I was fit. But I felt as if I could have died going up those steps at a terrific rate of knots. My mate, poor Bill, vent his feelings with bad language profanities and the air turned blue. A voice from the rear, with a roar like a bull, shouted: 'Shut that filthy mouth and keep it at the double!'

'Jesus,' I thought,''What have I let myself in for?'

For the first six weeks of my training we had two temporary Petty Officers in the Nozzers Annexe; they didn't make much impression on me and I don't remember their names. Then we were moved to Blake Division, number four mess, and I certainly remember the names of those Instructors. They were both characters, one more than the other. Number four mess had the best polished floor in Ganges. It was a holy floor, no shoes nor sweaty feet should touch it; walk down near the beds, mark it at your peril. The only one that did not abide by the rule was John Spriddell, our Instructor. He would stride down it with his hob-nailed boots on as if it didn't exist. I can still see a picture of him in my mind of his first appearance in our mess. He came through the doors, dressed prim and proper, everything looked so sanitary about him; his voice was loud and clear. We all shot up two feet when he spoke.

'Good evening, lads!' This was seven p.m. at night.

We replied: 'Good evening, SIR!'

He spoke again: 'Oh, dearie me! Who have we here? Do you know who I am? Well you bloody-well *will* know me!'

He was darned tooting! He was right. What a character! For all my life I will love that man. He was strict, so severe that up to a point that it seemed like cruelty. But then there would come the thought: he has never put us on the quarter deck with our hats off. He was mad on sport, his love was boxing. I had joined Ganges about three weeks before the I.S.B.A. competitions were about to take place. At the same time there was a young boy, Hill, who was the Amateur champion in 'civvy street. On my reference for joining the navy the police had stated that I was quite good at boxing, so it was arranged for me to fight Hill to see who was the best to be chosen to go to Pompey for the championships. I beat Hill quite easily. Spriddell was over the moon about this.

Hill and I became quite good pals along with Bill Webster. Hill had trained hard for the privilege of boxing for Ganges, so I could see that he was in agony about losing and he couldn`t stand not representing Ganges. I just couldn`t take his place, so I shammed sickness. I fooled the doctor but not Spriddell. He made my life hell at times, and Tiggy Eaves was none too light with me. Tiggy had an old boxing glove which he called `Little Henry.` Boxing gloves, in those days, were filled with horse-hair and, with age, it would go hard and lumpy, and what Tiggy used to do, he would ask you why you did something wrong, and at the same time he would be hitting you on the jaw, swiping it, making it go from side to side, making your teeth ache. Afterwards your jaw would be very sore. At times I thought how much I would have liked to have given it to him the same way, and I could`ve done! But I was getting used to Royal Navy discipline, I didn`t like it much, but couldn`t do much about it. But when I think of those two Instructors, I am thankful that I did not oppose them. With Spriddell you dare not.

I remember the time I happened to go over to the hockey pitch to watch the Ganges officers team play against the R.A.F. from Henlaw. The Ganges team were one man short. Spriddell was watching at the time and he called over to Lt. Blake: 'You need another man, sir?' The Lieutenant replied, 'Yes. Do you have one, Petty Officer?'
'Yes, sir. Could he go in goal?'
'Yes,' replied the Lieutenant.
'Right, Kent.' he said to me. 'Put those pads on.'
'But I`ve never played hockey, sir! Do I have to?'
'Yes, you do. You are going to play today, laddie. The only rule you need to know is to keep that bloody ball out of the bloody goal!'
I played the game of my life. We won. And from that game I was included in the Officer`s team, and we travelled out to different places. Here`s an example of the man, Spriddell: the hockey team was drawn to play at Ipswich and I was broke. I must have shewn what was wrong by the look on my face. Spriddell asked me why I looked so down in the mouth and I told him.`'I`m broke, sir.'
'Right,' he said. 'Take this half-a-crown. If you keep the ball out of the goal it`s yours. If you should fail, you owe it.' **We won.**

Tiggy Eaves and Spriddel were great Instructors. Every so often the Ship`s Company held a dance in the Gym. We boys could hear the voices - and the music. There would be a lot of laughter, it would be one of those moments when you would miss the company of a female, and we would do all we could just to get a glimpse of those lovelies going to the ball. Then one particular evening our Instructors came into our mess about a fortnight before a dance was due and we asked Spriddell and Tiggy: 'What were the dances like'` And other quesions that only future sailors would ask. One or two of us suggested that on the night of the dance they could fetch one or two ladies round to the mess. Both Instructors poised the question: 'Do you want us to get court-martialed?'

'Oh, no, sir, we would not like that to happen. But all the same, fetch them round and let`s see what women look like!' All good fun. Well, this particular evening we were preparing for to turn in, when we heard the voices of females. Then the mess doors were flung open and lo` and behold, there stood our two Instructors with five lovely ladies who, no doubt, were a few year`s older than us lads; but nevertheless they really looked glamorous in their lovely hair-do`s and gorgeous evening gowns. They stayed for about 15 minutes, chatting to us. We lapped it up. The two Instructors enjoyed it, I`m sure, and all in one voice we shouted: 'Thank you, sirs! And have a good time at the dance!'

'Happy at Ganges...'

My own thoughts at the time were, 'It`s not such a bad life after all, but roll on for the time when I might be able to do likewise.' A couple of days after I asked P.O. Spriddell why he brought the ladies round to the mess to talk to us.

He replied: 'Oh, nosey! I just wanted to let them see how a polished floor should look!' He was joking, of course. He and Tiggy were just being human and kind. Not many days go by that I think to myself,`'I wonder where all those folks are today, bless them all for they gave a little happiness into the lives of us young sailor-boys at the Ganges. I was happy at Ganges. When I got into the swing of things. Yeah, I did jankers, I swung the lead at times, and got caught, punished, cursed the person who dished it out, but I was enjoying the life all the time I was looking forward to going to my first ship, H.M.S. Enterprise, East Indies Cruiser Squadron where I met John Spriddell again with more lovely ladies on his arm.

Later, through the grapevine of Ganges, we heard that he had offered his services to the Indian Navy. When he had done with us he went away in 1931. I joined H.M.S. Enterprise of the East Indies Squadron in the same year. We were lying alongside in Bombay at the time, and one afternoon in the heat of the day, I was having a good nap on the Pom-Pom deck. I was awakened suddenly by a poke in the back. I sat up and couldn't believe my eyes. Towering above me was Spriddell, accompanied by two lovely English ladies.

Wet eyes..

Spriddell was a very attractive man, always dressed well, even to his hands. I had always noticed his finger-nails were trimmed. He said to his ladies: 'This was one of the boys under my training at H.M.S. Ganges. He was an excellent boxer and won many important fights. He also played in goal for the Officers team. A good man and a good seaman.' I have to admit that I was a little embarrassed. I had no idea he thought so highly of me. On leaving the ship he shook hands with me. I am not afraid to say there were wet eyes - they were mine. Many a time I think of him, and if he was still around I would travel with a good heart to meet him again. I often talk to my wife about Petty Officer Spriddell and Tiggy Eaves, and wet eyes come out again. As I said before, I loved the man. He was great. The half-a-crown he gave me is not the reason. Our mess were always tops in all the competitions at Ganges. We had to be - for Spriddell and Tiggy Eaves."

"Wait 'til I get hold of you.."

It must be human nature to lump everyone together, tar them with the same brush etc. When someone states that their Instructor was a bully, etc., there's always someone who thinks the statement covers all Instructors. It doesn't work that way, people only look at their own point of view and seldom, consider that of others. If their own Instructor was the acme of kindness, then all Instructors were of the same ilk. If one had a bullying Instructor, then all Instructors were bullies! And vice-versa. **W.W. Hills** says:

"I did not think the Instructors were sadists and bullies, they were strict but fair, what young person likes disclipline? This is my story about my Instructor: I was a boy at Ganges from June, 1925 till April 1926, my Gunnery Instructor was Petty Officer Joe Phipps. He chased us around and taught us how to look after ourselves in all ways, clean-liness and tidy-ness, and he used to serve out his own punishment rather than report to the Divisional Officer. Now here comes the twist in my story. In 1941 my ship went alongside another ship of the same class in Grimsby. I was a three-badge Petty Officer myself by now. I heard a voice call out on the ship alongside: Chief Petty Officer Phipps!!!'

I thought: 'I wonder if that is Joe Phipps they're shouting?' So I went aboard the other ship and asked if they had a Chief Petty Officer Joe Phipps. They did. Could I see him? I could, and did. When we met, he said, 'Do I know you?'

I said, 'I was in your class at Ganges in 1925.' I also told him what us boys would have liked to have done to him at the time." *If the Instructors were fair etc., as W.W. Hills says they were, why did the boys want to do him harm at the time?*

"Anyway, he took an old notebook out of his pocket, thumbed it open and said: 'Now I know you, you're name is Hills, and you were in 99a class.'"Then before I could say anything he said, 'Well, it didn't do you any harm did it?' I had to agree with him."

The Instructor, in a veiled statement, admits that he was hard on the boys, and excused his actions by playing down the issue and excuses any dubious and previous actions by saying, "It didn't do you any harm did it?" Mr. Hills says not all Instructors were bullies, but he only gives an example of one encounter, and even that is suspect. His Instructor was fair but strict, he says, then when he meets him later, much later, when time has erased most of the bad moments, he tells him to his face what he and others would have liked to have done to him in those Ganges days gone by. Perhaps it had been instilled into W.W. Hills' memory, whilst in Ganges, that he would have liked to have got his revenge on his Instructor, but the passing of time erased the reasons why. It doesn't make sense. But time blots out bad memories, and diminishes those memories to a lesser magnitude and, tho' we are left wondering what it was we should be annoyed about - w-e-e-e-ll, it wasn't so bad at the time - was it? Or was it? And if Mr. Hills wants to remember it that way, as most ex-Ganges Boys do, he has every right to do so.

"They're not bad all the time..."

Jock Elder, 1949, also has a good word to say for the Instructors, or Petty Officers of the Regulating Staff:

"Our class was retard party during the Christmas leave 1950. We were due to join H.M.S. Wrangler early in January so it was decided we'd better be back in good time. The result was that I spent about a week, which included New Year, as 'assistant mess-man' to the R.P.O.'s mess. In reality, this meant that I did all the work. The day started with lighting the fires at 0700, and, from then, time ground on with unrelenting pressure until about 2100. Fires, tea, breakfast, wash up, tea, deck polished, fires, dinner, wash up, dust, tea, fires, supper, wash up, fires, tea.....I staggered to my dormitory to prepare for the next day.

Two things stuck in my mind about that experience: One: Petty Officers did not shout and scream all the time and sometimes they even spoke kindly and joked with the lower orders. Two: Petty Officers messes were much more comfortable and offered privacy not available on the mess-decks of sailors. I vowed that I'd better make sure that I became a P.O. quickly if I wanted to share their comforts. And I did. I was in the P.O.'s mess at Whale Island in 1955 before I picked up my first good conduct badge!"

"Six cuts...couldn't sit down for ages!"

Bill Molloy, 1935, has many stories to tell but he doubts they will be of book material! "During my time as a boy at Ganges the Heads had no roof and two entrances. This is where we used to go whenever we were lucky enough to find a cigarette butt, which we used to light by means of scraping shavings off a bone-handled tooth-brush with a razor blade and then scratching a flint for a spark to smoulder the shavings.

It must have been the luck of the Irish on my behalf as I was only caught once. I used to pass the butt-end to my mate, Ginger Dors and go out one of the entrances to keep a look-out. I did this one day and went out of one of the entrances, when in the other entrance came the Jock Marine sentry. Poor old Ginger had been caught so many times before that it was decided this time that jankers wasn't doing the trick for he got six cuts, the poor devil couldn't sit down for ages.

The only time I was caught with Ginger the sentry said: 'Carry on, I want to see what you're doing.' So we showed him how we got the cigarette-end alight, and he said: 'Well done, but if you poor little bastards have to go to so much trouble to have a burn, I'm going to shove off and let you have it in peace.' He went out and, seconds later, over the wall came a full cigarette. We thought we were kings of England! We found out later that he had only joined Ganges a few days before."

"Yes," says **J.B. O'Neill.** "On the whole I hadn't much bother, and never got into a great deal of trouble and never having been caught, which was a miracle. The one outstanding case was Lofty, my friend, and I were underneath the mess having a fly smoke when we saw a pair of size 12's. The Marines had landed! So we slipped out the other side and ran like hell down the Long Covered Way to the sports field and just kept running. But the big Marine kept coming, so we

199

went right along the north side and back round to the mess, giving him the slip. However, what baffled me was that he was my drum Instructor and should have recognised me, but he never ever mentioned it again! We were not allowed to smoke, but we tried everything to get a fag or two. We were only allowed up the road outside the gate for a couple of hours on Sundays. The trick was to beat the Instructors on duty to the cigarette machine about a mile on the road towards Pin Mill, and put our sixpence in and have a smoke. I was once tempted by one of my mess-mates to get a packet and smuggle it in. I fell for it and slipped them down my front. On entering the gate I was told to go into the Guard Room and strip off. I knew what the punishment would be, six cuts, and I dreaded it. But as I was stripping the R.P.O. said:

'I've never seen you before.'

I told him, 'I have only been here about two month's sir.'

'What Division are you in? he said.

'Hawke, sir.'

He looked at me a bit curiously, then said: 'Is there another O'Neill in Hawke Division?'

'Yes, sir, there is.' I wasn't sure at the time but by sheer luck there was, and he had stolen some of my kit, but his mistake was that he had to cut the 'B' out of my clothes and it was noticeable.

'O.K.' he said. 'Put your clothes back on.' Relief beyond relief! But I'll tell you - never again!''

The Instructor's story.

"I was not a boy at Ganges," says **Dick Hotchkiss,** an ex-Chief Petty Officer Telegraphist, "But served two periods as an Instructor there in 1954-55, and again in 1959-60. So possibly a story or two from the outside looking on, from the Instructor's point of view, will vary your stories from boys only."

Quite true. Many letters were received in response to a nationwide request for humorous stories but most of those told of atrocities, bullying, and mis-use of authority and power by Instructors. That included Badge-boys - Instructor Boys, Schoolies - School teachers, Regulating Petty Officers, Masters-at-Arms, Marine Corporals - etc.

Dick continues: "I joined as a boy in 1937 and did my training at the Rosyth base onboard H.M.S. Caledonia - the ship eventually caught fire in 1938 and became a wreck. From then on the boys were trained at Ganges. When I eventually was drafted to the Ganges as a C.P.O. Tel. in 1954, the routines were almost identical. We on the Caledonia were on a ship, Ganges boys were in barracks, Caledonia boys did not suffer the bitterly cold weather experienced at Shotley; neither did we Caledonians suffer chilblains, or the early hike down to the laundry, but most other things were similar. Instructors, on joining, were usually given a week or so to settle in, and what I remembered from an introductory lecture was that the Instructors aim was to achieve character-building from which would develop first-class sailors who would be proud of the Senior Service, and this story of one of my 1954-55 class of budding Telegraphists fits that aim.

When messes were cleaned up for 9 p.m. rounds, the duty Instructor would appear about 8 - 8.30 to check everything was ship-shape and all boys accounted for and turned in. One particular evening two of my boys were absent. The duty P.O. Boy told me: 'They're both at the sick bay, sir.'

'Anything serious? Illness? Injury?' I enquired. At that moment one of the missing boys entered the mess. I directed my questions at him. He replied quite honestly and without hesitation: 'I had to take the other boy to the sick bay, sir, and packed his small case with his toilet stuff, pyjamas and so on, as I knew he would be kept in, sir.'

'What are you?' I demanded. 'A Sick Bay Tiffy?'

'No, sir. The boy seemed to have a grudge against me and kept pestering me all evening to fight, so I asked the P.O. Boy to keep him from me as I felt there was going to be trouble.'

'What happened then?' I asked.

'Well,' he continued, 'There *was* a fight, but not a *real* fight as I was a member of the Ganges boy's boxing team, and I knew I had to watch what I was doing, but he came at me and I had to defend myself. I only hit him once and knocked him out, so I took it upon myself to carry him from the mess to the Sick Bay.'

I looked sternly at the duty P.O. Boy: 'Is this true?'

He said: 'Yes, sir, That's completely true. The other boy was obviously spoiling for a fight for some reason.' He nodded towards the other P.O. Boy. 'It wasn't *his* fault, sir,' indicating the other P.O. Boy. 'He acted quite reservedly, in the circumstances...'

Needless to say, because of his honesty, he received a rather lenient punishment from the Divisional Officer."

Moving on to the 1959-60 draft, again at the 9 p.m. rounds in the Long Covered Way messes, Dick remembers this incident: "On the humorous side, I recall the duty officer - no doubt with a few nips inside him to keep out that always howling wind - decided he would inspect my mess for washed feet. At that time there were one or two black boys joining up and we had a shiny, shiny black boy in our mess. So it was 'On lights!' and the order was given: 'Out of your beds! Stand by your lockers and roll up your pyjamas for feet inspection!'

Along the row of beds went the duty Marine, followed by the duty officer, followed by me. The duty officer examing the boys' feet with a dull, glazed look, muttering more to himself than to the boys. Finding nothing amiss, he gave the order: 'Back to bed!' Then he shone his torch on the blackest pair of feet which he or I had ever seen. There was a pregnant pause until he gathered his wits and shone the torch slowly upwards and the light showed the shiniest black smiling round face looking straight at him.

He switched off the torch, and, obviously peeved, he grunted to me: 'That's not funny, Chief,' and stormed off back to the Wardroom, no doubt to sink another few pink gins.

Just after this, on the playing fields on a sunny Saturday afternoon in May, the cricket season had started and I was umpiring a cricket match, not on a voluntary basis, because on this particular afternoon it was either the Scotland or England football International on television. I desperately wanted to watch the match and that desperation was the cause of perhaps one or two wrong decisions!

The Captain of Ganges at that time used to mix with the boys very much and thought nothing of lying on the grass, in civvies, talking to the boys waiting to go in to bat. He was a keen cricketer - which I wasn't! To speed the game up, so that I might at least see the second half of the football - some of my decisions of being 'out' were not quite correct. One boy had been bowled out, according to my umpiring, and we were waiting for the next one to come - but nothing happened. Then the boy who had been declared out returned, came up to me and said, for all to hear: 'I've to tell you, sir, that a bigger 'sir' reckons you know very little about cricket and I've to carry on batting, sir.'

Looking over to where the boys were lying about, up stood the 'bigger sir' who gave a lovely wave - and shouted: 'Now Chief, let's see a proper umpiring!' I never did get to see the football.

Although Ganges has been described as second only to the Foreign Legion, it rightly produced men of character. I'm much the better for having been there."

Good! Let us hope that 'declaration' also means that you've stopped

cheating to get your own way!
"No atrocities or ill-treatment.."
Trevor Huggett was a boy at Ganges who returned later as an Instructor. He says: "During my time as a boy I witnessed no atrocities or ill-treatment of the boys, and, as an Instructor, later, I did not mis-treat those in my class."

When asked for explicit details of his Ganges` days as Boy and Instructor, Trevor says: "What do you want me to say? I can only give my opinion. Of all the Instructors passing through Ganges what percentage were unbelievably cruel? Very few. Look at the situation: a class of boys, an Instructor, Officers. The boys from all walks of life. Good, bad, rich, poor and the majority anything but angels, up to all sorts of mischief. The Instructors have a job to do, to take those boys, make them into men, good citizens and naval personnel of the future and the officers to ensure that boys and Instructors achieve their aim."

The directive to would-be Instructors was, `*The boy will change from boy to man anyway, but what he should become is the man that the Service requires.*` It is believed that further instructions as as to how this should be brought about is not very clear.

"Very few were cruel.."
Trevor made the statement: "What percentage were unbelievably cruel?" The answer could be: Very few; but `**very few**` is still too many, and it is those `*very few bad ones*` who give the `*very many good ones*` a lasting impression of cruelty, bullying and sadism.

"The end result," Trevor continues: "Despite good and bad on both sides, it was rewarding to the majority. On many occasions I was called out at all hours of the night to check noise from the boys` messes within the division, usually caused by clashes of personality, fights, etc. I was called out on one occasion about 2 a.m. On investigation I discovered one of my boys was selling chocolate and drinks bought from the canteen and was selling it at twice the price - enterprising, yes, but not allowed. What do I do? Slap his wrist and tell him not to be a naughty boy? Or take the goods and be considered a thief. Then I would have been accused of being as black as black."

I have to interrupt Trevor`s story again because a similar incident happened to me - I was the `enterprising entrepreneur,` and the tale I have to tell explains why we entrepreneurs operated in the manner which we did. It happened thus:

When I joined Ganges in September, 1947, I was a non-smoker. I had

had tried a nub-end or two, discarded by my father, but I didn't like smoking. Then Rita took a hand in this. I met her one Summer's leave. She was stricken with love for her heroic sailor-boy in his uniform, and who could blame her? I was sixteen years and nine months old, blond hair, blue eyes, good-looking, lots of personal charm, and, in my uniform, standing at a magnificent height of five feet two inches and almost eight stones in weight, I was a man of the world and soon to be a fully-fledged Jolly Jack. Rita decided that I was too good a catch to miss, so she decided to send to me forty Woodbines every week to retain first claims on my affections. I saw the transaction as profit rather than emotion, because the value of the cigarettes represented very near two weeks wages; four shillings and eight pence against my half-a-crown pocket-money.

Cadgers made me a fag baron

Just ten years before my time in Ganges the act of receiving them in a parcel would have warranted six cuts of the cane, even though I did not solicit for the cigarettes and didn't smoke, and, because I didn't smoke, I gave away the cigarettes to my closest friends. By the end of the first week, in a mess of about sixty boys, I had fifty-nine friends. Before that I had only three. Every week afterwards, when my parcel of cigarettes arrived - and the occasion was, by now, looked forward to by the whole mess, I was to dread waking on Thursday mornings, knowing I was going to be mobbed by fifty-nine 'close friends.' The mess echoed to the pitiful cries of: "Give us a couple of fags! Go on, matie! I'm your best oppo!"

Well, being a jam-tart and ginger-biscuit maniac, spending my weekly half-a-crown on twelve jam-tarts every pay-day, or ten jam-tarts and a couple of large ginger-biscuits, I decided to increase my jam-tart and ginger-biscuit intake by selling my unwanted fags to those who craved them. At first the price was tuppence each. The saying: 'They sold like hot-cakes' should be replaced by: 'They sold like contraband fags to Ganges Boys.' I thought I had fallen down a gold-mine. I could hardly believe it. I upped the price gradually, to stop the mad scramble every Thursday dinner-time until it reached a level of sixpence each. Twenty cigarettes cost two shillings and fourpence. That was just over one penny each. I was charging, and getting, more than five times as much. My attitude and opinion of the situation was, and still is, if people want to pay silly money for their vices, it's tough on them. But why should I also be subjected to derisory remarks because I was more enterprising?

"On another occasion," Trevor continues, "one boy caused a few problems, he went missing. He was later found and brought back. He had been on his way home - no money, but a case full of bread from the dining-hall. He wasn`t used to being away from home, or used to such discipline. He was punished, obviously, and no doubt he blamed us, the Instructors, for bringing him back."

Trevor confesses: "As a boy at Ganges, I had no real affection for Instructors or officers. I survived, and in many ways was grateful for my training - as an Instructor I understood what my Instructor had gone through. It`s not an easy job, believe me. I met my own Instructor later, and we had a pint together. Cannot write any more, I did not keep a diary. There were little incidents, but neither as boy or Instructor did I see or do anything cruel."

Trevor`s story should be believed, but a niggling doubt lies in his words, *"There were little incidents..."*

Some boys had a happy existence at Ganges with kind, understanding Instructors. That state of euphoria was not the experience of most of Ganges Boys. **John Riordan** remembers only happy memories, starting in July, 1962: "I well recall an expedition to Dunwich with the rest of my class. It was our first taste of freedom, apart from one run-ashore to the fair at Felixtowe. We cooked over an open fire, skinned rabbits, and lived under canvas, and, to round it off, our Instructors took myself and another oppo to a couple of pubs and gave us our first taste of under-age bevying. We had a few pints and ended up quite merry 15-year olds. I met some characters and fine oppo`s and will always recall my stay at Ganges with great affection."

And so can many others, particularly the next story of an ex-Boy who adored his Instructors:

An Instructor bends the rules.

"In October, 1931, I joined class 278 for the Boy Signalmen and Telegraphists course, and we dwelt in mess 24 at the bottom of the Long Covered Way, then later we moved to 28 mess. Our Instructors were P.O. Tel. Hines and Chief Yeoman of Signals Avernel. He was a fine man, small, neat and, like most of the small Chief`s and P.O.`s I ever met, a strict disciplinarian. He was a Lion with a golden heart. When our final exams arrived to pass out and be available to go to sea - a moment we all yearned for - you will be aware that the class results reflected favourably, or otherwise, on the Instructors so I believe the exam results worried them as much as they did the boys.

At this time, smoking was forbidden and anyone caught doing so was cautioned the first time, then six cuts of the cane in the Gymnasium on the second offence. Most of us smoked after `pipe-down,` `lights out` at 2100. Look-outs were posted in the wash-room and he who had a cigarette would share it in winter by the dying fire-light around the stove. One fag on the end of a pin would be drawn into eager mouths! In my time no boy was caught, we always got away with it. I used to pop along to the parade-ground, and climb up to the button, sitting there for a draw, and sometimes my dear Mother used to send me ten Players` cigarettes buried deep in a jar of home-made strawberry jam. This was a useful supplement to my 3/6d per week pay. I sold some of them for 3d each!

We all passed our exam with high marks, and, after mustering on the parade-ground for evening quarters, we returned to the mess to find, tucked under each pillow, a packet of **five woodbines!**

We puffed ourselves silly that night. Did any of us consider, however, that our Chief Yeoman risked everything on his arm to show his appreciation of our passing-out results? Selfishly, no! He was a lovely man. I heard later, sadly, that he was killed in the battle of Jutland."

Chapter ten.

Injustices

In the Royal Navy, punishment for the most trivial of offences was very severe, sometimes barbaric and cruel. The cat o' nine tails was frequently used, and eighteen strokes of the birch, soaked in brine to stiffen it so that it would lacerate the flesh, was awarded to boys who absconded.

An extract from the book, 'H.M.S. Ganges,' written in 1966, commemorating 100 years of Boys' Training, by Instr. Lt. D.L. Davies, writing about the sailing ship Ganges when it was anchored in St. Just Pool, Falmouth, in the late 19th century, states: "At 11.40 a.m. each day instruction finished and the boys fell in to witness punishment. This occasion was the only one on which they saw the Captain of the ship and so it had a particularly impressive aura about it. The usual instrument of punishment was the cane which was whipped at both ends with waxed twine to prevent it from splitting. It was the standard punishment for a variety of offences, the most common of which were: failing to have a chin-stay sewn on a cap; having a button off the trousers; or being slack in falling in. For the punishment to be carried out, hammocks were lashed horizontally and perpendicularly to form a cross, the best position for the caning. The boy's shirt was then drawn up around his waist leaving him with only a thin pair of duck pants stretched tightly across the buttocks. It was customary to give six or nine cuts, and the weals often took ten days to heal.

The cat o' nine-tails was abolished as a naval punishment in 1881, but the birch - up to a maximum of twenty-four strokes - was still used on boys for such serious offences as theft and desertion. Incidents frequently occurred during a birching which caused a local member of Parliament to raise questions in the House of Commons. In 1892 the birches on board the Boscawen at Portland were pickled in brine to leave the flesh torn and lacerated. Moreover, the ship's corporals took it in turn to administer alternate strokes to the boy under punishment, _laughing as they did so._ Immediately after watching this public administration of punishment, the boys went to dinner."

Parliament tried to reduce the birching to a maximum of 12 strokes, and to stop the Royal Marine Corporals carrying canes. It was some years before this actually came about. It seems that the main culprits

"MEDIC,—BOSUN'S
PULLED A MUSCLE!!"

208

for meting out punishment to the boys, by way of random whacks across the backside or elsewhere, were Marine Corporals.

Another extraction from the same book states, regarding Ganges again at Falmouth, that two local boys, Earle and Finch, were unjustly birched; the mother of one, Mrs. Finch, a fish woman, had been drinking, and lay in wait for the Captain `armed with a bludgeon.` This incident led to an investigation where it was claimed by the prosecution that the birch had been pickled in vinegar to stiffen it and so cause lacerations, but the defence claimed that `the birch in question had been soaked in water, not vinegar, to soften it!` The boys finally escaped to the freedom of `civvy street because Mrs.

" HANDS TO WITNESS PUNISHMENT "

Finch had already induced her son and his luckless friend to return home, depriving the recruiters of their catch!

The birch and cat o' nine-tails were not used at *Ganges*, Shotley. The maximum number of strokes allowed of the cane was 36, later reduced to 12. But imagine 36 strokes of a bamboo cane and the damage it would cause! Recall the recent case of the American youth caught vandalising cars in Singapore, he received just four strokes - and that had been reduced from six because of the adverse world-wide publicity. The American Ambassador who inspected his bottom was horrified at the `bloody wounds of lacerated flesh, so cruelly administered in cold blood cannot be condoned.` Even so, caning was no light matter, despite the joviality of Marine Corporals those 50 years hence; the cane left ugly red, blue and bloody weals across the backsides of the boys, and the drawing of blood was common rather than rare. There is no evidence to support the stories that the Captain would give the unfortunate boy one shilling for each `cut` which bled; perhaps that would have been too many and therefore too expensive for the Captain. It could have been a feasible statement, and true only if it was to keep the victim`s mouth closed and silent against such barbaric treatment!

It was not always the boys who were punished in such fashion. An extract from the log of H.M.S. Ganges the warship, the last of the sailing-ships to carry an Admiral of the Fleet and justify the honour of being known as Flagship, carries this entry from its log of 19th August, 1831: *"0900 George Beeks, seaman, punished with 36 lashes for absenting himself from duty. Chas. Breech, for theft, 36 lashes. Noon. Light breeze."* This harsh punishment is dismissed lightly with a brief mention of the prevailing weather.

Not all of the boys who received `cuts` deserved them; and some of those who did, seemed to have received more than they rightfully and justifiably should have done. But, proceeding onward to comparatively modern days of the 1930`s, Jim Lawlor, who has a story elsewhere in this book, describes his punishment lightheartedly, but with jocular overtones to disguise his underlying resentment of gross injustice. His crime was stealing. It was only an apple. But it *was* stealing. The Captain compared the offence to Jim stealing his, the Captain`s, gold watch. Misdeamenours were seldom explored in depth, and if the Captain had delved a little deeper into Jim`s explanation, he may well have found extenuating circumstances.

Jim Lawlor: "There was never a dull moment in the Navy, and I often think it`s a good job the future`s not ours to see. For instance, I`m working in the Boys` Cook-house, and that day, for sweet, or `afters` as we called them, it was apples. A boy`s voice near me said, 'Bet you daren`t pinch one.' Without hesitation, or very little, thinking it was something of a lark, I took an apple out of one of the dishes and put it inside my naval jumper. And next thing I know is I`m on the Quarterdeck in front of an officer and the charge against me is `stealing.` He gave me Commander`s report and he gave me Captain`s report. All this fuss over an apple; I`ve scrumped dozens

210

from orchards without all this malarky.

Soon, I am standing before the Captain himself, fully expecting to be cautioned. He asked me why I stole the apple. So I told him someone dared me to pinch it. So he said, 'If you were standing in my office with another boy dusting and sweeping, and my gold watch was on the desk, and this other boy dared you to pinch it, would you?'

'No, sir,' I said.

But that didn't help me any, for the Captain said: 'I punish you to Nine Cuts with the cane.'

So I'm marched to a Prison cell and strapped to a box-horse, as used in the Gymnasiums, with my hands on one side and my feet the other, but I did manage to stuff my clean white handkerchief into my mouth before being strapped to the box-horse.

The Captain sat in the cell. He read out the charge, and added, 'For which I did punish him to Nine Cuts with the cane.'

Somehow I had a feeling I wouldn't enjoy the caning..

Swishhhhh-**thhhhwaackkk!**...went the cane, and the humiliation of being strapped to a bloody box-horse was forgotten in the horror of the pain as the first stroke hit my backside. I could hear the Captain's voice counting.

'One!' he said. Bloody hell, my backside felt on fire.

Swish.

'Two!' Jeesus, the stinging is unbearable.

'Three!' Dear God. It was only a 'dare!'

'Four!' Cor, aren't I glad I put my handkerchief in my mouth.

'Five!' Oh, God! It's not fair! Come on, get it over with.

'Six!' I'll never be dared to do anything again.

'Seven!' I can feel tears of pain running down my face.

'Eight!' Come on! Come On!

'Nine!'

Thank God!

My trousers were lowered after I was unstrapped to see if blood had been drawn. It hadn't. Later I learned that if blood had been drawn, I'd have been awarded five weeks pocket money. Imagine. Five Whims, five bars of chocolate, and five bottles of pop. Quart bottles, too! What a lesson that punishment taught me."

Could a little more questioning of the culprit have revealed that the crime could have been converted into a meaningless, boyish prank? No. The mentality of those days, Captain or Nozzer, the thinking was that stealing was stealing, whether it was a farthing or a fortune.

"The flog `em brigade.."

Paul Nolan says: "I was an `inmate` at Ganges, Rodney Division, 1962 - 63. There is a saying that you only remember the good times, but I suppose things were pretty tough. The further you go back the harder the times were. I can think of many of the tough times at Ganges, but I`m going to concentrate on something that`s been in my mind lately, and that is, `cuts.`

There has been a lot of discussion lately about corporal punishment, in fact, there was a letter from a local councillor in my local paper only the day before, extolling the virtues of it. Whenever I hear someone saying `bring back the birch,` or `flog `em,` I think of the time I got the dreaded `six` at Ganges.

It was kit-muster time and I couldn`t find one of my caps. I asked an oppo to lend me one of his and, yes, the Divisional Officer asked to see my caps! I passed it to him, he frowned, and said:

'This isn`t your cap.' Well, *that* was pretty obvious.

'I know, sir,' I answered, 'I had to borrow one because I have mislaid one of my own.'

'See me on the quarterdeck in five minutes,' he said, and walked away.

I was given Commander`s report; *he* gave me Captain`s report; and the Captain said: 'Six cuts. Carry on.'

The sentence didn`t bother me too much, I had received the cane a few times at school, so, although apprehensive, I wasn`t terrified. But no-one could anticipate what was about to happen.

First I was taken by a Patrolman for a medical, then marched to the Master-at-Arms office, where, waiting for me was the Master-at-Arms, the `Jimmy` and a great big wooden chair without a seat. I was ordered to bend over the chair from the back and grip the frame. A Patrolman on each side then turned out the lining of my pockets and gripped them, stretching my number eight trousers tight across my bottom. I wasn`t allowed to wear underpants.

I waited, a bit apprehensively, then:

'One!' shouted the `Jimmy.`The Joss-man wielded the cane.

THWACK! I`m sure that me, the chair and the two patrolman went forward six inches. It hurt, it *really* hurt, and it was nearly as bad as waiting for the next one as the Master took his time selecting the next cane for the next stroke. Anyway, I gritted my teeth, closed my eyes, and got through it without shouting out or crying. And I was proud of that."

It is very obvious that the Master-at-Arms responsible was eking out the time between strokes to deliberately apply not only pain but mental anguish and torture to the offender/victim. No matter how thorough the vetting of would-be Instructors, or the Regulating Petty Officers and others involved in Boy's training, the boys were always at the mercy of the sadists who filtered through and who delighted inflicting pain or torture. It was known and admitted by another M.A.A. that some who volunteered to carry out the punishment in such a manner were sadists. Fortunately, that kind, humane M.A.A. denied the pleasure of inflicting such obvious pain to those who volunteered, and gave the dubious pleasure of handing out the punishment by Regulating Petty Officers who *did not really want to do it.* It follows that the cane would not then be admistered so heavily or viciously.

Paul continues: "The point I would like to make to the `flog `em` brigade, who are of the opinion that this sort of punishment is a deterrent and humiliates the victim, is, five minutes later I was down the mess-deck showing off my `stripes` to my oppo`s. It was rumoured you got two-and-sixpence for every crossed cut, but I never heard of anyone getting it.

Anyway, I can`t see that sort of thing stopping the joy-riders and muggers. They would regard those stripes as a medal!"

To digress from Paul`s story: that treatment would cause some to become more rebellious. To others it would deter them ever again from committing an offence which carried the sentence of painful corporal punishment.

Paul Nolan displayed his criss-cross cuts as medals or trophies, but trophies - cigarettes were considered as trophies - were not allowed in Ganges. Ex-boy **Frank Phelps** recalls the delivery of parcels from home which led eventually to a similar display of the trophies of six cuts, wielded by an Instructor who was delighted to satisfy his sadistic and perverted urges by inflicting pain on the bottoms of young boys: "When mail from home included a food parcel," Frank writes, "It had to be collected from the mail office. The Petty Officer in charge would open the parcel to check for cigarettes. Cakes were cut open because some of the boy ratings would ask their parents to hide a packet of cigs inside. We had a couple of boys in our class who were caught with cigs and matches in their ditty-boxes shortly

before we were due for leave. Our Instructor said to them:
'Do you want my punishment, or go on Commander's report?'
Commander's report meant waiting another couple of days - which meant the offender would have to lose two days of their leave waiting to see the Commander. Then the Commander might give fourteen days' jankers, taking up all the rest of the offender's leave.

The answer could only be, 'Your punishment, sir,' which is what they said. They took his punishment.

The next morning at breakfast the two culprits were lined up.

The Instructor commanded: `Bend over the beds!`

In turn, they each received six cuts from the Instructor.

'That's it, then!' said the Instructor, 'Carry on and eat your breakfast.'

After they had gone, the two ratings dropped their trousers and let us see the result. The bruises were already visible and they were looking like zebras. That made sure no-one else in the class handled cigarettes or matches."

Instructors were not allowed to carry out corporal punishment. They were not allowed to lay hands upon any of the boys. It can only be assumed that the Instructor concerned enjoyed chastising the bottoms of young boys. (He probably smoked like a chimney himself!) If the foregoing story is true, is it possible to assume that some Instructors applied for the job to enable them to carry out their own personal fetishes of taking the merest and simplest opportunity to deliver pain on the simplest of misdemenours. If that is so, then it degrades those Instructors who's only aim was to teach and instruct Boy Entrants for the purpose for which they had joined.

Frank continues: "Some of the boys at Ganges would buy a packet of Woodbines from a workman in the establishment for 2d., and during stand-easy charged others one penny each for a draw on a cigarette. They also sat in the front row at the cinema on film night, doing the same thing, until the film was cut and the lights switched on. Instructors then pounced and caught them smoking. Those ratings were known as the `draggers union.`

Doing a runner..

We had a Scots boy who could not face the routine any longer. He was going to do a runner up to Ipswich and jump on a train to London. It was a Sunday night, very cold and wet. He let us know of his intentions, so we each gave Jock a penny from our weekly shilling and wished him the best of luck as he climbed out of the mess window and into the darkness at about midnight.

At 6 a.m., just before reveille, the topic of conversation was Jock, and how far he might be away from Ganges at that time. One of the boys, who had gone to the galley to fetch cocoa and ship's biscuits, came running in.

'Help!' he cried. 'I've just seen Jock, hanging on the fence! He's been there all night on a spiked railing, stuck through the back of his jumper!'

Five of us rushed to the fence where we found Jock hanging on the spike, his feet just two inches from the ground, unable to move. We released him from the railings, he was freezing and stiff with cold but we got him back into the mess just before roll-call by the Instructor. He escaped punishement because he didn't get found out, and later he passed the course with the rest of us. But I wonder why the Boy's Service was shut down? After all, we were the forerunners of what is called The Professionals in the armed forces."

It is not clear what he means by 'The Professionals,' but one certain 'professional' in one occupation is Ivan Johnstone who had a 'brush with the Ganges discipline.'

Ivan Johnston joined Ganges in 1957; later, he became one of the youngest peace-time Petty Officers, leaving the navy to become a Detective Sergeant in the Thames Valley police. He is also an author and current sales manager of a large, Bristol-based international company. A good showing for a man whom Ganges discipline branded as a thief, but he doesn't seem to mind that wrongly-applied stigma, and tells his story thus:

"My mess was in the Short Covered way, 35, I think, the one at the bottom of the hill that led down to the playing fields. Lieutenant Commander Blake was my Divisional Officer. What an impression he must have made on a boy of 15 that his name jumps clearly to mind just like that, and it was 1957 when I started my sentence. Well, he decided that because we had been warned once or twice about the noise we had been making after lights out, he would have us lay out our kit at the most inconvenient time - after lights out, a suitable punishment to fit the crime. At that time I was in charge of the scran-bag, so I had the keys to the cleaning store which housed that item.

Horror of horrors! When I got my kit laid out I found I was missing a clothes-brush. I searched everywhere for that brush, but I could not find it and I knew that, with Blakey, it was for sure a dose of number tens, or some such, because they did not like you losing any part of your kit. If I had known of the outcome, and the subsequent consequences, and the pain and suffering of being honest in telling the truth, I would have left things as they were and gladly done any amount of number tens, compared with the punishment meted out for such a minor misdemour. However, I remembered that in the scran-bag there was a clothes brush that had been lying about in the store. It had been there long before we moved into the mess, and did not, in effect, belong to anyone, except a long-gone ex-member of the mess. I went and had a look at it, and it looked good enough to include in my kit on a temporary basis, although down one side of it was a name stamped very faintly, but still discernably upon it. I decided to borrow it for the kit muster and laid it out just below my pyjamas and in line with the housewife, as per Admiralty Instructions etc.

The tannoy sounded off. Out lights. Bugle softly playing the meloncholy notes of the Last Post. 'Boys turn in. Out lights.'

Then it was our kit inspection time: Lieutenant Commander Blake strode into the mess, red beard bristling and he began to systematically tear kit after kit apart. Boy's who had only just washed underpants etc, were sent off to wash them again. Others were given a date to re-muster their kit. I mean, let's face it, anything which inconvenienced us was the name of the game wasn't it?

Finally, he got to me. I was feeling quite chuffed because I knew my kit was in good fettle. I had worked hard at it and it was a good kit, but the bastard came straight to me, picked up the clothes brush, and said: 'Whose brush is this, boy?' he boomed.

My father had always taught me to tell the truth, so I replied: 'Sir, I mislaid my own brush, and borrowed that one from the scran-bag. It's been there since before we occupied the mess, sir. It probably was left behind by someone of a previous draft, sir.'

The Divisional Officer looked at me, brandishing the rogue brush. 'Stole it, you mean.' He looked at his side-kick, the sub-divisional officer, a young, tall, Sub-Lieutenant, probably no more than 12 months older than myself.

'Take him to my office!'

I was led away by the pimply-faced young Subbie, who lectured me that I had let the side down and that Her Majesty's Navy did not like thieves. But I was no thief. By then, in the near and recent past, I had done so many leg-aching bunny-hops with a .303 rifle that I had learned to keep my cake-hole well and truly shut when there was trouble brewing. So I never said a word. It would have been hopeless anyway.

The duty crusher was sent for and duly arrived and led me away with a twist of my ear all the way to the main gate where I was banged-up whilst they got the Officer-of-the-Watch out so that I could be charged with theft - which is what happened.

Eventually I appeared in front of the Captain and the charge was read out by the Master-at-Arms: 'Boy Johnston, sir. He was found with a brush in his possession which was not his own. It had the name of another boy stamped upon it.'

The Captain, taking his eyes off the Jaunty, looked straight at me like a snake hypnotising a rabbit.

'What do you have to say to that, Johnston?' His voice was toneless, disinterested, asking the question only because he had to. It was obvious he wasn't interested in the answer, or that he would even consider it. It was asked only as a matter of naval protocol.

Even then, thinking that my excuse was valid, I was sure my case would be dismissed. I said, innocently: 'I borrowed the brush from the scran-bag, sir. The owner of it must have gone on draft several months ago. I didn't steal it, sir, I had mislaid mine and didn't have time to order another from slops. I was going to put it back after the kit inspection, sir.' And that was the honest truth. The honest and valid excuse was not even considered.

The Jaunty piped up: 'That's an admission of guilt, sir.'

'Anything to say, Johnston?'

'No, sir.'

'Three cuts. Take him away. Next case.'

It was as simple as that. No in-depth investigation to determine guilt or innocence, my case was dismissed almost as if it was nothing more than a nuisance to be gotten out of the way as soon as possible with the least trouble to everyone involved - except myself. Well, I hadn't been given a keel hauling, but not far short. A little while later after Captain's Table, I was led back into that office across the quarter-deck, the back of the guard-room, and was held down across the back of an old wooden chair that must have come from the Victory. On each of my arms I had a Crusher holding them down tight onto the

217

arms of the chair whilst the Jaunty slowly swished the cane about in a deliberately menacing fashion, obviously and purposely trying to add to the fear I was now feeling. I was sweating with terror, droplets of moisture were dripping from my forehead. Then, whilst I sweated with fear, although I was expecting it, the cane came crashing with sudden, unexpected violence and searing pain, down onto my backside with all the force of a 4.5 shell hitting the target.

Bloody hell! Did it hurt!!? Much more than I had even expected, or could reasonably stand. But I was determined that they would not get the pleasure of hearing me scream, grimace, whimper or call out. I never even flinched, although my whole body wanted to fight back and wrench myself from the grasp of those who held me.

When it was over I knew better than to show any facial expression which would possibly bring even more punishment, so I stood up to attention and was immediately dismissed and told to double around the parade-ground twice to get the circulation moving again.

After, I approached the quarterdeck, saluted it, and scurried off to the Short Covered Way to change into my number three's, and, thankfully, there was no one in the mess. I went into the cleaning cupboard, locked the door, took the mirror from the wall and pulled my number 8 trousers down and looked at the blood weeping from my wounds.

I allowed myself a few minutes to cry. Not with the pain, but with the sheer humiliation of such barbaric punishment administered for such a minor crime of borrowing a brush which did not, technically belong to anyone. I mean, Christ, I was only a young boy who had merely borrowed a brush, and for that I was taken by three strapping men, held down like an animal, and beaten until the blood was drawn. I was hundreds of miles away from my family, and I think I deserved a few tears for myself. So I cried."

He goes on to say that Ganges must have taught him something because he has no hang-ups and enjoys life to the full. He also has the envious disposition of being able to differentiate between those who are right and those who are wrong. Ganges itself was not wrong, it was the interpreters of the regime of Ganges who were wrong. And there were very many, too many, who *were* in the wrong.

A personal comment by the author: It's funny how the Divisional Officers could pick the one item of kit which was defective, crabby or torn. I remember on our last kit-muster, held in Nelson Hall and attended by the Commander, I was unable to get the whole thing to come together at once. I mean, after all, how can you present a fully-dhobeyed kit, ready and unblemished and un-dirtied when you have to wear some part of it in trying to get the rest of it up to standard? I managed this final kit-muster quite well apart from one pair of blue woollen stockings. I looked at the items in the kit and decided it was about a sixty-nine-to-one chance, with seventy items of stockings, that he would pick up on a pair of crabby stockings. Or should I wear the smelly, long-worn, unwashed, pussers-stockings, the soles hardened to shininess, and lay out the clean ones? I chose to lay out the renegade stockings and wear the clean ones.

In the meantime, the Commander reported to the Regulating Office where they had a crystal ball, used solely by Kit-inspecting officers prior to kit-inspection. The crystal ball showed that Boy Sig. Douglas had a pair of crabby stockings in his kit, second pair from the left. With this information, the Commander strode into Nelson Hall, tossing off salutes at all and sundry as they toadied around him, and located Boy Sig. Douglas about two-thirds along the row. He sort of slow-marched along the row, casting cursory, seemingly disinterested glances at the kits of others. I felt a lot easier, no chance of him picking up on my stockings out of all fifty-eight boys, multipled by about seventy, making the odds around five-hundred-to-one that he would pick upon my crabby stockings. But the Commander had backed an outsider. He stopped by my kit, pointed at the stockings. 'Let me see those, boy.' I handed him the stockings.

The Commander leaned forward, hands behind his back, doing a Prince Philip; peering, sniffing, and looking generally unsatisfied. He nodded his head. 'Petty Officer! See this boy is stopped draft, re-muster in two week's time. His kit is an absolute disgrace.' *On the basis of one pair of stockings?*

I couldn't believe it. The kit was clean and he had made his decision on just one item. Did the Navy teach it's officers to make such decisions? I was ordered to wash the whole of my kit, iron it, roll it up as per same width as Seamanship Manual, etc. You know the score. I refused to do it. Not openly, or verbally. But whilst my mess-mates went on draft, I had the mess to myself. I threw away the offending stockings, ordered a new pair, placed them with the rest of my kit and never touched the rest of it. In the bedding store I parted the middle lockers about six inches and spent the next two weeks, back against the wall, looking directly down into the opening of the entrance to the mess, practising my mouth-organ. From this position I could see any Patrolman entering the mess, which they did on several occasions. From that distance they couldn't hear the mouth-organ, and it gave me time to stow away the mouth-organ and busy myself with my kit. Why they never queried that it should take two weeks to get a kit ready for re-muster I cannot guess. I bought in a stock of nutty bars, pop, cigarettes from my accumulations of money gained from my 'Fag-Baron' days and experienced the best time and the freedom of Ganges for two weeks. Walks on the foreshore, almost to Pin Mill. Sunbathing on the sands of the banks of the Orwell, it was like being on leave, except that I had to be back in the mess before 2100. Fourteen days later I laid my kit out again for Commander's inspection alongside those of a Seaman's class who were due for draft. The Commander came in and when he reached my kit the report came: 'Signal Boy Douglas, sir. He was stopped draft because of his kit and ordered to lay it out today, sir.'

'Now,' said the Commander, trying to remember the incident. Now isn't that one hundred percent better, lad?'

You stupid, ignorant prat. How could it be a hundred percent better when I've only added one pair of new stockings and ditched the pair which you picked up on? I replied, with false enthusiasm: 'Yes, sir.'

'Good. Carry on.'.

So I did, and caught up with my 'oppos' in 'Viccy Barracks II' a few days later. The 'system' was so easy to get the better of!

A green rub for a green stamp..

Nine cuts for stealing an apple, three for borrowing a cap and six cuts for being in possession of a hair-brush with someone else's name upon it. Harsh? Injustice? How about six cuts and fourteen days' jankers for finding a ha'penny stamp?

Nobby Hill was the unfortunate victim:

"A Wednesday afternoon, Autumn 1934, and the tanner I'd doffed my lid for tucked in my belt pocket. I'd been back to the mess to stow my bar of pusser's hard, and was making my way across the parade ground to the canteen, slavering at the thought of the two 'Charlies' I was going to pouch in my ever-starving belly, when, on the ground I spotted something green. I bent down, picked it up and put it in my belt pocket with the tanner and promptly forgot all about it.

A day or so later I was in the heads at the top of Laundry Hill having a 'dump' and a five-minute dream of home, when the small hole, drilled in the bog door for observation, was obscured by the dreaded 'Turkey's Eye' - the Royal Marine sentry who was posted to patrol

220

the traps to see if anybody in there was having a `smoko` or `handy`-shandy, both of which were forbidden. A sigh of relief as he passed on. Suddenly all hell was let loose, he'd caught somebody smoking, and before I'd even got time to polish my `duck-run,` the Crushers had descended, and everybody in the Heads was lined-up on the Quarter-Patch for a strip search. I was feeling quite smug when it was my turn to face the Joss-man, I knew I was clean. There was no evidence on me. One of the favourite places for them to look for fag-ends or `baccy-dust was your belt pocket, a sign of either - a few strands of tobacco - and you was a `gonner.`

'What`s this?' the Joss-man chirped, holding up the green stamp.

As quick as a flash, and wet as a can of wee-wee, I replied: 'Oh, only a stamp, sir, I picked it up on the parade-ground, sir.' I'd nothing to worry about or fear. Without further ado he wiped the smirk off my face with an aside to the crusher: 'Divisional Officer`s report. Stealing by finding. Dismiss!' I was shaken rigid and went back to the heads for another quick dump. Naval justice took it`s remorseless course: Commander`s report, Captain`s report, **six cuts and fourteen days jankers. A green rub,** I thought, if ever there was one. In all the years since, if ever I've had a dodgy deal and scored off it, I always remember with some trepidation that bloody ha`penny stamp and the price I paid for it. And fourteen day`s jankers to look forward to. Oh, the agony astern! **My bum was like a hot-crossed bun!**

*Or, more appropriately: **'A hot-crossed bum!'*** Sorry....!!

Chapter eleven
Varying views of H.M.S. Ganges.

The Instructor's story...

There are very few accounts in this book from Instructors who give their point of view, as opposed to the views of the ex-Boys. The following in-depth record by an Instructor, portrays the many and diversive opinions, other than those of the detrimental, sadistic and/or masochistic reports, so it is considered fair and proper that it should be included. He was never a Boy, and not, initially, an Instructor, but a member of the ship's company. Later, he did become an Instructor.

"It may interest ex-Ganges Boys to read of H.M.S. GANGES as remembered by others to whom that rather isolated corner of Suffolk also holds memories, albeit from a different angle or point of view. I refer to the hundreds of officers, Chief and Petty Officer Instructors and others of the ship's company who passed through those famous gates. Although I was never a Ganges Boy, I did, however, spend a total of three years and six months there between 1958 and 1967. My first spell started in August, 1958, when, as an Able Seaman UW (2) waiting for my 'hook,' I was drafted to Ganges as ship's company. I had an introductory talk from a Lieutenant Commander who welcomed me to Ganges by informing me that the Ship's Company are expected to, and must at all times, set an example to the boys. No smoking in front of the boys, no swearing. All messes and recreational areas were strictly out of bounds and I was not to engage the boys in idle chatter. The only contact would be during the course of duty. As far as dress was concerned I was informed that there would be no bleached collars, no split silks, no bow-waves in caps, no overalls, no tiddly-bows and that I could expect a kit-muster every six months.

I began to think this may not, after all, be the best of drafts. However, on finally reporting to the duty coxswain down at the pier I was informed of my duties, also, I would be watch-keeping 24 hours about with every other week-end off. I only lived about 50 miles away so this suited me, although I was warned not to damage any of the boats!

I survived my 16 months at Ganges without actually damaging any of the boats; I also survived without having to endure a Ganges kit muster."

More fulfilling..

That period in Ganges was uneventful, but his next draft to that place was more interesting and self-fulfilling: "My next stint at H.M.S. GANGES commenced in July, 1962. I had just completed a U.W.I.'s course at H.M.S. Vernon as a Leading Seaman when I saw an `advert` on orders of the day, asking for Petty Officers to volunteer as Instructors on H.M.S. GANGES. I decided to volunteer, and, much to my surprise, I found myself in an office at GANGES being informed that I was to be made Acting Local Petty Officer to take effect immediately and was to pick up a class from the Annexe in the very near future. This was the start of what I can only describe as one of the periods of my naval service which gave me not only days and nights of very hard work, long hours, intense self-discipline, but also probably the job which gave me the most `job satisfaction` I have ever encountered.

I was briefed by the Personnel Planning office what the aims of H.M.S. GANGES were; namely, character-building, school instruction and professional training. All new Instructors were advised to read `Captains Standing Orders and Commander's Orders` which were the bibles of H.M.S. GANGES.

The following extract from a copy of `Joining Instructions for Instructors` (circa 1962) may well differ from the memory of many ex-Ganges members who were at Ganges long before myself. However, with the benefit of hindsight, I think they were extremely apt for the early 1960's. This is how the instructions were laid out:-

THE JOB. `For eleven months you will be everything to the Juniors in your class, your example, your interest, your authority and particularly your enthusiasm will be the dominant influence in their lives, and may well determine whether they are to be a success or failures in the service.`

INSTRUCTORS RESPONSIBILITIES. `As a Class Instructor you are responsible to your Divisional Officer for your boys in two ways: as a Mess Instructor and as a Professional Instructor. The first means you will be held responsible for the spirit, bearing and cleanliness of your class. The second, that you have to teach your boys so that they may take their place usefully in the Fleet when they leave H.M.S. GANGES.`

YOUR TASK. `Drop any resolutions that because you were made to `go through the hoop` that you'll get your class to jump even higher and further. The old, `This is how you do it and never mind why` methods are dead and gone, they make today's boys sullen and hostile.`"

That former attitude prevailed long before the `60's, believe me!

To continue:

"YOUR EXAMPLE: `Lead by example, during his year here any normal youth will grow in self-confidence. He will change from a boy to a man with or without Service influence. What you have to do is mould that self-confidence so that the man he becomes is the man that the Service requires.`

The Joining Instructions continued in respect of `The Instructor,` `Interest,` `Firm Authority,` `Enthusiasm,` `Helping the weaker link,` `Encouraging weaker links,` etc.

Armed with this advice, together with my co-Instructor, Petty Officer Pedlar Palmer, we were eventually introduced to our new classes - Blake 75 and 76, who were to occupy 8 Mess in the Long Covered Way for the best part of the next year.

Pedlar Palmer was the Seamanship Instructor whilst I was the Domestics Instructor who, as most will remember, was responsible for Parade and Rifle drill together with the T.A.A. Training of selected Juniors from, in addition to Blake, Juniors from Exmouth, Duncan and Rodney Divisions.

I still have vivid memories of striding across the Parade-ground from the P.O.'s Mess, fully booted and gaitered at some unearthly hour, together with other Instructors and entering a very quiet Long Covered Way, which, within minutes, would erupt into a hive of activity with boys milling about everywhere.

During the period at GANGES, I think it would be true to say all Instructors got to know every lad in the mess very well as of course did the lads themselves get to know each other, and the `esprit de corp` and pride in the class and mess grew as the weeks went by. I have never witnessed or experienced such pride in any other group of youngsters since, which of course is borne out by the strength of the GANGES Association which is now over 2,000 members strong, founded by John Douglas, author of, "H.M.S. GANGES (Roll on my dozen!).

Pride in his class or mess was not restricted to the boys. The Instructors, too, developed a great sense of pride in their respective messes. Although I doubt if all ex-Instructors would admit to it. It was not unknown for one to stroll into a mess, perhaps when the class was at school, to find a fellow Instructor slapping a coat of paint on a door or repairing some fixture or other that had been broken.

Talk in the Instructor's Mess and Bar was invariably about 'my class,' it's achievements, its problems or how an Instructor had solved a certain problem. Although good-natured rivalry abounded, a new Instructor could always rely on obtaining tips and advice from the more experienced Instructor. At times it appeared almost comical to see a couple of Instructors in the bar discussing the finer points of the rules of Softball or hockey.

There were many impromptu 'socials' which were not organised or planned but just happened. These also were times memorable, but then, that was typical 'Ganges,' work hard, play hard.

On reflection, I wouldn't have missed it for the world!"

Vic Duncan says that just hearing the name of Ganges "Opens a floodgate of memories, unfortunately not all memories are of the kind I wish to recall with any fondness."

Vic joined in June, 1956, "And," he states, "Apart from the odd fishing trip as a schoolboy on my Grandad's trawler, it was the first time I was on my own away from home.

Well, like all other new entrants I did not pass through the imposing Main Gates of Ganges, but started in the Annex, some half a mile up the road. We were issued with our Ship's Book numbers and Official numbers; I will never forget number 962005, a chap called Blowers from Lowestoft, and 962007, a chap called Bluett who came from Hall. We suffered the hardships of basic training till we could pass out as a somewhat disciplined body of young boys.

Boxing was compulsory and you fought opponents, based rarely on weight. I was all of seven stones, five foot three inches, so you can gather there wasn't too many my size.

I battled through three preliminary bouts and made the final. My opponent a big five foot six inches, eight or nine stone boy - Bluett, my best friend.

All the pleading to our Boy Instructors or C.P.O. meant nothing, we had to fight each other. Came the big day. The Skipper, Captain Lefanu, his good lady, all other officers, wives and all the other new entrants who, through good fortune, were beaten earlier, made up an audience.

The running sequence of fights were decided on weight, the lightest went first, DUNCAN v BLUETT. We were warned that if we didn't try we had to fight the P.T.I. This option scared me more than an equally nervous Bluett did and to end the saga, I knocked Bluett out of the ring onto the table with the Certificates and medals - and into the Captain's wife's lap, much to the delight of all present except Bluett and the Captain's wife.

Luckily, Bluett recovered, but he never spoke to me again, and when we passed over to the Main Camp, he went to his signalling training and I went with more of the lads of my branch.

Unfortunately, my worst memory was nine months into my term at Ganges with only three months to go. I took ill. I blame it on standing on the parade-ground with a damp shirt for three hours, and wearing the shirt again later in fear of failing an inspection because of wearing a dirty shirt, the consequences for that would have been very incomprehensible Next morning, whilst the lads were getting ready to start the day, I could hardly get up, my chest was on fire. I had sweated all night. I really was in agony. Our Chief, when he came on the scene, allowed me to miss the first lesson of the day and go to Sick Bay. How I made it there under my own steam I'll never know, but I made it. Whilst waiting, the Sick Berth attendant took our names and class numbers. Within five minutes I was taken into a room by the S.B.A. who said I was swinging the lead. I had committed a cardinal sin. I had gone sick whilst my class was at P.T. Again my pleading met no response. I was given a 'bumper,' a big lead weight on a long handle covered with rags. The corridor which I had to polish, which I saw through tear-filled eyes, looked a mile long. I had to polish it whilst waiting for the Surgeon Commander to appear.

My chest, head, every muscle in my body ached as I tried to swing the 'bumper.' I was at it for twenty to thirty minutes when I collapsed. Again, after taunting, kicking and my head slapped about by this S.B.A., I woke up in a hospital bed twenty four hours later, a temperature of 103, I had pleurisy and pneumonia. I spent four weeks in Sick Bay which, after the illness started improving, was the best four weeks I spent at Ganges. The irony of it for me was that I loved P.T. That's one lesson I would not dream of missing on purpose. I had colours at Ganges for boxing, sailing and football. I played for the Home Air Command at football, I was sports daft, but I was back-classed to 110 class, and made up my missing month at Ganges. Luckily they were also in Blake 10 Mess, so I knew them, and I passed out in July, 1957, and went to H.M.S. Gamecock at Nuneaton for my trade training, aircraft mechanic.

My class-mates and I looked for that S.B.A. to seek revenge, but he never appeared again. Whether he was drafted because of me I'll never know. I believe he was a lucky man that our paths never crossed again in my 12 years in the R.N.

Ganges is a memory now, I will never forget it. The well-worn cliche, 'it never did you any harm' is a load of toot. I and thousands of boys were brain-washed. To this day anyone in authority speaks or shouts at me I still jump!''

Yet another sad case of a large, small-minded person-in-charge of a small boy, this time an S.B.A., with a super ego, fed by a massive inferiority-complex, causing him to act 'Mister Big' with those whom he knew he could bully without fear of complaint. What a great pity that such a miserable, pathetic wimp should be allowed by his immediate superiors to brain-wash a boy so that forever afterwards the boy would react to authority in such a negative way.

Perhaps the actions of the Sick Berth Attendant was the result of those boys who had nothing wrong with them and were 'swinging the lead,' 'loafing,' 'scheming,' or just trying to dodge out of a lesson - like physical training. Whatever the reasoning of that S.B.A., the immediate reaction should have been to give the benefit of the doubt first, and then issue the punishment if the 'patient' was found to be scheming, swinging the lead or just loafing - even then, the punishment could not have been justified.

I can equate the above incident with a similar one of my own. I was a Boy Signalman onboard H.M.S. Mauritius, a colony-class Cruiser, performing speed-trials on the measured-mile off Portland in May, 1949, prior to setting sail for the East Indies for two-and-a-half years. The order was given: 'Batten- down all hatches and port-holes.' I was ordered to clip the port-hole in the cable flat, starboard side. To enable me reach up to it I had to climb upon a barrel. After clipping the port-hole I jumped down into the semi-darkness and my right foot landed on a ring-bolt protruding from the diamond-patterned iron deck. I have never before, or since, experienced such excruciating pain. It was so intense that it caused me to feel nauseous, sick and weak and I broke into a bilious sweat, limping my way back to the Boy's Mess, just a few yards through the hatch-way.

I had never suffered from-sea sickness and I had always jeered with jocularity at my fellow-boys when they showed signs of queasiness on previous rough sea-trips. This caused me to be the target of derision as I sat at the mess table, head in hands, sick with pain. In the sick bay I was treated as a 'schemer,' swinging the lead to get out of flag-deck duties, and was ordered to buff up the bright-work in the Sick Bay. After several attempts to complain, the Chief Sick Bay 'Tiffy told me that the Surgeon Commander had ordered that my so-called painful ankle be X-rayed, and if there was nothing wrong with it I was to be slapped in the rattle.

The 'Mauritius' bounced and slewed, bucked and rolled, and it took fourteen X- rays to determine the state of my painful ankle.

The Chief Sick Bay 'Tiffy' approached me with an X-ray in his hand: "Douglas!" he ordered. "You'd better get into bed. It seems you've got a bit of bone chipped off your ankle. It's broken." He made it sound as if I was at fault for not knowing that fact.

The ankle played up for several years after that, I could cause it to sprain by just looking at it, but every time I complained I was told not to be so petty and silly. I found out later, three days before my demobilisation. I could have asked for my ticket at any time. This information was imparted by one-time S.B.A 'Ginger' Brooks, by now demobbed and serving me pints of cheap 'scrumpy' in the canteen in Mercury. 'Ginger' had been a sympathetic Sick Berth Attendant at the time of my injury. He told me that if I had, at any-time, insisted on being discharged because I was not a complete person, I could have insisted on immediate discharge with a pension.

The culmination of this matter was, in later years, showing my young, foot-ball mad children how to do a Georgie Best swerve one Boxing Day morning on an icy foot-ball pitch, I twisted my ankle and ended up in hospital having a muscle transplant to strengthen my ankle, and later a compensation of £300. It was welcome at the time, but I think I would prefer that it had never happened at all.

"I am rubbish!"

R.R. Daniell, 1960-61: "My Division was Exmouth, 45 Mess, - (shanty town) - right on the edge of the parade-ground. I remember leaving the mess one morning to go to breakfast, and seeing in the middle of the parade-ground one of the famous highly-polished mess dust-bins. I heard someone shout: 'I am rubbish!' and when I looked again I saw a boy who was standing in the dust-bin with the lid on his head. He then promptly crouched back down inside the dust-bin, replacing the lid. He was still there when I returned from breakfast, and still shouting: 'I am rubbish.' I never did find out why his Instructor had made him do this. That incident would probably, today, be called bullying and is an example of the discipline we were subjected to. But it didn't seem to do us any harm, and I have to agree that Ganges turned out the world's finest sailors."

The hardened Instructors, who gave the boys hell, did not repent of their treatment, tho' be it unfair, when the Royal Navy recruited adults to replace the innocent young boys. Old habits take a long time to break, they are hard to erase, as it was with the methods of the salts of the old school. The raising of the school-leaving age from fifteen to sixteen, heralded the end of the intake of innocents of fifteen years, and brought about the beginning of the recruitment of the older, but just as unfortunate, sixteen years plus, mostly around the seventeen years age. At that point in their lives they had almost reached manhood. No one could expect a person, almost a man, to be treated as a junior, a boy, an inferior - or could they? Of course they could!

"I am a....."

"I was fortunate, or unfortunate, to have gone through Ganges in the summer of 1974, 4th June", reflects **Pete Diaper**. "I was then seventeen and half years old and my class was one of the first 'Adult Classes' to pass through the hallowed gates of Ganges. We were unique in being the only mess to be made up of solely Medical Branch personnel. There was approximately some 30 to 40 of us from every walk of life, but we had one thing in common: we were all apprehensive, or, to use the proper naval terminology, shit-scared, because there, standing before us, was a rather large Chief Petty Officer Gunnery Instructor, swagger-stick under his arm, and growling. He then gave us a lecture on the do's and do not's, mainly the do's. We were also the only Ceremonial Guard, for passing-out parade work, made up of Medical Personnel. This was some-what of a unique thing, because under the rules of the Geneva Convention, Medical personnel are not allowed to carry arms. But we were all honoured and we turned out a very smart and praise-worthy guard.

We were not allowed to wear a branch badge, as, unlike Baby Stokers, gunners, Fleet Air Arm, etc, we had to earn our badges, that meant six weeks at Ganges, 32 weeks initial training at R.N.A.S. Haslar, then on to specialist training of three years to become a State Registered Nurse. Anyway, back to Ganges where our basic training consisted mainly of rifle-drill and marching procedures. We were constantly being picked-up for improper dress, which wasn't surprising, we were, after all, Medics, not square-bashers. One poor chap who answered a Chief back, regarding this issue, was forced to double up and down the infamous steps of Faith, Hope and Charity for half an hour.

I was on the receiving-end of similar punishment after a misdemeanour in which I dropped my rifle on the parade-ground. I was told not to drop my rifle again and ordered to do bunny-hops all around the parade-ground, rifle held above my head, shouting: `I AM A C..T!`

It was bad enough doing this but it became much worse and more humiliating later on when a squad of lady W.R.N.S. marched onto the parade-ground. Naturally, being a gentleman, I lowered the tone of my voice as I hopped past them, but the Chief GI shouted: `I cannot hear you, Diaper!` Or words to that effect. So I had to increase the volume, shouting at the top of my voice as the W.R.N.S. passed by me: `I AM A CUNT!` They all turned their heads, some giggling, some smiling and one or two looked very shocked. But not as shocked as I was. I have never felt so embarrassed. I never dropped my rifle again!"

"As much use as a man's tits!"

`First Impressions` is the title ex A.B. **R.Wyatt** chooses to call his 1959 memories of Ganges. "Apart from feeling as if I'd journeyed to another planet with the sudden application of rigid discipline, the freezing cold, the highly-polished mess-deck, and the sudden realisation of what I'd let myself in for, the one moment that will always remain in my memory is the first encounter with a real live R.N. Chief Petty Officer, Chief Loveday!

I had led a fairly sheltered up-bringing in some ways. My parents were very Edwardian in their outlook on life, sex and bad language were things that were discussed between members of one's own peer group at the far end of the school playing-fields. Suddenly, in Ganges, I was confronted by this adult, old enough to be my father, whose very first words were: `You're about as much f.....g use as a man's tits!`"

Mr. Wyatt lists his likes and dislikes:

"Instructors: Many horror stories are circulated about the staff of Ganges. In the main most of them were true, as I both witnessed and suffered. There were many cases of sheer brutality that made Borstal seem a much better prospect, but on the whole, I must have been extremely lucky. My Instructors, through that terrible 12 months, were C.P.O. Loveday during my time in the Annexe; P.O.`s `Nobby` Hall and Ted Roe for the remainder of the course.

Of course there were the usual very early morning cold showers,

230

rowing on the Arctic wastes of the river, and happy hours spent naked in the sub-zero temperatures of the laundry. Why did we have to wash our clothes naked? There were also many memorable hours spent attempting to flatten out Laundry Hill and Faith, Hope and Charity, which added to the nausea of returning to the mess to find your bed and locker up-ended because something had been found out of place.

These nightmares tend to remain at the forefront of the memory but on reflection, in my case, they were the exception rather than the rule. Generally, my Instructors were usually very fair, dependable and thoroughly professional and I look back with much affection, knowing in hindsight what they had to put up with from us.

Hawke's Divisional Officer, Lt. Cdr. McKiver was extremely strict, but he was a gentleman who, I am sure, is remembered with much respect and affection. He was a very keen sailing man and I've crewed many a victorious whaler in the inter-divisional sailing regatta's with the help of his expertise, the odd bucket tied to the bilge rail of the competition and a handful of thunderflashes to lob into the other boats.

Parade-ground G.I's:

Who remembers Chief Tansey, the Parade Chief G.I.? His voice used to frighten the passengers off the Dovercourt ferry! No marching pace was ever sharp enough, no uniform was ever smart enough, and no rifle-drill was ever crisp enough, but I am sure that nobody remembers him as a bully. I ran into him later at Whale Island whilst training for a Royal Guard for the Belgian King and Queen and he treated us exactly the same as he used to with the Sunday guard at Ganges.

On the other hand, there was one particular specimen, a so-called Instructor who should have been in Broadmoor! Unfortunately I cannot remember his name as I would have loved to have seen it in print. Here's just one of the disgustingly atrocious things which he did to one boy: I had been invited by the Commander to join the lucky boys on number 9 punishment in their afternoon 'constitutional' around the parade-ground. One of the lads, albeit a fairly weedy character, was wearing a cap that was too tight and he attempted to ease it by pushing it back on his head. Every time we ran past this Instructor he smashed his fist down on the lad's hat, pushing it back to the correct position. After four or five of these 'dress corrections,' the boy's forehead was cut open and streaming with blood. He finally passed out and was left lying on the parade-ground. This act was witnessed by the good ladies from the N.A.A.F.I. who downed their tools in protest and officially complained to the powers-that-be. We never found out the result of this, but that particular swine was in need of treatment."

Leaving for a moment this story at this point and referring to similar stories of an Instructor smashing his fist down upon the cap of a boy, causing it to cut into the bridge of his nose; a similar occurrence is seen in the stories of Dave Van der Weele and Harry Vann. From the dates given of both those offences against the boys, it is not possible that the same Instructor was involved because the time lapse is about ten years.The treatment of an Instructor smashing his fist down upon the caps of young boys was not only *not* isolated, but a general principle, learned by some from others. A good example of this `learning by the methods of others` syndrome is very prevalent in the numerous and different stories of the "I am rubbish!" treatment of Instructors humiliating boys who dropped their rifles.

Back to A.B. Wyatt:

"Never stir up anything you cannot drink!"

"During school one day, whilst misbehaving boyishly in some way or another, a certain very tall, thin Lt. Cdr. Schoolie struck me from behind around the side of the head with the black-board T-square. Although it felt very painful at the time I thought no more about it until that night when my ear became even more painful and started to bleed. I reported to the Sick Bay the next morning and was asked how it had happened. Without thinking of the consequences, and being very green, I told them I had been struck by an officer.

Bad news! Before I knew it I was being questioned by a senior medical officer who informed me of the levity of my complaint which could lead to a court martial. Panic! I knew what he meant by `levity.` They were of the opinion that I was being frivolous about a slight smack around the ear, making much more of it than had really happened. I was being made to consider that I was making a mountain out of a molehill. But I wasn't! He had smacked me about the head with the T-square, and I really was in pain. But, luckily, I thought at the time, I was invited to `have another think` about what had occurred, which I did. I had been smacked on the ear with a T-square, and my head ached and my ear bled. That was that. But I knew I could not win against the officers, so I dropped the case and never heard anything more about the matter, but that certain

'Schoolie' was never quite so physical after that.

It pays to keep your head down when you're a Nozzer!

One of the lasting impressions I have of Ganges was being constantly HUNGRY! Probably caused by the surfeit of exercise and fresh air. The food from the galley definitely wasn't Cordon Bleau. In fact, it could be fairly disgusting at times but I never remember leaving a scrap. A Junior Seaman at Ganges was likened unto a jungle scavenger, always on the look-out for something extra to eat and stuffing his face with 'nutty' from the N.A.A.F.I. Who remembers sneaking rounds of bread from the galley, taking them back to the mess and having a nocturnal toasting session, using the messdeck iron for a grill? Somebody always forgot to clean the iron afterwards which resulted in some poor soul spreading his white-front with burnt crumbs and butter the following day?

When I joined Ganges I had the usual teen-age foibles about food, lots of likes and more dislikes but after a few weeks, and ever since, I have been able to eat anything and everything! What good training for later when meals would be prepared in a ten-foot square galley beneath the heaving decks of some Frigate or Destroyer, tossed upon the heaving seas of mighty Atlantic or the non-pacific Pacific? The results could be daunting, but with the help of the naval tot and gastronomic training of H.M.S. Ganges, very little would be wasted.

Years later, I returned to Ganges as a member of the newly-formed Diving School. I remember going to the Sick Bay for my three-monthly diving medical and being confronted by a retired Surgeon Captain. After a routine examination he told me that I'd been drinking too much, having too many late nights and probably ungirthing my loins and exercising them to excess! He recommended that I cancelled my Long Week-end leave, partake in some long, healthy walks, get a few early nights and come back the following Monday for a re-examination. I took no notice, indulged myself to the full in all the forbidden things which he had suggested for the next three days, and, after re- examining my completely debauched shagged-out and weary body, he took a pace to the rear and said: 'Well done, lad. I can see that you have taken my advice and I can now pass you fit for diving.'

Nothing had changed since 1959!

Writing this has brought it all back, and if it was 1959, and I was 15 years old again, I wouldn't hesitate to do it all over again. I remember going home on my first leave and my older brother said: 'Where the 'ell did you get that chest from?' I think that says it all. They were interesting times and I'm sure that everybody who went through the experience feels that, **'Gentlemen in England, now abed, shall think themselves accursed they were not here.'"**

"Fond memories of Ganges..."

Well, there is one fellow who was there, in Ganges of course, and glad of it, according to **Robert Andrew Gradon,** who joined in 1970. After reading all the other stories on Ganges, one wonders if Bob Gradon was indeed at that place! He does not say he had a hard life before Ganges, but the way he describes what can only be an existence deprived of the benefits and privileges of Ganges, he considers himself very fortunate to be one of the lucky few who were chosen to join Ganges as a boy entrant. He loved it, so he says. Then, in parts, he says the opposite, and one begins to wonder.

"I have very fond memories of Ganges, it was, without doubt, the only period of my life when I had nothing better to worry me than ensuring all my kit was of the same dimensions and had my name on display. I had gone to Ganges from a very depressed area, and, as a child, I never had much in the way of personal possessions or money, but I was still a happy youth. And here I was, a spotty, 15 year-old, minus my long flowing locks of hair, my arms making a good impression of a pin cushion after numerous vaccinations, with more clothes - be them ill-fitting - and more money than I knew what to do with. £3 per week was a King's fortune to me. Those first four weeks as a nozzer in new entry were heaven; hot water when I wanted, good food, although the tea was dodgy. New friends, sewing, washing, playing football, and marching. Marching was not such heaven. New boots, the introduction of gaiters and a sadistic Gunnery Instructor who's vocabulary consisted of: 'Chests out, back-sides out, stomach in, dig those heels in, swing those arms, heads, up, bull-shit'" and 'A piece of cake,' turned my dream into a nightmare."

So he **didn't** like it then?

"Little did I know that life was to take enormous steps in a downhill direction. New entry completed, it was onto the reality of survival of the fittest. Thankfully, I was amongst the fit, and could give as much as I could take. Establishing a hierarchy was painful, I didn't want to be one of the 'Tufty Club,' laying down the rules that everyone had to adhere to, nor did I want to be dominated, I had to fight for my freedom of movement, choice and a bed nearer the door. The nearer the door in the mess you were, the more esteem you had, and the more blankets you needed, youthful logic!

"Rapped knuckles..."

Many a night was disturbed by the raid from the other mess-decks followed by the inevitable double-march, wearing oilskins, boots with no laces and carrying a full kit-bag, up and down the Long Covered Way. Woe betide anyone who spoke during this activity, each mutter resulting in another length of the covered way and a black eye for the culprit.

Another of the sadistic tortures for minor infringements was the 'Burma Walk,' mattress thrown back, bare-footed, with wooden ditty-box ar arms length, slow mark time on the bed-springs until we were exhausted. There was, of course, a little deterrent should you try lowering the ditty-box to lessen the pain. A broom handle rapped upwards against the knuckles. Yet although these little niceties were trying, they were far out-weighed by the good times; skulking from church on Sundays, sailing, movies and the camaraderie. I don't think I'll be able to give justice to an establishment I think should be re-opened and all young men put through those paces. Remember Gilbert Green, or Green Gilbert, depending on who told the tale, of the World War II sub-mariner who's mini-sub sank off Ganges. Apparently, Gilbert was captured and held in the laundry; during the bitter winter's night he climbed into one of the huge spin-dryers for warmth. and some disconcerting sailor switched it on, turning poor Gilbert into mincemeat. It is said that he was left in that condition and began to decompose, hence the name Green, and ever since that tragic night the spin-dryer mysteriously turns itself on and the screams of Gilbert can be heard around the establishment. As a 15-year-old boy I was never in the laundry alone.

I was entirely and unashamedly in love with the navy at this stage, I had been chosen to spend a week aboard H.M.S. Dittisham, an inshore minesweeper. I was to have my first taste of foreign lands, France. We went to Cannes for Bastille day. The Dittisham was another romantic adventure for me, after watching film after film during naval history lessons. I envisaged myself on the open bridge of one of the escorts on the Russian convoys. It was just as cold and wet as I had envisaged, and my buddy, standing next to me, crying because he had lost the use of his digits. He was so cold the couldn't move and was eventually carried from the bridge. God, I loved it! I loved the stomach-churning smell of warm diesel, the salt water and everything and the peeling of spuds during the middle-watch. The week was over in a second for me.

Back to reality and 50 times up and down Faith, Hope and Charity. Why? Because my kit, which had taken a hammering during my week at sea, was not up to scratch. I sometimes think that I probably annoyed those who tried administering punishments out to me. I was enjoying myself and no-one was going to stop me being a sailor. No one could hurt me because I was not going back to civilian street where I had no prospects.

Remember the Gym? In white sports kit, to distinguish your recruitment as not being worthy of wearing blue, that honour had to be earned, anymore than two creases in the front and back of your shorts was horrifying, and dirty pump laces would see you laying your kit out. I`m trying to remember the Rudyard Kipling poem that adorned the wall in the Gym: `If you can keep your head while others around you lose theirs etc.` "

(If you can keep your head when all about you, are losing theirs and blaming it on you).

"If I had any bad memories of Ganges I think it would be of the dentists, and of course there was no choice, if the dreaded white appointment card was handed to you, then you either kept the appointment, or went in front of the Commander and took whatever punishment he deemed fit for not going. I think the dentist must have completely rebuilt my mouth, I was always there. This man was no artiste, an ex coal-miner, I think.

Leave? Main seasonal leave. I hated it. All my ex-friends in civvy-street would be working or would have no money to go anywhere and the £19.00 I had got for 3 weeks leave never seemed to get past week 2. I was always in a hurry to get back."

Amazing! He is the only ex-boy ever to admit that he hated seasonal leave.

"However," he continues: "I remember my Workship week with fond memories. Once again I came up smelling of roses. I was to be the 1st Lieutenant`s messenger. No Galley for me. I had to deliver the morning newspapers to the officer`s married quarters and chat up the daughters who would be waiting for me each morning. I didn`t **have** to chat them up, but I felt it my duty to make the galley boys, not only green with the slops, but green with envy too.

Friday night routine: never before, or since, have I seen so much achieved by so many with so little to do it with. Not being one for shirking hard work, I never missed a Friday night. There were those who wouldn't have known a day's graft if it jumped up and bit them on their backsides, but the faithful handful would scrape the old wax off the wooden decks with wire wool, scrub it with soapy water, then lay the orange wax with one hand and buff it with the other, using a boot brush. The dust-bin and spit-kid both being chrome had to be brasso-polished and the Heads and bathrooms scrubbed with the most revolting grey paste I have ever come across. It was impossible to get it off once it had been applied - as some less-than-hygienic sailors found out."

Sometimes the most cruel and degrading `punishments` were meted out by the boys themselves. Robert Gradon continues:

" If you thought not to be taking showers regularly, every day at least once, then the `Tufty Club` would go into action.

I witnessed two of these forced `showers,` no laughing matter for the poor subject; long-handled, hard-bristle scrubbing-brushes were used to ensure the grey paste had good effect, together with any other cleaning-agent they could get their hands on, turned the `not-so-clean` a very healthy pink colour, and it always ended in tears. The unclean would also awake to find they had been removed from the mess, bed as well, and left outside overnight."

No-one liked kit-musters, for varying reasons, but Robert Gradon, true to form, actually loved them!

"Kits! My kit was, on the whole, immaculate. I had bought extra kit from slops to cover the items I wore most, and so did not need to disturb my locker, blues down one side, ships book size, whites down the other, shoes, boots highly-polished and pumps under the bed in line with the bed edge, ditty-box on top of the locker, yellow duster upon it, name showing, and my best cap on top of the duster. Blankets folded with no edges showing and sheets folded into the blanket folds, but a third of the width. So, it was with the utmost of horror, when one day I found my best cap spiked on the bed post with a `love letter` from my Instructor stating that the top of my cap was not completely flat. I spent ten shillings for a new one. When I think of some of the caps I saw worn at sea, it was nothing short of criminal to spike mine.

I also spent hour upon hour in the ironing-room, pressing the five creases into my blue serge trousers, being too short for seven, mercifully. Those hours struck up friendships with boys from all kinds of backgrounds. I remember my best pals were a lad from

Bristol and a Scots lad, one as smart and ambitious as myself, and the other a right scare-crow. I never saw either again once we left Ganges. The Scots boy went to Collingwood and my friend from went to Bristol to Vernon.

There are many more memories, but if I were to keep going I would probably be best writing my own book."

**Jim Lawlor`s** claim to fame was not as an ex-Ganges boy, or later as a Petty Officer. Many famous and a few infamous people passed through the magnificent main gates of H.M.S. Ganges, but Jim Lawlor wasn`t in either category. He was one of the should-have-been-famous, but the bad luck which sank an unsinkable ship on the day of his birth, seemed to attach itself to him in at least one aspect of his exciting and varied life.

As the Titanic slowly disappeared so tragically beneath the icy waters of the Atlantic, Mrs. Lawlor was giving birth to young Jimmy. It was May 7th, 1912, and Jim spent many frustrating years trying to gain recognition as a natural champion boxer. Most of the boxers of his weight shunned him, they were afraid of his special punch. He was the eighth-rated Welter-weight in the world, but never made world champion, in fact, he never made British Champion. The noted boxers of his day, who stood between him and the title, made various excuses, "not available," "indisposed," etc., and refused to fight him because he was too good. Although they would not have given that reason as the real excuse.

At his fighting best he weighed ten stones four pounds, and stood half an inch short of the one-fathom mark. He perfected what came to be known as the `Lowestoft Loop,` a short six-inch cork-screw jab to the solar plexus, the gathering of vital nerves just below the sternum, the breast-bone. In fact, being a boxing fan during the height of Jim`s fame, I clearly remember reading about the boxer with the `corkscrew punch` which felled opponents with one short blow to that area which will put a man on his knees for more than the specified period of the ten seconds needed to score a knock-out. Jim practised delivery of his specialised punch for hours, and performed it to perfection.

He had ten first-round knock-outs, the longest of the shortest rounds lasting seventy-five seconds, the shortest was seventeen seconds including the count, and he holds the record in the Guinness Book of Records for that feat. Jim is also a poet and author, writing his own autobiography.

Jim Lawlor joined Ganges in 1927 when he was fifteen; the following is an extraction from the book of his life story:

"A chest like a fourpenny rabbit.."

In the recruiting office an officer came to see me. Running to keep up with his big strides, I said, "Please, sir, do you think I will pass the exam, sir?"

"Let's look at you, he said. I stood as erect as I could. "Yes, you have a chest like a fourpenny rabbit, you'll pass."

I did too, I remember going on a train for the first time in my life, from Horncastle to Birmingham, in August, 1927. When I arrived I found six more boys waiting to take the medical exam. Only two of us passed, so the next morning five boys returned to their homes, and two boys were feeling on top of the world. Gee, real sailors we were going to be.

H.M.S. Ganges was our new abode and we soon found out it was more like a prison than a holiday camp. But while I was there I soon was taught the difference between right and wrong. And I was always saluting, every time I saw an officer, or running onto the quarterdeck. H.M.S. Ganges was a huge training ship. Mast, 150 feet high, and up one side, down the other in bare feet. We had to climb it early every morning before getting our enamel bowl of ship's cocoa and very hard ship's biscuits. Then tragedy. A boy fell off the mast onto the quarterdeck and died. So the climbing was stopped.

My pay as a Boy Seaman was a shilling a week, and of that I only received sixpence pocket-money every Wednesday. The money went to our credit until we became seamen at the age of 18.

As a Boy Seaman we were always hungry and our sixpence pocket money was soon spent in the Tuck Shop, and every boy asked for the same, "A Whim, a bar and a bottle of pop. The Whim was a big doughnut, full of jam and cream; the bar was a big bar of chocolate, and the pop was a quart bottle. Real value. Wednesday afternoons were Make-and-Mend days for us boys, and we had to watch sport on the playing fields, or else take part ourselves. Our tea, on Wednesday only, was always the same - two slices of bread, a little knob of butter and a basin of tea. None of us boys saw a cup, saucer or a crock plate. We all had enamelled tin plates and tin basins and an inferior knife, fork and spoon.

I remember just one boy who never spent his sixpence. Every Wednesday he sat in the Tuck Shop with us and he had his tanner slotted in between a piece of cardboard to send home to his folks to save for him. I still remember his name, Peafold. But he may have changed it now to Rothschild!

Wednesday evening, after tea, we were marched down to the gymnasium for a free film show. On the gymnasium walls in big letters was the greatest poem I've ever read. Rudyard Kipling's "IF." And I was always thinking about walking with Kings and never losing the common touch. Or losing one game of pitch and toss. And making one heap of all your winnings and never breathing a word about your loss. Yes, a really great poem. Absolutely great. I rate that poem.

In those tough old days, imagine a sailor boy going home on leave with no ribbon round his cap and no overcoat to wear - and at Christmas time! Well, to get a ribbon to put round your cap, in gold letters, H.M.S. GANGES, you only had to become a first-class boy and that meant passing an exam in seamanship, boxing the compass: N, N by E, NNE, NE by E, is only part of it; knots and splices, anchors and cables, signals, rules of the road - at sea. And to get an overcoat as part of your kit you only had to pass your swimming test, and that was three lengths of the baths, wearing a sailor suit, and then float on your back for four minutes. Three times I went on leave with no overcoat. But if you don't succeed, try again, so three times I failed and the fourth time I won, and when I put my overcoat on for the first time, I felt I'd won it for swimming the English Channel!

Each boy had a kit-bag and his kit was valued at £40; they had to be marked on each article of clothing with a type with his name on, then sew through each letter with white or black cotton. The lads with the longest names had to keep going and I remember a lad with a name like Scattergoodenough, F., and I bet he thought *There ain't no justice.* And here is a four-letter word for life in the Royal Navy as a boy, **G-R-I-M.**

The Chief Petty Officers in charge of us boys at Shotley Barracks were like very strict fathers to the different messes where we ate and slept. Our Chief gave me a whole penny for winning the boys' Lightweight Boxing Title in 1927. Often you felt like answering back to the stern Chiefs but you didn't, because you see, he and all the other C.P.O.'s kept a stonnicky in their trousers' pocket, so, I'll tell you: it's a half fathom of rope, three feet, with a huge knot at the end of it and it was used on our backsides at every opportunity.

"One for luck with a stonnicky..."

In bed at 9 p.m. every night, everyone of us boys had to wear a big

240

yellow flannel and in big letters on the back it said: NIGHTSHIRT. If a boy was caught in his bed not wearing his nightshirt, or still had his socks on, he was belted out of bed with the knotted rope. And twice a week, bath nights, we had to be inspected by the Chief P.O.'s and although we scrubbed our bodies spotless, we still got one for luck on our bare backsides.

I never forgot - nor ever shall forget - our Chief's favourite words to all of us. They were: 'If you see Harry Tate struggling, help him. And when you're struggling, Harry Tate will help you.' The Chief was right. His philosophy worked for me all the time I was in the Royal Navy. But, in civvy street, well, it never worked out that way, Chief.

When he took us for Seamanship lessons, he was always telling us boys, 'A sailor without a knife is like a woman without a fanny.' And he was always telling us that, 'A girl who thinks a sailor is her only sweetheart, doesn't know her ABC.' (Know her A.B., see?)

We were always having lectures and being shown films about

venereal disease at H.M.S. Ganges. It scared me stiff and I'm glad it did, because on one ship I was on, a sailor I knew caught it and he went beserk and smashed his fists at the full-length mirrors on the Mess-deck and cut his hands dreadful. He finished up as a Mental Case. But I'm more than willing to bet that out of every hundred boys at Shotley who saw the VD films, and heard the lectures, there wouldn't be more than one boy who caught it.

I can see that Chief P.O. now. All powerful. All wise. When I told him I wanted to be a world Champion Boxer he put his hand on my shoulder and said, 'Son, never ride in a car if it`s less than a ten mile walk, don`t drink, don`t smoke, and put between your lips a piece of chalk and always keep it handy for your appetite' And that Chief P.O. was one of the Unforgettable Characters in my life. I still chuckle to myself thinking about that penny he gave me for winning that boys` boxing title. Nor will I forget that all of us boys had convict haircuts, whether we liked it or not.`'You`re in the Navy now,' they told us, and they wasn`t kidding.

Some time later and two of us boys are on the Quarterdeck. We had been caught fighting each other. So we were marched from the Quarterdeck to the Gymnasium. Boxing gloves were put on our hands, and we were in a boxing ring for the first time.

'Seconds out...Time!' the officer shouted and there we were fighting like mad. Bang! Bang! Bang! I`ve drawn blood. And my opponent staggers. He`s down. And now I hear the words. 'Have you had enough?'

It was the officer speaking.

`Yes, sir,` my opponent said.

'Get up then, and shake hands with Boy Lawlor.' So he did, and my opponent and I, Boy Ellis, became great friends all the time we were at Shotley.

Soon after this encounter we were both getting special tuition in the Gymnasium, and when we had become `old salts,` with twelve weeks service in, Boy Ellis was the runner-up in the Boy`s Welterweight Championship, and Boy Lawlor won the title, Boy`s Lightweight Champion of H.M.S. GANGES.

The Chief Petty Officer in charge of us was delighted when I won the title. He said: 'Congratulations, son. Here`s a little present for you.'

As I mentioned earlier, it was then that he placed a penny in my palm. One Penny! I can never forget that. My first taste of money for fighting! One Penny. Still, a penny was a penny in those days, almost a day`s pocket-money to Boy Sailors.

But when I told Boy Ellis that our Chief had given me a penny for winning the title I could see he was disappointed. He had not been given a penny for being the runner-up. So I bought a toffee-bar in the Tuckshop and gave him half. We became real buddies and helped each other in many ways. I remember writing his letters for him and he would copy them out to send to his Aunt and Uncle. They had a shop and when a food parcel came for him he always shared it with me. I was never lucky enough to get a parcel from anyone, so I always felt glad when he insisted that I share his parcels.

Yes! That fight we had was great, because it was the beginning of an eight and a half month's friendship. Then, alas, he went to one ship and I to another, and although we often say, 'It's a small world,' well, for Boy Ellis and Boy Lawlor it turned out to be the biggest of Big Worlds, and we never saw each other again.

After nine months at Shotley, I'm still the Lightweight Champ, and still have the medal to prove it. Then I'm sent to a real great Battleship in the Third Battle Squadron, H.M.S. EMPEROR OF INDIA. One of the last warships that ran on coal..."

This was extracted from a book written by Jim Lawlor, "SECONDS OUT - TIME!" And although the following has nothing to do with Ganges, it is felt that the foregoing story, because of it's interesting content, warrants a brief mention of the sequel.

Jim Lawlor progressed rapidly as a boxer, from Lightweight to Welterweight, and was bought out of the Navy by a syndicate of Boxing Promoters so that Jim could turn professional. He was ranked as eighth in the World Ratings, but he was so good, knocking out several within 75 seconds of the first round with his famous 'Lowestoft Loop,' a six-inch punch to the solar plexus, that those boxers of his weight, and above, who stood between him and the British title, which would have eventually led to a World Title Fight, either refused to fight him or were 'not available,' or 'indisposed' at the time.

In 1939 Jim was recalled to the Navy and demobbed as a Petty Officer at the end of the war. All through the war he was looking for fights, and he managed quite a few, but on demob. he had lost six valuable boxing years, fighting for another cause, freedom of his country. After the war, he was told by boxing managers: "There's no way that we'll put any of our boys against you!" Although he had many more fights, he never managed to get a chance for a crack at the British or World titles.

Jim is in his eighties now, still fighting fit, and lives in Lowestoft.

"Was it as bad as I remember?"

Mike Hancock joined Ganges as a Boy Seaman Second Class, transferred later to what he calls the 'Hairy Fairy' branch, and reached the rate of Petty Officer, Electrical Air Weapons branch. The electrical branch, and perhaps allied branches, were known as Hairy Bog-trotters, and Mike titles his story as such:

"A Hairy Bog Trotter, plus Small Boats, plus One Class of Greenies - equals Disaster!!"

If you cannot work that out, explanatory details follow in his own words, thus: "I'm looking forward to reading your forthcoming book to learn the views of others to see if it was really as bad as I remember. I had the dubious pleasure to serve in H.M.S Ganges from the 27th of June, 1966 to the 7th June, 1967 as a Junior Rating in number 85 recruitment. I cannot say they were the happiest 12 months of my life but then, at 15 years old, the whole thing was of a magnitude sometimes too big to comprehend.

It was a bit of a triad really, concerning (1) a small boat, (2) a 32-foot cutter and, (3) later, an M.F.V.

The Hairy Bog Trotter was Chief Coxswain Kavanagh, an ancient mariner, probably nice to his wife and kids when teaching them to play cricket or soccer, but with Nozzers, Sprogs and Trogs of the lowest order, viz: boy entrants into His or Her Majesty's Royal Navy, he portrayed a very low tolerance level when it came to teaching boat-work to boys who were totally ignorant about boats and water.

After the preliminaries of boat-work in the class-room, accompanied by several dire threats of what would befall us if we failed, came the fateful day to put theory into practice - a wholly, uncomfortable, wet, dreary and dismal morning spent pulling oars on the mighty River Orwell. Oh, the pain, the cold!

I shall always remember the Orwell as a grey, choppy stretch of water and invariably cold, especially if you happened to fall in, and a biting wind which continually gusted at near gale-force - or so it would seem.

Exmouth 451 class, out in the divisional cutter, catching more crabs than the local fishermen, whilst our Instructor, poor old Chiefy Kavanagh, may his socks rot and his teeth and hair fall out, was getting consistently more and more frustrated as we consistently caught more and more crabs. In the end we rowed, well, tried to row, back to the pier-head. The last straw came when we tried to toss our oars. The tossing of oars should be carried out like this: On the order: `Toss your oars!,` each member of the boat should take his sixteen-foot long oar, weighing about sixty pounds, lift it from the water, place it between his knees and hold it there in a vertical position whilst drenching himself and his oppo's with cascades of water dripping in gushing streams directly down upon the holder(s) of the oar(s), making sure that the coxswain, usually the Instructor, received an equal amount in the struggle and strain to cause oars to rise to the vertical. And if each oar had been in the process of `catching a crab,` or, in land-lubber`s jargon, stuck in the black slimy mud of the Orwell, then great gobs of gooey, glutinous mud would enhance the distress already caused by the icy drenching.

Strangely enough, that is just what happened. Being subsequently knackered from our exertions on the river, that effort was, well, an effort. We were weary of mind and muscle, and raising the oars, always a laborious chore, was more than we could properly manage. We were waving the things all over the place, trying to do it as efficiently as we had been taught, but the resulting clash and final entanglement and collapse of oars was more than poor Kavanagh could stand. We had broken every rule in the seamanship manual. Execution was pending, and inevitable.

With faint hearts and dire despair, we disembarked, hoisted the cutter onto the davits, and began the long-established relationship with the infamous steps, `FAITH, HOPE AND CHARITY`

I recollect that most of my boat-work instruction was spent doubling up and down this famous landmark. I never could see, and I still cannot see to this day, several years later, why or how, running - well, staggering, up and down those flights of concrete steps, could ever make us better seamen than we were. We had tried our best, and, though it wasn`t good enough at the time, I`m sure all my mess-mates were of the same mind as myself: to try better next time, and be proud to do so. Being punished for trying our best only brought out resentment in the boys."

It would seem that the essence of Ganges` basic rule, or perhaps that of the Instructor concerned, was: If they don`t get it right, an hour doubling up and down Laundry Hill, or Faith, Hope and Charity etc., will somehow cause them to do it properly next time, no matter if they have already decided, as good seaman and responsible boys, to try their hardest to get it right.

Mike continues:

"I think Chief Kavanagh must have had a Brain Storm the day he took us sailing. I imagine it was a decision which haunted him the rest of his life. It was the last time I went out on the Orwell in a 32ft cutter, boat-work instructions after that event consisted entirely of trying to wear Faith, Hope and Charity flat.

246

We successfully rigged the cutter for sailing - much to his surprise - and we pushed off from the shore-side part of the pier. We got the sail up O.K., and then Chief Kavanagh started shouting something about dropping the keel. The shout turned into a strangled scream and then, looking at it from his point of view, I suppose it must have been the ultimate humiliation to someone as respected as our Chief with a title as grand as that of `Chief Coxswain,` because we ran onto a mudbank and got well and truly stuck in the thick, glutinous sucking mud.

Chief got over his amazement first, then his horror. It was seconds after that when he turned purple, changing gradually to puce, streaked with purple blotches. He ordered me to push us off the mud with an oar. Very unwieldly things, oars, and, after successfully missing everyone's head I got the oar over the side and managed to get us afloat again. I do not recall getting any accolades for that feat, then, or later, but Chief did seem to mellow a little and was going to give us another chance when I brought the oar into the boat. I had neglected to wash the black, sticky Orwell mud from the blade and managed to shower all those including the Chief in the blunt end with icy water and thick gobs of mud. Without a word he ordered us back to the pier where we stowed and cleaned the boat, and then onto the dreaded concrete steps **for the rest of the sailing lesson.**

Having tried and failed with oars and sail, our next adventure involved the Motor Fleet Vessel, BEMBRIDGE. Until I met the mighty Bembridge the full implications of hull design had eluded me. As usual, the Orwell was looking green and angry and the sky was typically and characteristically overcast with clouds which threatened rain.

The destination was Ostend, my first trip abroad and my first trip in a boat where I would leave the sight of land and, to add to the excitement, no oars, no sails, just marine diesels to do all the work.

At last a chance to enjoy the water again, which is why I had joined. Down below in the forward hold to stow my kit and make up my bunk then back on deck to enjoy the departure from Harwich Harbour.

At last we shed our ties with the pier and we powered out with a thunderous roar of engines towards the gap to seaward between Harwich and Felixstowe. The wind was strong and the normally choppy estuary was beginning to make small waves. Was it an indication that outside the harbour things could be worse? Whatever it forebode it didn`t stop Chief Kavanagh, who had taken on the role of Chief Cook; he was in the Galley cooking up one of his reknown pot-messes: corned-dog, peaches, tomatoes, everything and anything which was edible. The list of ingredients was endless and the pot became a gourmets nightmare.

We passed the row of Light-ships which were anchored off Harwich and headed for the open sea and our destination. It was around that point where we had our first casualty. One of the junior ratings was sea-sick over the back-end. The gurgling messy morass concocted by Chief in the galley may have had something to do with it. To me the whole situation was wonderful, we were at sea, and I realised that this is what I wanted.

What a contrast from a choppy Orwell to an extremely lumpy North sea. Some of the lumps were like glassy mountains, majestic in their splendour. This was it, this is why I had signed that piece of paper. At last the open sea and some real excitement.The Bembridge was having a rare old time, one minute we were at the top of the waves, the next in the deep gully`s surrounded by giant mounds of water towering above us.

The number of people on deck began to diminish as it became colder and wetter, and it began to get more and more rough. The actual sea could not have been that bad for, as a ferry steamed past us, she seemed to be hardly rolling at all, although being several hundreds of tons heavier and bigger than us, I was not surprised. It was at this stage someone explained the disadvantages of having a flat-bottomed boat.

Up front two of my fellow travellers were clinging onto the mast and no amount of persuasion would make them let go. They were getting the full brunt of the weather, and sea water was funnelling through the stove pipes and gushing over them in great plumes.

I went below to secure my kit. What a sight, groaning, writhing bodies everywhere and the smell of hot vomit filled the already stale air of the mess-deck. My orientation was going quickly. The sound of someone being violently sick sent me hurrying back onto the deck.

Chief Kavanagh, the Coxswain, was now at the wheel and there were about seven of us left on deck. Two clinging to the forward mast, one on the bridge and the remainder, including me, between the wheel-house and forward-hold doors.

We were becoming cold, wet and hungry, but salvation was nigh: mugs of Chief Kavanagh`s pot-mess arrived. It was wonderful, I shall never forget it, and at that moment I forgave him for all his sins. I can still recall the peaches.

We spent the rest of the trip singing every song we could think of and drank copious amounts of pot-mess. Even the two stalwarts up front managed to hold on and drink at the same time.

Then the bad news; the forecast was that the storm was getting worse and we had been ordered back to Shotley.

We stuck it out on deck and all too soon we had passed back through the gap and into a choppy Orwell, which now looked pretty calm and tame by comparison to us hardened matelots of the sea.

As we neared the pier someone put a rope in my hand and said: `As we draw near the pier, someone will be waiting to receive this on the jetty.` I was to throw it so that we could be tied up. I was stationed on the back end, getting more and more nervous as we approached the pier which got bigger and bigger as the dreaded moment arrived.

The order was given, 'Throw the line!' I looked and spied a pair of eager hands outstretched, ready to receive the line. The dream of the ecstatic trip was rapidly turning into a nightmare of reality.

I threw the line. It missed. But before it did, it described a glorious arc and the free end disappeared under the pier to lasso and latch firmly and unmovedly onto one of the cross-braces.

There was a lot of shouting and cries of obscenities proclaimed with anguish as I was shoved aside. Chief Kavanagh was there, clutching and clawing at his beard, muttering his favourite catch phrase: 'Festerin` `ell!' Or perhaps more obscene words to that effect.

`Oh, no,` I thought, `My weekend in Ostend was going to turn into a marathon on Faith, Hope and Charity.` And for once, I was right.

From parades to hades, but the trip, short though it had been, had been worth it. An experience that no one could take away. I blew all my Ostend money in Felixstowe. We were excused Sunday Divisions and we may have actually been allowed to lay in on the Sunday morning. Those details are trivial, and anyway, would have been eclipsed by the sheer enjoyment of the aborted voyage to Ostend.

H.M.S. Ganges, what did she give me? An appreciation of my freedom, a sense of adventure, the tenacity to overcome my obstacles. But my career was marred for a time by the fear that someone would make me man a sea boat or throw a heaving line. I later transferred to the Electrical Branch and was happy to be a Hairy Fairy and take the looks of scorn from those nautical types who knew about such things."

One boy was saved from the complete rigours of Ganges by the intervention of the war. But first he tells a tale of his Instructors whose bullying was backed up by an equally-bullying Instructor Boy. Instructor Boys were allocated to a mess or Division after completing their own course, or part-way through their training. Most were sympathetic to the boys; they were, after all, only either six or nine months older, or that much further advanced in the Ganges regime, and treated their underlings with compassion. Unfortunately, the power of rising three rates above the most junior rating, went to the small brains in the big heads of some of them. It is unfortunate that certain types, who`s character lacked substance, were of a tyrannical nature, and treated the boys like slaves.

Jack Thwaite from Liverpool joined Ganges in June, 1939, and takes up the story.

"A three ton lorry took us from the station to Shotley and having arrived at the gate to the Annexe the driver of the lorry, a stoker, implored us to think again and offered to lend us our fares home if we changed our minds. He told us of the rigours of Ganges, but the worse it sounded the more we liked it. We were sailors, we were tough and, although we listened, we heeded not a word. We had joined the navy to see the world, and the world we intended to see.

Having signed on the dotted line again we were allocated to messes named after Admirals; I was in Tyrwhitt Mess.

We were issued with uniform clothing and taken to the Bath House for a shower where we were inspected by our Instructors to see if were were as clean as was expected.

The first day wasn`t too bad, but for the rest of the six weeks in the Annexe we were badgered, bullied and given general hell to fit us for the Utopia of the Main Establishment.

"You will enjoy being punished.."

As well as the usual Instructors we were allocated an Instructor Boy. One nasty habit which the Instructor Boy had was to arouse us just as we were going to sleep. He would turn on the lights, shouting orders and obscenities, then he would chuck a bucket of water over the recently-polished floor. This happened just as the warmth of sleep and cosiness was seeping through our bodies, and sleep was beginning to overcome us. He would make us turn out and dry the water off the deck, then re-polish it all over again. This task was urged on with a liberal dose of the rope`s end which he carried.

We had been told by the Instructors that we were being trained as men and sailors, so few of us complained - if any at all.

However, one lad wrote home and boasted to his Mum of the hard life. She took a dim view of her son being belted at any old hour, and wrote to the Commanding Officer of H.M.S. Ganges.

The result was that the lad who had written was, quite unfairly, ostracised and made to feel like an outcast because, as the Instructor said, if we were to be men and sailors we should not write home to Mum and tell her of the nasty things which were happening to us, only that we were in good health and enjoying every minute of our life in the Royal Navy.

The routine in the Annexe didn`t worry me too much. I was not upset with home-sickness as some of the boys were. I had worked away from home previously and was used to it.

What did get me down was getting up at dawn to wash down the covered ways in barefeet. The Training Ship boys, (from Arethusa etc) took it in their stride, being used to swabbing the decks every morning, but the rest of us found it extremely painful, especially when we were made to double across the Parade Ground, which was composed of sharp grit, to sharpen us up.

Six weeks later we moved into the Main Establishment, having been turned into men! But not yet sailors! Or so we thought. We were soon disillusioned and put into our place as NOZZERS by the rest of the lads.

This position we would hold for the next sixteen weeks when we would become Boys 1st Class with a rise in pay from one shilling a week to one shilling and sixpence.

Whilst in the Annexe I had opted to be either a Boy Signalman or a Boy Telegraphist, and joined 203/204 Class in number six mess, Blake Division.

After twelve weeks I chose to become a Signal Boy in 204 class.

Our Instructors were a Chief Yeoman of Signals and a Leading Telegraphist.

Soon after joining the Main Establishment we went on Summer Leave, and whilst on leave war was declared. We returned to Shotley on the ninth of September, worrying ourselves sick that the war would be over before we could be trained as men and sailors and prove ourselves heroes.

Instructor Chief Yeoman went to sea when war was declared and our new Chief Yeoman, C.Y.S. Nash, a kindly man, had retired on pension in 1936, fought valiantly for us and on one or two occasions saved us from the dreaded Shotley Routine. The Leading Tel. stayed with us until we left, and, with the war, that was fairly soon.

Wednesday afternoons were devoted to sport. I enjoyed sailing in the Whalers and the excitement was intense during the obstacle cutters race when we sailed and rowed alternately dropping the mast and stowing the sails each time. Unfortunately, I was at Shotley during the cold part of the year and the bitter East winds cut through the sportswear we had to wear in all weathers, rain, hail, snow or shine.

"Shotley Joe..."

One morning a week we were up at dawn, about 0400, to do our dhobeying, supervised by one of our Instructors and a gentleman called Shotley Joe, who joined the navy in 1897 and had worked in

251

the laundry at Shotley ever since his demob.

Another morning we were up about five o'clock for a bath. On completion of which we would stand naked in front of our Instructor with our arms raised. The Duty Instructor usually carried a small cane which brought tears to the eyes when brought down on to a wet bottom if the lad concerned had left a 'tide mark.' The bathing and dhobeying routines were also carried out during evening sessions during the week.

Smoking was one of the most serious crimes at Shotley, and to be caught meant certain caning, even to be caught in the vicinity of boys who were smoking was to be found guilty and you were punished, even if you didn't smoke!

Yet the hardier souls smoked blatantly after 'lights out,' and in the Heads and on the Playing Fields.

For most of my time at H.M.S. Ganges the only liberty we were allowed was four hours Shotley Leave, when we were allowed to walk around the village and country lanes. As we set out on our Shore Leave, Instructors would mount bicycles and pedal furiously to places where there were cigarette machines, some three or four miles away.

Discipline was maintained by punishment implied as well as punishment given. A boy was reputed to have been killed when a Field Gun went out of control as a bunch of lads on jankers were running down Laundry Hill with it. He didn't die in vain as that was the last of the Field Gun punishment routine. Shotley Routine was greatly feared but most other punishments we took in our stride. We were always threatened with punishment. If we made a mistake we were punished, if we couldn't do a task we were punished and, of course, if we broke the rules we were punished. Caning was the most severe punishment. I can well understand the need for strict discipline. With two thousand youths under training, given an inch they would have been uncontrollable.

Some of the Instructors were sadistic bullies, but most did their best and shielded us from our own and others excesses; even if they were a bit too robust at times with their discipline.

The officers were a different kettle of fish; they were 'gods' surrounded by a mystique which was to remain with them as far as I was concerned, to a greater or lesser degree, until I left the Andrew in 1954. Routine training went on and a new and much appreciated innovation had been instigated. Once a fortnight we were allowed either Harwich or Ipswich leave and could spend all afternoon and evening until half-past seven, completely free from all routine and discipline in one of the two towns. Wild were the boasts of the women we had 'conquered' and the beer we had drunk - out of one shilling and sixpence - when we returned to the messes.

A month or so after returning from Easter Leave, Holland fell to the invading armies and it was decided to move all the boys from Shotley. It must have been decided at very short notice.

Our class was marching down to the Signal School when we were suddenly told to return to our mess where we changed into working rig, then we were doubled down to the jetty and spent the rest of the day and well into the night loading kit-bags and hammocks into the lighters, taking them across the river and loading them into railway wagons.

Most of the boys packed their kits and were entrained for Liverpool and the Isle of Man to join H.M.S. St George, which was the old Cunningham Holiday Camp. Classes which had almost finished their courses were sent to their Port Divisions, Portsmouth, Devon and Chatham for sea service.

The following day, those of us who were left, packed our kits and entrained for Liverpool and the old Southern Hospital which was being taken over by the Royal Navy with an ultimate destination of H.M.S. Impregnable at St. Budeaux, near Devonport.

I must, at this stage, say something about the renowned mast at Shotley. Climbing the mast was, like bathing and dhobeying, a twice-a-week routine, once early in the morning and once in the evening. Occasionally the mast had to be climbed at Divisions with the whole of the Establishment looking on. Woe betide the boy who failed the Devil's Elbow. He had to climb the mast again the following day at Divisions and keep on doing it until he had conquered it. Due to lack of maintenance after the war broke out, the mast became unsafe and was put out of bounds after several boys fell from it.

What did H.M.S. Ganges do for us?

On the debit side it made us fear authority to such an extent that we would lie and cheat rather than admit we were wrong. Indeed, there was only one law: 'Thou shalt not get found out!'

On the credit side, it gave us a strong and undivided loyalty to the ships we served on, our Officers and Shipmates. The external discipline, although it was disliked, was probably essential for a fighting force to go through a war that was to last another five years. The inner discipline, however, will last us all our lives and perhaps they did make those that passed through H.M.S. Ganges into men and sailors.

All Shotley Boys like to think so anyhow."

Chapter twelve.

"My Finest Hour"

To recap and go over old ground to jog the memory: If it could be possible to pose the question to anyone who attended Ganges as a boy entrant: "What is, or was, your opinion of H.M.S. Ganges?" Their answers would fall into several categories. The main category would be strongly allied to their own experiences and opinions. What happened to *them*, they may opine, is *exactly* what happened to *everyone,* and that is a strongly, self-opinionated biased answer, embracing all and everything without giving thought to the importance of considering the opininions and experiences of events which happened to others.Whatever those events, which may, and did, occur to several others, did not happen to them, personally. Many narrators of tales contained in this book have not taken into account the widely differering experiences which took place between the ill-treated boys in one mess and the cossetted, comforated boys in any other mess: nor have they compared the kind actions of their Instructor to those of a bullying Instructor elsewhere. To put the matter into the right perspective, each of us is the centre of our own world, and, because of that, our personal experiences are more important and interesting - to ourselves - than the relative, minor, not-so-important recollections of others. It is because of the latter that we incline to regard our own memories as superior and more appealing, and play down the importance of the memories of others.

Personal experience..

My opinion of Ganges is that I can truly believe and acknowledge the problems of the Instructors: 2,000 different boys from 2,000 different homes and 2,000 variously and assorted characters, acting in 2,000 separate ways, all trying to prove, subconsciously maybe, that they are individuals and, as they are of the male gender, attempting at that age to prove themselves, even if *only* to themselves, that they are men in a man`s world. They were boys, young boys, teenagers approaching manhood, and they would certainly attain the status of `man` - with or without the help of Ganges, a known factor which seems to have been overlooked by many who quote: **"Ganges made a man of me."** Ganges made them tough, or tougher and more able to cope with the traumas of life than they might have done otherwise. It is an opinion of most, that if a person successfully survived Ganges, then most other hard or traumatic happenings in life could be considered trivial by comparison. It could also be an admission that their passage through Ganges was the testing ground, and an admittance that nothing could be worse than the Ganges regime. If that is so, it is an admission that Ganges, and all it stands, for, was nothing more or less than a downright nuisance and despairingly awful most of the time! That does not mean to say that the regime of Ganges was right. It was right in the intention that it`s aim was to turn green young boys into competent sailors, 'To take their place as seaman/communicators/ stokers/etc. in the fleet.` What is surely suspect is the manner in which some Instructors interpreted, or misinterpreted, the briefs and rules given to them to carry out their tasks, difficult tho` those tasks may have been. It is true that some boys, attending a school of naval training, would welcome the most trying and toughest of ordeals so that they could overcome those ordeals and prove they are really men - and hard with it, admitting they enjoyed the ruggedness and frugality of Ganges - believing it would prove they were equal to the tasks demanded of them. I know by personal experience that no matter how many times, or how grisly the descriptions told to me to discourage me from joining as a Boy, the gorier it was, the braver I felt, thinking I would be able to cope with it. And I did. There were many who didn`t, as the reader will have read about in previous chapters.

Interests of the Boys...

This chapter is about an Instructor who was personally concerned about the interests of `daddy`s boys,` as his own children had referred to them, and it is a relief and nice to know that there were some Instructors, and there were very many who were of the same opinion, who were capable of doing the job properly. Conversely, there were Instructors who had the, `as it was done to me so shall I do to you to get my own back` attitude. This was an opinion of which I have first-hand experience of when writing my first book on Ganges. It is an approach which was absolutely forbidden in the 1960`s naval issue called: `Instructions to Instructors,` explained more fully elsewhere in this book. Another book, "H.M.S. Ganges, 100 years of boy`s training" by Instr. Lt. D.L. Summers, on the subject of Instructors, writes, mentioning Ship`s Police, or `Crushers,` "..frequently came in for criticism in the training ships for their often quite brutal treatment of the boys. Questions were periodically asked about their conduct in the House of Commons. They all carried canes which were about three feet long and as thick as a man's thumb. The ratings, who acted as the boys' Instructors, carried a piece of rope - called a Stonnicky - with a Matthew Walker knot near one end. When the bugle for the Assembly sounded, the police would lash out indiscriminately at the boys in an attempt to hurry them up. This practice was discontinued only when a boy lost his sight after one such blow. To the modern generation this treatment may sound savage, but at the time it was thought that the *'frequent use of a rope's end was the only method to teach a boy to be a man'.* In H.M.S. Ganges, the ship, it was not until the 1890's that the use of the stonnicky was severely restricted by successive Captains." *Note that the phrase 'severely restricted' does not mean 'abolished.'*

Another extract from the same book: "Looking back on his time at Shotley in the 1930's one boy commented that 'the discipline would have made the French Foreign Legion look like a Sunday School.' Another: 'Instruction in all subjects was carried out by senior ratings, most of whom had volunteered for a training job. There is no doubt that having had a hard introduction to the navy themselves, they tended to treat the boys in the same way, and boys who had not been to a preliminary training-ship must have found the life hard, and from time-to-time cruel. Many of the younger boys went to sleep crying and sobbing away their fears.'

That aspect of Ganges never did change. Some boys still cried at night when seemingly alone and lonely in their beds. At least one boy obtained his discharge because he could not stop the flow of tears.

Tough guys and bullies...

Those who have to outwardly prove to their contempories that they are tough, are not tough at all. There are personal memories of hard-cases, from the tough Gorbals of Glasgow and the equally tough Liverpool Docks, who were braggarts and bullies during the day, picking on the lesser-endowed of muscle and stature, then sobbing themselves to sleep at night when they thought no-one was listening. Trying to teach others by force and loud-mouthed vociferations, violence, bullying and the pain, humiliation and degradation which violent punishments bring, is not an indication that the sufferer or victim is at fault, it is solid proof that the perpetrator of violence is lacking sadly in the correct way in which to treat his fellow-man, over whom he enjoys a sense of power. He knows they cannot retaliate for fear of painful consequences. The Instructor, in that case, being the owner of a massive inferior complex, has to make others seem inferior to make himself look superior. We have met these people many times in the course of our lives, but do not always recognise them.

The Instructors - most Instructors in fact - and some officers, of H.M.S. Ganges, are guilty of those accusations. But not all. Some were excellent Instructors and officers. My experience of Instructors contains no cruelty, bullying - a bit of shouting perhaps - a dash up and down Faith, Hope and Charity once, maybe twice because we had unsuspectingly committed a misdemenour, whatever it was, but nothing which came anywhere near to cruelty, or the merest fraction of it, and nothing more, and often less, than some of the tales of violence and bullying which I have learned of since leaving Ganges and writing this book.

It is very refreshing, therefore, to learn from an ex-Instructor - reluctant though he was to take on that task, and a hard task it proved to be, that he was not only a natural psycho-analyst, but understood the needs of the young boys within his care. He had experienced Ganges as a Boy himself, and knew the requirements of the boys, their hopes, their projected expectencies, and treated them as he would have liked to have been treated himself. He admits that when he was a Boy Seaman in 1921, he thought all Instructors were monsters, but, as an Instructor himself, and living intimately with other Instructors, he admits that most had soft spots for the boys in their care. In researching this book, the proportion of letters from ex-Instructors formed a small, inadequate fraction of those received from ex-boys, so it is refreshing to receive the `other point-of-view` from one of the exalted but misunderstood few.

"My Finest Hour..."

This man, Frank Henry Austin, is a denial of the myth that all Instructors were 'malicious, bullying, masochistic and sadists.' He describes his time as an Instructor at Ganges, as, **"My Finest hour."**

Frank Henry Austin:

"In 1937, as a P.O. Telegraphist, I returned to the U.K. from two and a half years on the China station, and, after foreign draft leave, was given the choice of going on another foreign draft or operating as an Instructor at H.M.S. Ganges. I chose the latter. After I left the Navy I gave lectures and after-dinner speeches; my main topic was what was nearest and dearest to my heart, and was obviously the high-light of my eventful life. Here, in my own words, is an account of what amounts to a transcript of the lecture which I gave to many enjoyable meetings."

'I'm hoping to interest you to what, to me, was my finest hour. Needless to say, as an ex Petty Officer Telegraphist, that it concerns the Royal Navy. But one side of it is that not a great many people experience. This is the Boys' Training Service. I have to begin by telling you how I became an Instructor at the Boys' Training Establishment, H.M.S. Ganges, Shotley, near Ipswich. In November 1936 I returned from my second commission in China, serving in H.M.S. Kent, and we paid off in Chatham dockyard. I had my foreign service leave and returned to the R.N. Barracks to find I was on draft to H.M.S. Ganges as an Instructor. I protested and was given the option of going there or else another foreign commission. As I had a wife and two young children, the youngest was only 19 days old when I had gone to China, but was able to come running to meet me when I came home, needless to say, I went to Shotley although with considerable misgivings. Arriving there I found I was to take over, with another Instructor, 28 Mess, classes 257 and 258. This consisted of 50 boys who had been in the R.N. but six weeks and were just coming out of their preliminary training, having been selected for visual signalling and wireless telegraphy training. I must digress here to give you some idea of these things. My knowledge of Boys' training establishments was limited to my own experience as a boy at the same place in 1921. Thoughts of climbing the mast bare-footed, no matter what the weather; stonnickies, that is, a knotted rope's end across the backside, and many other little torments. I had lots to learn. It was with some misgivings that I entered my new job as a Ganges Instructor. If I remember rightly we were given some idea of the routine and what was expected of us as Instructors in a couple of interviews with various officers, masses of orders and regulations and that was that, except that we would be required to attend classes on seamanship with boat sailing in particular, and, of course, parade-ground drill. We, that is my opposite number, Chief Yeoman of Signals and myself a Petty Officer Telegraphist, were not expected to know a great deal about such things, but until we could satisfy the officers concerned that we were proficient in those arts, we were not entitled to Instructor's pay of six old pence per diem, per day. We had, I believe, a couple of days to get our Boys' mess fitted-out with the necessities; bedding, mess-gear, knives, forks, spoons etc., and generally organise things ready for the great day when we could begin.

That day duly arrived and we took over our classes, which came over

258

from the Annexe that afternoon, on the Quarter-deck. The boys had been kitted up and generally had the first rough edges rubbed off. It was now up to us to train them to be useful members of the Royal Navy. We belonged to Anson Division under the command of Lieutenant Commander Burgel Nugent known more familarly by Instructors as Nutty Nugent, because of his big head. A very likeable and efficient officer, with a second-in-command, a Mr. Wade, Gunner, R.N. The Boys' mess, 28 mess, was at the bottom of the Long Covered Way. The Long Covered Way was a road with a covered canopy of a roof, a quarter of a mile long with messes leading off from it on either side, together with the ships' galley half-way down on the right-hand side, with stores and other communal buildings. Our mess was alongside of the chapel. I mention this because we were to find that it wasn't an asset being in close proximity of a chapel. In addition, 28 mess was the furthest point from the P.O.'s mess, which was, at the very least, a half a mile away. This was another snag from the Instructors point of view because of the time spent in getting to and from the boys mess to our own in the very limited time available for meals.

Well, we got the boys settled in that first day without too much trouble. They were feeling strange and wondering what was in store for them, it being the first time any of us had met. They thought we knew all the answers, little knowing that it was as new to us as to them, except that we had the great advantage, of course, of having quite a few years experience of the R.N., and, as you all know, experience and common-sense is always a great help.

Now, an idea of the general routine for the boys: Rise 6.30, wash, cocoa and biscuits and make up beds. 7 a.m., assembly and away to instructions for forty-five minutes. 7.45: breakfast, clean into the rig of the day, clean and tidy the mess etc., and general assembly on the parade-ground at 9 a.m. One Instructor would be present at assembly in charge of the boys, and the other Instructor in the mess seeing to the final touches ready for the daily inspection by an officer. After assembly and prayers, instructions for the boys until 11.45. Then the tannoy would pipe: 'cooks to the galley,' which indicated dinner at noon. 1.15 p.m. assembly and instructions until 4 o'clock. Then tea-time and afterwards either night instructions for an hour or organised games in the summer. As Instructors we worked every other day on duty and had to take the responsibility of the mess from noon on one day to noon the next. 24 hours. This entailed responsibility for the care and comfort of 50 Boys, any special duties, if you were duty division or duty mess Instructor, or, if bath night, mustering the Boys through the bath. If it was wash-day, or dhobeying-day, it meant getting up at 5 a.m. to wake the Boys and get them, with their washing, over to the laundry. Our mess was only excused normal routine until 9 a.m. divisions. Well now, life at Shotley both for Instructors and boys was a full life. Every minute of every day was carefully planned to make these boys into men with a sense of responsibility and moral courage to bring out the best in them by a good healthy life, good food and leadership, sports of all kinds, where they learned self-reliance and unselfishness by the team spirit and the art of living together. Their spiritual life was catered for by the Chaplains of whichever denomination they belonged to, so they attended that church. Which brings me to one interesting point of the draw-backs of our mess. It was next to the C-of-E chapel where early communion was held every Sunday and Feast Days for anyone who wished to attend. We were always in trouble because of the noise made by our mess during services. To try and keep 50 healthy boys quiet was no mean task. After one complaint by the chaplain I remember the next week we had to clear the mess and put sentries on the door to deny the boy's entering, except for meals, as punishment. As you can imagine, the Parson wasn't very particularly welcome.

To tell all that happened would take far too long, but the thrill of seeing those boys grow, their characters develop, their keen-ness to learn and get on, the trust they put in me as their Instructor and they confided in me of their troubles and worries, for I was the centre and hub of their life at this period. I realised that it was me who was responsible for moulding their character and who can, if he is worth his salt, refuse them? It is something that has to be experienced to really understand, something that to me, at any rate, became part of life itself. Of course, life was not a bed of roses for Instructors, or boys. It was hard work all the time. I well remember my first month or so until one became physically tuned to the pace. Come the end of the day the duty officers' rounds at 9 p.m., boys all tucked in for the night, I reported to the officer: '28 mess, sir, all correct. 47 boys, 2 sick, one on leave.' Then, afterwards, one staggered literally to one's dormitary, off boots and laid on the bed, too tired to move. It was not unusual to fall asleep when I first started the job, to awake at one or two a.m., cold and stiff, then to undress and crawl in between the sheets until 5.30.

As their training proceeded, so of course our duties were eased, for the boys responded, surprisingly, to the trust we put in them. I honestly think that their trust in us, their Instructors, was equalled by the trust we placed in them. Obviously there were black sheep, but they weren`t very troublesome after a while. They responded to treatment and the boys themselves saw to it that their Instructor was not hauled over the coals because of the odd one or two. So you see, another part of their character was developed.

Loyalty, well, leaves came and went, and what excitement there was just before leave days, especially the boys` first leave. No need to call them that morning! But as the period of training lengthened, annual leave dropped into its right perspective: a break from the arduous training period. After the first leave, the majority of the boys were homesick for a while, but again, as they got older, they were anxious to be back again to get down to the business of final examinations. The great landmark between training and their being drafted to sea-going ships, with all the romance that has ever been in our island history of exploring and adventure. On the day the results were announced, possibly one, or maybe two, failed to make the grade. The latter to be encouraged to do better next time, the others to congratulate. The day finally comes when you know your ways must part. The boys will go on draft to ships, establishments and even foreign stations in the Far East, East Indies, West Indies, Home Fleet, perhaps, or even the Reserve Fleet on the Clyde estuary. But we knew it had to come, but somehow we never thought about it because we knew from previous experience that it would be like paying-off a ship after a commission. Saying `cheerio` to your shipmates, `Been good fun serving with you, we`ll meet again.` But no, it wasn`t like that. We felt that we were losing something we had come to love. They were OUR boys. We had done for them nearly as much, or more, as their father`s had. In some cases, a lot more. And they were going out of our lives. We would no doubt see some of them again, maybe in some far-flung corner of the world, but now they were OUR chicks leaving the nest. How can I describe that morning when they were leaving the training establishment? When, at breakfast time, after seeing them settled, their appointed leader, with words that we knew meant they were leading up to giving us a parting gift. It was against the regulations, we didn`t expect it. A silk scarf and a pair of kid gloves. Somehow, I remember, losing my tongue, it just stuck, dry, against the roof of my mouth. My eyes filled, and I thought: I mustn`t let them see any tears. A mumbled few words of thanks, a short, halting speech of thanks, of hope for their future. 'One day, I hope, we shall meet again, then we will have a yarn, maybe a drink together, swap a few yarns about the old Ganges days.' I think I ended with: 'If we meet again, mine's a pint of bitter!' I had to get out, rush to the bedding store, our office, by now real tears and a good cry.

At sea, in bloody battle in World War Two, I have seen men slaughtered and maimed, my heart has been heavy and many times I have been afraid, but not so many tears were shed then as that last moment when I said 'goodbye' to my boys. Was I ashamed of those tears? No. never.

Yes, I met some of them afterwards. We laughed and talked of those days, exchanged many experiences since. Many of them, unfortunately, made the supreme sacrifice. Some are still serving. Occasionally, very occasionally, I see one now, but I am always remembered by those whom I meet, and I believe I would still know them all, every one of them.

My boys, '*Daddies boys*,' my baby sons used to call them.

Yes, they were right, they were '*Daddies boys,*' all fifty of them.

Can you see what I mean by "*My finest hour?*" Not the fighting that I had been trained for years at the country's expense, nor the medals and the cheering. No, nothing like that, but just fifty boys from fifty different types of homes, got together and organised into a unit, trained into useful and necessary occupations for their career in His Majesty's Royal Navy. I finish this narrative with Lieutenant Commander Nugent's farewell message to 28 mess from the Shotley magazine for the term ending Christmas, 1937.

ANSON DIVISION NOTES.

'I think you will agree that this has been a cheerful and eventful term., etc. Class 257/8, 28 mess, have developed into a pretty hefty lot of pirates, but they will be a great loss to the Division when they go to sea in the new year. They have won the senior Inter-Class Boxing, the thing most worth winning this term, provided most of the Anson Rugger team, and all the Water Polo Team, done well at Soccer, W/T and Flag Hoisting, and at everything else they have gone in for, and are doing extremely well in their P.T. Exams. But more important than all this is that they are a really keen, cheerful and fit lot of boys, ready to do their best at anything - and a jolly good best, too. I shall be really sorry to see the last of them next term. I think they have enjoyed their time at Shotley, too - but how many of them will admit it? The very best of good luck to them at sea. If they keep up their present standard they will all get on well, enjoy the Navy and be of real use to it as well. Their wireless Instructor, P.O. Tel. Austin, is going off to the Signal School to qualify for his A.C. Star, and Chief Yeoman Brown will soon be off to a well-earned pension. Good luck to both of them. They have every reason to be proud of their class.'

There were, of course, many others involved in the training of these boys, to whom tribute must be paid, even the cooks and supply staff played their part in providing sustenance necessary for the arduous training. To mention them all is not possible, for this is but a short, personal report of : **'My Finest Hour.'**   <u>Frank   Henry   Austin.</u>

And finally........
There cannot be a more apt, more befitting statement, or sincere declaration to end this book, than to admit that for anyone who had attended Ganges, as Boy, Instructor, Staff or Officer, that *they* may also say:

<u>'It was *my* finest hour, too!'</u>

John Douglas
8th, September, 1995

Info of Ganges memorabilia over the page....

Another book with the same theme is planned. If the stories in this book have jogged your memory and caused you to recollect similar experiences, or experiences which would conflict or agree with stories herein, please, in the first instance, write to the author:

John Douglas, Douglas House. Penmarth. Carnmenellis. Redruth. Cornwall. TR16 6NX, enclosing a stamped addressed envelope if you require a reply.

Stories should be typed, although that is not essential, but please try to write as clearly as possible. Don't worry about punctuation, grammar or spelling. It is preferable that stories should contain as much detail as possible, i.e: time of the year, month or day if it relates to the story; sights, sounds, smells, speech, reactions of the characters, etc. etc. It is possible to edit out that which is not necessary, but not possible for the editor to write details into a personal story belonging to another. As long as the story has a beginning, a middle and an end, and, preferably some re-action to the ending, that is all that is required. Most people think they cannot recollect in detail stories of their past. It is surprising how many start to tell a small anecdote, realise that they could, in fact, write a book!

Inscribed Boatswain`s call-pipes, nickel, gold and silver-plated, book and video of *Ganges*. *Also access to the `slop room` of the Ganges Association which provides various memorabilia of H.M.S. GANGES, ties, badges etc.* Details available from the address above.

The video is 60 minutes long and takes in all aspects of Ganges before it`s demolition. It is titled: 'H.M.S. Ganges, The Final Farewell.' detailing *Ganges* as it used to be. *Nelson Hall, Parade Ground, Quarterdeck, Long and Short Covered Way, Benbow Lane, Signal School, Gunnery School, Boat-pulling/sailing etc. etc.* shots of boat-pulling, sailing, manning the mast, etc. etc.

Write to the address above for further details and prices.